Siegel's

CORPORATIONS

Essay and Multiple-Choice Questions and Answers

By

BRIAN N. SIEGEL

J.D., Columbia Law School

and

LAZAR EMANUEL

J.D., Harvard Law School
General Counsel, Emanuel Publishing Corp.

Siegel's Series

Published by

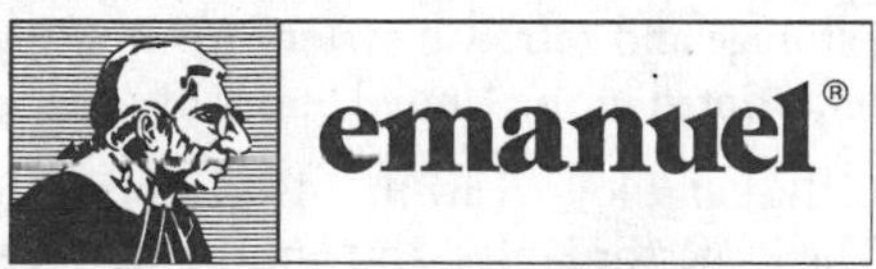

Siegel's Corporations, 2nd Edition (1998)
Emanuel Publishing Corp. • 1865 Palmer Avenue • Larchmont, NY 10538

ISBN 1-56542-352-6

About the Authors

Professor Brian N. Siegel received his *Juris Doctorate* from Columbia Law School, where he was designated a Harlan Fiske Stone Scholar for academic excellence. He is the author of *How to Succeed in Law School* and numerous works pertaining to preparation for the California Bar examination. Professor Siegel has taught as a member of the adjunct faculty at Pepperdine School of Law and Whittier College School of Law, as well as for the UCLA Extension Program.

Lazar Emanuel is a graduate of Harvard Law School. In 1950, he became a founding partner of the New York firm now known as Cowan, Liebowitz & Latman. From 1960 through 1971, he was president of Communications Industries Corp., multiple licensee of radio and television stations in the Northeast. Since 1987, he has served as Executive Vice President and General Counsel of Emanuel Publishing Corp. He has edited many of the publications in the Professor Series of study aids and in the Siegel's series of Essay and Multiple-Choice Question & Answer books.

Acknowledgment

The authors gratefully acknowledge the assistance of the California Committee of Bar Examiners which provided access to questions upon which many of the questions in this book are based.

Introduction

Although your grades are a significant factor in obtaining a summer internship or permanent position at a law firm, no formalized preparation for finals is offered at most law schools. Students, for the most part, are expected to fend for themselves in learning the exam-taking process. Ironically, law school exams ordinarily bear little correspondence to the teaching methods used by professors during the school year. They require you to spend most of your time briefing cases. Although many claim this is "great preparation" for issue-spotting on exams, it really isn't. Because you focus on one principle of law at a time, you don't get practice in relating one issue to another or in developing a picture of the entire course. When exams finally come, you're forced to make an abrupt 180-degree turn. Suddenly, you are asked to recognize, define and discuss a variety of issues buried within a single multi-issue fact pattern. In most schools, you are then asked to select among a number of possible answers, all of which look inviting but only one of which is right.

The comprehensive course outline you've created so diligently and with such pain, means little if you're unable to apply its contents on your final exams. There is a vast difference between reading opinions in which the legal principles are clearly stated, and applying those same principles to hypothetical exams and multiple choice questions.

The purpose of this book is to help you bridge the gap between memorizing a rule of law and ***understanding how to use it*** in the context of an exam. After an initial overview describing the exam writing process, you will be presented with a large number of hypotheticals which test your ability to write analytical essays and to pick the right answers to multiple-choice questions. ***Do them — all of them!*** Then review the suggested answers which follow. You'll find that the key to superior grades lies in applying your knowledge through questions and answers, not rote memory.

In the sample answers (both to the essays and to the multiple choice), you will notice references to *Emanuel* on *Corporations*. The reference tells you where in the outline to find the relevant discussion. Thus, a reference to "Ch. 4–VI(A)(2)(d)" means Chapter 4, section (Roman numeral) VI, capital letter A within that section, number 2, paragraph d. This notation is perhaps less convenient than page numbers, but it helps us keep the reference constant from one edition of a book to the next.

GOOD LUCK !

Introduction

Table of Contents

Preparing Effectively for Essay Examinations

Essay Questions

Essay Answers

Multiple Choice Questions

Answers to Multiple Choice Questions

Index

Preparing Effectively for Essay Examinations[1]

To achieve superior scores on essay exams, a student must (i) learn and understand "blackletter" principles and rules of law for each subject, and (ii) analyze how those principles of law arise within a test fact pattern. One of the most common misconceptions about law school is that you must memorize each word on every page of your casebooks or outlines to do well on exams. The reality is that you can commit an entire casebook to memory and still do poorly on an exam. Reviewing hundreds of student answers has shown us that most students can recite the rules. The ones who do ***best*** on exams understand how problems (issues) stem from the rules which they have memorized and how to communicate their analysis of these issues to the grader. The following pages cover what you need to know to achieve superior scores on your law school essay exams.

The "ERC" Process

To study effectively for law school exams you must be able to ***"ERC"*** (***E***lementize, ***R***ecognize, and ***C***onceptualize) each legal principle listed in the table of contents of your casebooks and course outlines. ***Elementizing*** means reducing the legal theories and rules you learn, down to a concise, straightforward statement of their essential elements. Without a knowledge of these precise elements, it is not possible to anticipate all of the potential issues which can arise under them.

For example, if you are asked, "what is self-defense?", it is ***not*** sufficient to say, "self-defense is permitted when, if someone is about to hit you, you can prevent him from doing it." This layperson description would leave a grader wondering if you had actually attended law school. An accurate elementization of the self-defense principle would be something like this: "Where one reasonably believes she is in imminent danger of an offensive touching, she may assert whatever force she reasonably believes necessary under the circumstances to prevent the offensive touching from occurring." This formulation correctly shows that there are four separate, distinct elements which must be satisfied for this defense to be successfully asserted: (i) the actor must have a ***reasonable belief*** that (ii) the touching which he seeks to prevent is ***offensive***, (iii) the offensive touching is ***imminent***, and (iv) the actor must use no greater force than she ***reasonably believes is necessary under the circumstances*** to prevent the offensive touching from occurring.

1. To illustrate the principles of effective exam preparation, we have used examples from Torts and Constitutional Law. However, these principles apply to all subjects. One of the most difficult tasks faced by law students is learning how to apply principles from one area of the law to another. We leave it to you, the reader, to think of comparable examples for the subject-matter of this book.

Recognizing means perceiving or anticipating which words within a legal principle are likely to be the source of issues, and how those issues are likely to arise within a hypothetical fact pattern. With respect to the self-defense concept, there are four ***potential*** issues. Did the actor reasonably believe that the person against whom the defense is being asserted was about to make an offensive contact upon her? Was the contact imminent? Would the contact have been offensive? Did the actor use only such force as she reasonably believed was necessary to prevent the imminent, offensive touching?

Conceptualizing means imagining situations in which each of the elements of a rule of law have given rise to factual issues. ***Unless a student can illustrate to herself an application of each element of a rule of law, she does not truly understand the legal principles behind the rule!*** In our opinion, the inability to conjure up hypothetical problems involving particular rules of law foretells a likelihood that issues involving those rules will be missed on an exam. It is therefore ***crucial*** to (i) ***recognize*** that issues result from the interaction of facts with the appropriate words defining a rule of law; and ii) develop the ability to ***conceptualize*** fact patterns involving each of the words contained in the rule

For example, an illustration of the "reasonable belief" portion of the self-defense principle in tort law might be the following:

> One evening, A and B had an argument at a bar. A screamed at B, "I'm going to get a knife and stab you!" A then ran out of the bar. B, who was armed with a concealed pistol, left the bar about 15 minutes later. As B was walking home, he suddenly heard running footsteps coming up from behind him. B drew his pistol, turned and shot the person advancing toward him (who was only about ten feet away when the shooting occurred). When B walked over to his victim, he recognized that the person he had killed was not A (but was instead another individual who had simply decided to take an evening jog). There would certainly be an issue whether B had a reasonable belief that the person who was running behind him was A. In the subsequent wrongful-death action, the victim's estate would certainly contend that the earlier threat by A was not enough to give B a reasonable belief that the person running behind him was A. B could certainly contend in rebuttal that given the prior altercation at the bar, A's threat, the darkness, and the fact that the incident occurred within a time frame soon after A's threat, his belief that A was about to attack him was "reasonable."

An illustration of how use of the word "imminent" might generate an issue is the following:

> X and Y had been feuding for some time. One afternoon, X suddenly attacked Y with a hunting knife. However, Y was able to wrest the knife away From X. At that point X retreated about four feet away from Y and screamed: "You were lucky this time, but next time I'll have a gun and you'll be finished." Y, having good reason to believe that X would subsequently carry out his threats (after all,

> X had just attempted to kill Y), immediately thrust the knife into X's chest, killing him. While Y certainly had a reasonable belief that X would attempt to kill him the ***next time*** the two met, Y would probably ***not*** be able to successfully assert the self-defense privilege since the "imminency" element was absent.

A fact pattern illustrating the actor's right to use only that force which is reasonably necessary under the circumstances might be following:

> D rolled up a newspaper and was about to strike E on the shoulder with it. As D pulled back his arm for the purpose of delivering the blow, E drew a knife and plunged it into D's chest. While E had every reason to believe that D was about to deliver an offensive impact on him, E probably could not successfully assert the self-defense privilege because the force he utilized in response was greater than reasonably necessary under the circumstances to prevent the impact. E could simply have deflected D's prospective blow or punched D away. The use of a knife constituted a degree of force by E which was ***not*** reasonable, given the minor injury which he would have suffered from the newspaper's impact.

"Mental gymnastics" such as these must be played with every element of every rule you learn.

Issue-Spotting

One of the keys to doing well on an essay examination is issue-spotting. In fact, issue spotting is ***the*** most important skill you will learn in law school. If you recognize all of the legal issues, you can always find an applicable rule of law (if there is any) by researching the issues. However, if you fail to perceive an issue, you may very well misadvise your client about the likelihood of success or failure. It is important to remember that (1) an issue is a question to be decided by the judge or jury; and (2) a question is "in issue" when it can be disputed or argued about at trial. The bottom line is that if ***you don't spot an issue, you can't discuss it.***

The key to issue-spotting is to approach a problem in the same way as an attorney would. Let's assume you're a lawyer and someone enters your office with a legal problem. He will recite the facts to you and give you any documents that may be pertinent. He will then want to know if he can sue (or be sued, if your client seeks to avoid liability). To answer your client's question intelligently, you will have to decide the following: (1) what theories can possibly be asserted by your client; (2) what defense or defenses can possibly be raised to these theories; (3) what issues may arise if these theories and defenses are asserted; (4) what arguments can each side make to persuade the factfinder to resolve the issue in his favor; and (5) finally, what will the ***likely*** outcome of each issue be. ***All the issues which can possibly arise at trial should be discussed in your answer.***

How to Discuss an Issue

Keep in mind that ***rules of law are the guides to issues*** (i.e., an issue arises where there is a question whether the facts do, or do not, satisfy an element of a rule); a rule of law ***cannot dispose of an issue*** unless the rule can reasonably be ***applied to the facts.***

A good way to learn how to discuss an issue is to start with the following mini-hypothetical and the two student responses which follow it.

Mini-Hypothetical

A and B were involved in making a movie which was being filmed at a bar. The script called for A to appear to throw a bottle (which was actually a rubber prop) at B. The fluorescent lighting at the bar had been altered, the subdued blue lights being replaced with rather bright white lights. The cameraperson had stationed herself just to the left of the swinging doors which served as the main entrance to the bar. As the scene was unfolding, C, a regular patron of the bar, unwittingly walked into it. The guard who was stationed immediately outside the bar, had momentarily left his post to visit the restroom. As C pushed the barroom doors inward, the left door panel knocked the camera to the ground with a resounding crash. The first (and only) thing which C saw, however, was A (who was about 5 feet from C) getting ready to throw the bottle at B, who was at the other end of the bar (about 15 feet from A). Without hesitation, C pushed A to the ground and punched him in the face. Plastic surgery was required to restore A's profile to its Hollywood-handsome pre-altercation form.

Discuss A's right against C.

Pertinent Principles of Law:

1. Under the rule defining the prevention-of-crime privilege, if one sees that someone is about to commit what she reasonably believes to be a felony or misdemeanor involving a breach of the peace, she may exercise whatever degree of force is reasonably necessary under the circumstances to prevent that person from committing the crime.

2. Under the defense-of-others privilege, where one reasonably believes that someone is about to cause an offensive contact upon a third party, she may use whatever force is reasonably necessary under the circumstances to prevent the contact. Some jurisdictions, however, limit this privilege to situations in which the actor and the third party are related.

First Student Answer

"Did C commit an assault and battery upon A?

"An assault occurs where the defendant intentionally causes the plaintiff to be reasonably in apprehension of an imminent, offensive touching. The facts state that C punched A to the ground. Thus, a battery would have occurred at this point. We are also told that C punched A in the face. It is reasonable to assume that A saw the punch being thrown at him, and therefore A felt in imminent danger of an offensive touching. Based upon the facts, C is liable for an assault and battery upon A.

"Were C's actions justifiable under the defense-of-others privilege?

"C could successfully assert the defense of others and prevention of crime privileges. When C opened the bar doors, A appeared to be throwing the bottle at B. Although the "bottle" was actually a prop, C had no way of knowing this fact. Also, it was necessary for C to punch A in the face to assure that A could not get back up, retrieve the bottle, and again throw it at B. While the plastic surgery required by A is unfortunate, C could not be successfully charged with assault and battery."

Second Student Answer

"Assault and Battery:

"C committed an assault (causing A to be reasonably in apprehension of an imminent, offensive contact) when A saw C's punch about to hit him, and battery (causing an offensive contact upon A) when he (i) C knocked A to the ground, and (ii) C punched A.

"Defense-of-Others/Prevention-of-Crime Defenses:

"C would undoubtedly assert the privileges of defense-of-others (where defendant reasonably believed the plaintiff was about to make an offensive contact upon a third party, he was entitled to use whatever force was reasonably necessary to prevent the contact); and prevention-of-crime defense (where one reasonably believes another is about to commit a felony or misdemeanor involving a breach of the peace, he may exercise whatever force is reasonably necessary to prevent that person from committing a crime).

"A could contend that C was not reasonable in believing that A was about to cause harm to B because the enhanced lighting at the bar and camera crash should have indicated to C, a regular customer, that a movie was being filmed. However, C could probably successfully contend in rebuttal that his belief was reasonable in light of the facts that (i) he had not seen the camera when he attacked A, and (ii) instantaneous action was required (he did not have time to notice the enhanced lighting around the bar).

"A might also contend that the justification was forfeited because the degree of force used by C was not reasonable, since C did not have to punch A in the face after A had already been pushed to the ground (i.e., the danger to B was no longer present). However, C could argue in rebuttal that it was necessary to knockout A (an individual with apparently violent propensities) while the opportunity existed, rather than risk a drawn-out scuffle in which A might prevail. The facts do not indicate how big A and C were; but assuming C was not significantly larger than A, C's contention will probably be successful. If, however, C was significantly larger than A, the punch may have been excessive (since C could presumably have simply held A down)."

Critique

Let's examine the First Student Answer first. It mistakenly phrases as an "issue" the assault and battery committed by C upon A. While the actions creating these torts must be mentioned in the facts to provide a foundation for a discussion of the applicable privileges, there was no need to discuss them further because they were not the issue the examiners were testing for.

The structure of the initial paragraph of First Student Answer is also incorrect. After an assault is defined in the first sentence, the second sentence abruptly describes the facts necessary to constitute the commission of a battery. The third sentence then sets forth the elements of a battery. The fourth sentence completes the discussion of assault by describing the facts pertaining to that tort. The two-sentence break between the original mention of assault and the facts which constitute this tort is confusing; the facts which call for the application of a rule should be mentioned ***immediately*** after the rule is stated.

A more serious error, however, occurs in the second paragraph of the First Student Answer. While there is an allusion to the correct principle of law (prevention of crime), the ***rule is not defined***. As a consequence, the grader can only guess why the student thinks the facts set forth in the subsequent sentences are significant. A grader reading this answer could not be certain that the student recognized that the issues revolved around the ***reasonable belief*** and ***necessary force*** elements of the prevention-of-crime privilege. Superior exam-writing requires that the pertinent facts be ***tied*** directly and clearly to the operative rule.

The Second Student Answer is very much better than the First Answer. It disposes of C's assault and battery upon A in a few words (yet tells the grader that the writer knows these torts are present). More importantly, the grader can easily see the issues which would arise if the prevention-of crime-privilege were asserted (i.e., "whether C's belief that A was about to commit a crime against B was reasonable" and "whether C used unnecessary force in punching A after A had been knocked to the ground"). Finally, it also utilizes all the facts by indicating how each attorney would assert those facts which are most advantageous to her client.

Structuring Your Answer

Graders will give high marks to a clearly-written, well-structured answer. Each issue you discuss should follow a specific and consistent structure which a grader can easily follow.

The Second Student Answer above basically utilizes the ***I-R-A-A-O format*** with respect to each issue. In this format, the ***I*** stands for the word ***Issue***, the ***R*** for ***Rule of law***, the initial ***A*** for the words ***one side's Argument***, the second ***A*** for ***the other party's rebuttal Argument***, and the **O** for your ***Opinion as to how the issue would be resolved.*** The ***I-R-A-A-O*** format emphasizes the importance of (1) discussing ***both*** sides of an issue, and (2) communicating to the grader that where an issue arises, an attorney can only advise her client as to the ***probable*** decision on that issue.

A somewhat different format for analyzing each issue is the ***I-R-A-C format.*** The ***"I"*** stands for ***"Issue;"*** the ***"R"*** for ***"Rule of law;"*** the ***"A"*** for ***"Application of the facts to the rule of law;"*** and the ***"C"*** for ***"Conclusion." I-R-A-C*** is a legitimate approach to the discussion of a particular issue, within the time constraints imposed by the question. The ***I-R-A-C format*** must be applied to each issue; it is not the solution to an entire exam answer. If there are six issues in a question, for example, you should offer six separate, independent ***I-R-A-C*** analyses.

We believe that the ***I-R-A-C*** approach is preferable to the ***I-R-A-A-O*** formula. However, either can be used to analyze and organize essay exam answers. Whatever format you choose, however, you should be consistent throughout the exam and remember the following rules:

First, ***analyze all of the relevant facts.*** Facts have significance in a particular case ***only as they come under the applicable rules of law***. The facts presented must be analyzed and examined to see if they do or do not satisfy one element or another of the applicable rules, and the essential facts and rules must be stated and argued in your analysis.

Second, you must communicate to the grader the ***precise rule of law*** controlling the facts. In their eagerness to commence their arguments, students sometimes fail to state the applicable rule of law first. Remember, the "***R***" in either format stands for "Rule of Law." Defining the rule of law ***before*** an analysis of the facts is essential in order to allow the grader to follow your reasoning.

Third, it is important to treat ***each side of an issue with equal detail.*** If a hypothetical describes how an elderly man was killed when he ventured upon the land of a huge power company to obtain a better view of a nuclear reactor, your sympathies might understandably fall on the side of the old man. The grader will nevertheless expect you to see and make every possible argument for the other side. Don't permit your personal viewpoint to affect your answer! A good lawyer never does! When discussing an issue, always state the arguments for each side.

Finally, don't forget to ***state your opinion or conclusion*** on each issue. Keep in mind, however, that your opinion or conclusion is probably the ***least*** important part of an exam answer. Why? Because your professor knows that no attorney can tell her client exactly how a judge or jury will decide a particular issue. By definition, an issue is a legal dispute which can go either way. An attorney, therefore, can offer her client only her best opinion about the likelihood of victory or defeat on an issue. Since the decision on any issue lies with the judge or jury, no attorney can ever be absolutely certain of the resolution.

Discuss All Possible Issues

As we've noted, a student should draw ***some*** type of conclusion or opinion for each issue raised. Whatever your conclusion on a particular issue, it is essential to anticipate and discuss ***all of the issues*** which would arise if the question were actually tried in court.

Let's assume that a negligence hypothetical involves issues pertaining to duty, breach of duty, proximate causation and contributory negligence. If the defendant prevails on any one of these issues, he will avoid liability. Nevertheless, even if you feel strongly that the defendant owed no duty to the plaintiff, you ***must*** go on to discuss all of the other potential issues as well (breach of duty, proximate causation and contributory negligence). If you were to terminate your answer after a discussion of the duty problem only, you'd receive an inferior grade.

Why should you have to discuss every possible potential issue if you are relatively certain that the outcome of a particular issue would be dispositive of the entire case? Because at the commencement of litigation, neither party can be ***absolutely positive*** about which issues he will win at trial. We can state with confidence that every attorney with some degree of experience has won issues he thought he would lose, and has lost issues on which he thought victory was assured. Since one can never be absolutely certain how a factual issue will be resolved by the factfinder, a good attorney (and exam-writer) will consider ***all*** possible issues.

To understand the importance of discussing all of the potential issues, you should reflect on what you will do during the actual practice of law. If you represent the defendant, for example, it is your job to raise every possible defense. If there are five potential defenses, and your pleadings only rely on three of them (because you're sure you will win on all three), and the plaintiff is somehow successful on all three issues, your client may well sue you for malpractice. Your client's contention would be that you should be liable because if you had only raised the two additional issues, you might have prevailed on at least one of them, and therefore liability would have been avoided. It is an attorney's duty to raise ***all*** legitimate issues. A similar philosophy should be followed when taking essay exams.

What exactly do you say when you've resolved the initial issue in favor of the defendant, and discussion of any additional issues would seem to be moot? The answer is simple. You simply begin the discussion of the next potential issue with something like, "Assuming, however, the plaintiff prevailed on the foregoing issue, the next issue would be..." The grader will understand and appreciate what you have done.

The corollary to the importance of raising all potential issues is that you should avoid discussion of obvious non-issues. Raising non-issues is detrimental in three ways: first, you waste a lot of precious time; second, you usually receive absolutely no points for discussing a point which the grader deems extraneous; third, it suggests to the grader that you lack the ability to distinguish the significant from the irrelevant. The best guideline for avoiding the discussion of a non-issue is to ask yourself, "would I, as an attorney, feel comfortable about raising that particular issue or objection in front of a judge"?

Delineate the Transition From One Issue to the Next

It's a good idea to make it easy for the grader to see the issues which you've found. One way to accomplish this is to cover no more than one issue per paragraph. Another way is to underline each issue statement. Provided time permits, both techniques are recommended. The essay answers in this book contain numerous illustrations of these suggestions.

One frequent student error is to write a two-paragraph answer in which all of the arguments for one side are made in the initial paragraph, and all of the rebuttal arguments by the other side are made in the next paragraph. This is ***a bad idea***. It obliges the grader to reconstruct the exam answer in his mind several times to determine whether all possible issues have been discussed by both sides. It will also cause you to state the same rule of law more than once. A better-organized answer presents a given argument by one side and follows that immediately in the same paragraph with the other side's rebuttal to that argument.

Understanding the "Call" of a Question

The statements ***at the end of*** an essay question or of the fact pattern in a multiple-choice question is sometimes referred to as the "call" of the question. It usually asks you to do something specific like "discuss," "discuss the rights of the parties," "what are X's rights?" "advise X," "the best grounds on which to find the statute unconstitutional are:," "D can be convicted of:," "how should the estate be distributed," etc. The call of the question should be read carefully because it tells you exactly what you're expected to do. If a question asks, "what are X's rights against Y?" or "X is liable to Y for:..." you don't have to spend a lot time on Y's rights against Z. You will usually receive absolutely no credit for discussing facts that are not required by the question. On the other hand, if the call of an essay question is simply "discuss" or "discuss the rights of the parties" then ***all*** foreseeable issues must be covered by your answer.

Students are often led astray by an essay question's call. For example, if you are asked for "X's rights against Y" or to "advise X", you may think you may limit yourself to X's viewpoint with respect to the issues. This is ***not correct***! You cannot resolve one party's rights against another party without considering the issues which might arise (and the arguments which the other side would assert) if litigation occurred. In short, although the call of the question may appear to focus on one of the parties to the litigation, a superior answer will cover all the issues and arguments which that person might ***encounter*** (not just the arguments she would ***make***) in attempting to pursue her rights against the other side.

The Importance of Analyzing the Question Carefully Before Writing

The overriding ***time pressure*** of an essay exam is probably a major reason why many students fail to analyze a question carefully before writing. Five minutes into the allocated time for a particular question, you may notice that the person next to you is writing furiously. This thought then flashes through your mind, "Oh, my goodness, he's putting down more words on the paper than I am, and therefore he's bound to get a better grade." It can be stated ***unequivocally*** that there is no necessary correlation between the number of words on your exam paper and the grade you'll receive. Students who begin their answer after only five minutes of analysis have probably seen only the most obvious issues, and missed many, if not most, of the subtle ones. They are also likely to be less well organized.

Opinions differ as to how much time you should spend analyzing and outlining a question before you actually write the answer. We believe that you should spend at least 12-18 minutes analyzing, organizing, and outlining a one-hour question before writing your answer. This will usually provide sufficient time to analyze and organize the question thoroughly ***and*** enough time to write a relatively complete answer. Remember that each word of the question must be scrutinized to determine if it (i) suggests an issue under the operative rules of law, or (ii) can be used in making an argument for the resolution of an issue. Since you can't receive points for an issue you don't spot, it is usually wise to read a question ***twice*** before starting your outline.

When to Make an Assumption

The instructions on an exam may tell you to ***"assume"*** facts which are necessary to the answer. Even where these instructions are ***not*** specifically given, you may be obliged to make certain assumptions with respect to missing facts in order to write a thorough answer. Assumptions should be made when you, as the attorney for one of the parties described in the question, would be obliged to solicit additional information from your client. On the other hand, assumptions should ***never be used to change or alter the question.*** Don't ever write something like "if the facts in the question were ..., instead of ..., then ... would result." If you do this, you are wasting time on facts which are extraneous to the problem before you. Professors want you to deal with ***their*** fact patterns, not your own.

Students sometimes try to "write around" information they think is missing. They assume that their professor has failed to include every piece of data necessary for a thorough answer. This is generally ***wrong.*** The professor may have omitted some facts deliberately to see if the student ***can figure out what to do*** under the circumstances. In some instances, the professor may have omitted them inadvertently (even law professors are sometimes human).

The way to deal with the omission of essential information is to describe (i) what fact (or facts) are missing, and (ii) why that information is important. As an example, go back to the "movie shoot" hypothetical we discussed above. In that fact pattern, there was no mention of the relative strength of A and C. This fact could be extremely important. If C weighed 240 pounds and was built like a professional football linebacker, while A tipped the scales at a mere 160 pounds, punching A in the face after he had been pushed to the ground would probably constitute unnecessary force (thereby causing C to forfeit the prevention-of-crime privilege). If the physiques of the parties were reversed, however, C's punch to A's face would probably constitute reasonable behavior. Under the facts, C had to deal the ***"knockout"*** blow while the opportunity presented itself. The last sentences of the Second Student Answer above show that the student understood these subtleties and correctly stated the essential missing facts and assumptions.

Assumptions should be made in a manner which keeps the other issues open (i.e., necessitates discussion of all other possible issues). Don't assume facts which would virtually dispose of the entire hypothetical in a few sentences. For example, suppose that A called B a "convicted felon" (a statement which is inherently defamatory, *i.e.*, a defamatory statement is one which tends to subject the plaintiff to hatred, contempt or ridicule). If A's statement is true, he has a complete defense to B's action for defamation. If the facts don't tell whether A's statement was true or not, it would ***not*** be wise to write something like, "We'll assume that A's statement about B is accurate, and therefore B cannot successfully sue A for defamation." So facile an approach would rarely be appreciated by the grader. The proper way to handle this situation would be to state, "if we assume that A's statement about B is not correct, A can not raise the defense of truth." You've communicated to the grader that you recognize the need to assume an essential fact and that you've assumed it in such a way as to enable you to proceed to discuss all other potential issues.

Case Names

A law student is ordinarily ***not*** expected to recall case names on an exam. The professor knows that you have read several hundred cases for each course, and that you would have to be a memory expert to have all of the names at your fingertips. If you confront a fact pattern which seems similar to a case which you have reviewed (but you cannot recall the name of it), just write something like, "One case held that …" or "It has been held that …" In this manner, you have informed the grader that you are relying on a case which contained a fact pattern similar to the question at issue.

The only exception to this rule is in the case of a landmark decision. Landmark opinions are usually those which change or alter established law.[2] These cases are usually easy to identify, because you will probably have spent an entire class period discussing each of them. *Palsgraf v. Long Island Rail Road* is a prime example of a landmark case in Torts. In these special cases, you may be expected to remember the case by name, as well the proposition of law which it stands for. However, this represents a very limited exception to the general rule which counsels against wasting precious time trying to memorize case names.

---

2. The only subject to which this does not apply is Constitutional Law, since here virtually every case you study satisfies this definition. Students studying Constitutional Law should try to associate case names with holdings and reproduce them in their exam answers.

How To Handle Time Pressures

What do you do when there are five minutes left in the exam and you have only written down two-thirds of your answer? One thing ***not*** to do is write something like, "No time left!" or "Not enough time!" This gets you nothing but the satisfaction of knowing you have communicated your personal frustrations to the grader. Another thing ***not*** to do is insert the outline you may have made on scrap paper into the exam booklet. Professors rarely will look at these items.

First of all, it is not necessarily a bad thing to be pressed for time. The person who finishes five minutes early has very possibly missed some important issues. The more proficient you become in knowing what is expected of you on an exam, the greater the difficulty you may experience in staying within the time limits. Second, remember that (at least to some extent) you're graded against your classmates' answers and they're under exactly the same time pressure as you. In short, don't panic if you can't write the "perfect" answer in the allotted time. Nobody does!

The best hedge against misuse of time is to ***review as many old exams as possible***. These exercises will give you a familiarity with the process of organizing and writing an exam answer, which, in turn, should result in an enhanced ability to stay within the time boundaries. If you nevertheless find that you have about 15 minutes of writing to do and five minutes to do it in, write a paragraph which summarizes the remaining issues or arguments you would discuss if time permitted. As long as you've indicated that you're aware of the remaining legal issues, you'll probably receive some credit for them. Your analytical and argumentative skills will already be apparent to the grader by virtue of the issues that you have previously discussed.

Write Legibly

Make sure your answer is legible. Students should ***not*** assume that their professors will be willing to take their papers to the local pharmacist to have them deciphered. Remember, your professor may have 75-150 separate exam answers to grade. If your answer is difficult to read, you will rarely be given the benefit of the doubt. On the other hand, a legible, well-organized paper creates a very positive mental impact upon the grader.

Many schools allow students to type their exams. If you're an adequate typist, you may want to seriously consider typing. Typing has two major advantages. First, it should help assure that your words will be readable (unless, of course, there are numerous typos). Second, it should enable you to put a lot more words onto the paper than if your answer had been handwritten. Most professors prefer a typed answer to a written one.

There are, however, a few disadvantages to typing. For one thing, all the typists are usually in a single room. If the clatter of other typewriters will make it difficult for you to concentrate, typing is probably ***not*** wise. To offset this problem, some students wear earplugs during the exam. Secondly, typing sometimes makes it difficult to change or add to an earlier portion of your answer. You may have to withdraw your paper from the carriage and insert another. Try typing out a few practice exams before you decide to type your exam. If you do type, be sure to leave at least one blank line between typewritten lines, so that handwritten changes and insertions in your answers can be made easily.

If you decide against typing, your answer will probably be written in a "bluebook" (a booklet of plain, lined, white paper which has a light blue cover and back). It is usually a good idea to write only on the odd numbered pages (i.e., 1, 3, 5, etc.). You may also want to leave a blank line between each written line. Doing these things will usually make the answer easier to read. If you discover that you have left out a word or phrase, you can insert it into the proper place by means of a caret sign ("^"). If you feel that you've omitted an entire issue, you can write it on the facing blank page. A symbol reference can be used to indicate where the additional portion of the answer should be inserted. While it's not ideal to have your answer take on the appearance of a road map, a symbol reference to an adjoining page is much better than trying to squeeze six lines into one, and will help the grader to discover where the same symbol appears in another part of your answer.

The Importance of Reviewing Prior Exams

As we've mentioned, it is ***extremely important to review old exams.*** The transition from blackletter law to essay exam can be a difficult experience if the process has not been practiced. Although this book provides a large number of essay and multiple-choice questions, ***don't stop here***! Most law schools have recent tests on file in the library, by course. We strongly suggest that you make a copy of every old exam you can obtain (especially those given by your professors) at the beginning of each semester. The demand for these documents usually increases dramatically as "finals time" draws closer.

The exams for each course should be scrutinized ***throughout the semester***. They should be reviewed as you complete each chapter in your casebook. Generally, the order of exam questions follows the sequence of the materials in your casebook. Thus, the first question on a law school test may involve the initial three chapters of the casebook; the second question may pertain to the fourth and fifth chapters, etc. In any event, ***don't wait*** until the semester is nearly over to begin reviewing old exams.

Keep in mind that no one is born with the ability to analyze questions and write superior answers to law school exams. Like any skill, it is developed and perfected only through application. If you don't take the time to analyze numerous examinations from prior years, this evolutionary process just won't occur. Don't just ***think about*** the answers to past exam questions; take the time to ***write the answers down***. It's also wise to look back at an answer a day or two after you've written it. You will invariably see (i) ways in which the organization could have been improved, and (ii) arguments you missed.

As you practice spotting issues on past exams, you will see how rules of law become the sources of issues on finals. As we've already noted, if you don't ***understand*** how rules of law translate into issues, you won't be able to achieve superior grades on your exams. Reviewing exams from prior years should also reveal that certain issues tend to be lumped together in the same question. For instance, where a fact pattern involves a false statement made by one person about another, three potential theories of liability are often present — defamation, invasion of privacy (false, public light) and intentional infliction of severe emotional distress. You will need to see if any or all of these apply to the facts.

Finally, one of the best means of evaluating if you understand a course (or a particular area within a subject) is to attempt to create a hypothetical exam for that topic. Your exam should contain as many issues as possible. If you can write an issue-packed exam, you probably know that particular area of law. If you can't, then you probably haven't yet acquired an adequate understanding of how the principles of law in that subject can spawn issues.

As Always, a Caveat

The suggestions and advice offered in this book represent the product of many years of experience in the field of legal education. We are confident that the techniques and concepts described in these pages will help you prepare for, and succeed, at your exams. Nevertheless, particular professors sometimes have a preference for exam-writing techniques which are not stressed in this work. Some instructors expect at least a nominal reference to the ***prima facie*** elements of all pertinent legal theories (even though one or more of those principles is ***not*** placed into issue). Other professors want their students to emphasize public policy considerations in the arguments they make on a particular issue. Because this book is intended for nationwide consumption, these individualized preferences have ***not*** been stressed. The best way to find out whether your professor has a penchant for a particular writing approach is to ask her to provide you with a model answer to a previous exam. If an item is not available, speak to upperclass students who received a superior grade in that professor's class.

One final point. While the rules of law stated in the answers to the questions in this book have been drawn from commonly used sources (i.e., casebooks, hornbooks, etc.), it is still conceivable that they may be slightly at odds with those taught by your professor. In instances where a conflict exists between our formulation of a legal principle and the one which is taught by your professor, ***follow the latter!*** Since your grades are determined by your professors, their views should always supersede the views contained in this book.

Essay Exam Questions

Question 1

Space Corporation (Space), an aerospace manufacturer, had 100,000 shares of authorized common stock, of which 85,000 shares were issued and outstanding and 15,000 shares were unissued. In need of immediate cash, Space validly issued and sold the remaining 15,000 shares to Banco Corporation (Banco) at $14 per share. The next day Adams, Treasurer of Banco, was duly elected to fill a vacancy on the Space board of directors as Banco's "representative." At the first Space board meeting after his election as a director, Adams learned of a recent confidential study which showed that if Space did not receive governmental financial assistance, it would become insolvent. Adams immediately informed Banco's directors of the study.

One month later, Senator Jones, a U.S. Senator and a good friend of Mary Conn, Space's main lobbyist, told Conn that in two weeks' time the President would probably announce his support for the proposed Aerospace Act, then pending in the Senate, which would provide government-guaranteed loans to aerospace industry firms. That same day, Conn purchased 2,000 shares of Space stock on the New York Stock Exchange at $15 per share. The next day, through an agent who did not disclose that Conn was her principal, Conn purchased Banco's 15,000 shares of Space stock at the market value of $15 per share. In light of the earlier confidential study showing the need for financing, Banco was eager to unload its Space stock.

Two weeks after Jones's conversation with Conn, to the surprise of the general public, the President announced his support of the Act. Space stock immediately climbed to $25 per share.

Discuss the rights of Space and Banco.

Question 2

Aco, Inc. (Aco) and Target, Inc. (Tco) are corporations. All sales and purchases described below were conducted through a national stock exchange.

On December 1 of ***last*** year, Aco bought 120,000 Tco shares for $5 per share, thereby becoming a 12% Tco shareholder. Aco had never previously owned any Tco stock. Aco immediately notified Tco's chief executive officer, Dan, that it had made the purchase and that it was considering a tender offer for the rest of Tco's stock at $9 per share.

On December 2, Dan's personal lawyer, Leslie, warned Dan not to buy Tco stock until Aco's stock purchase and acquisition plans became public. That same day, Dan told his son, Sam, about the proposed acquisition. On December 3, Leslie and Sam each bought 10,000 Tco shares for $5 per share.

On December 4, Aco filed the appropriate disclosure documents with the Securities and Exchange Commission (SEC), and Aco and Tco separately issued press releases about the stock purchase and proposed acquisition.

On December 5, Leslie and Sam each sold their 10,000 Tco shares for $8.50 per share. Aco sold its Tco shares for $9 per share on February 15 of ***this*** year.

Dan has neither sold nor purchased any Tco stock since he learned of the acquisition plan.

1. Discuss Aco's liabilities, if any, under SEC Rule 16(b).
2. Discuss Dan's liabilities, if any, under SEC Rule 10b-5.
3. Discuss Sam's liabilities, if any, under SEC Rule 10b-5.
4. Discuss Leslie's liabilities, if any, under SEC Rule 10b-5.

Question 3

Paul owns 250 of the 1,000 issued and authorized shares of Durco, a State X close corporation. The Durco directors are Al, who owns 650 shares of Durco stock, and Baker and Carr, each of whom owns 50 shares. Al offered to buy Paul's Durco shares at a price substantially less than Paul had paid to acquire the stock. Paul refused Al's offer, claiming the offered price was "unfair."

Paul has brought an action in State X court against Durco and its three directors. His complaint alleges:

(A) The directors acted unreasonably in failing to have Durco distribute as cash dividends, approximately $5 million of accumulated earnings;

(B) The distribution is being arbitrarily withheld for the benefit of Al;

(C) There is an "invalid" agreement between the individual defendants as Durco shareholders, the purpose of which is to maintain Al in office as "managing director" to "supervise and direct the operations and management" of all of Durco's business;

(D) Paul has been consistently denied the right to inspect Durco's corporate records during regular working hours or at any other time.

By way of relief, the complaint asks that: (1) Al be removed as a director for misconduct, (2) the shareholders' agreement be found invalid, (3) the directors declare and pay a substantial cash dividend and (4) Paul be permitted to inspect Durco's records during normal business hours.

In their answer, the defendants allege that Paul's action should be considered a derivative action, and admit: (1) the existence and terms of the shareholders' agreement, (2) withholding of accumulated earnings of approximately $5 million, and (3) denial of access by Paul to Durco's records. They allege by way of affirmative defense that: (1) the discretion of the directors to declare dividends has been properly exercised (the business judgment rule); (2) the shareholders' agreement is valid and therefore Al cannot be removed as director, even for cause; and (3) the requested inspection should be denied because Paul only wants to inspect the corporate records for the "improper purpose" of bringing a "strike suit."

The defendants have moved for an order requiring Paul to post security for costs in the pending action.

State X law grants an unqualified right to shareholders of State X corporations to inspect corporate books and records, and requires plaintiffs in shareholder derivative actions to provide security for costs.

1. Discuss how the court should rule on the defendants' motion for security for costs.
2. Discuss how the court should rule on each of Paul's requests for relief.

Question 4

The bylaws of Dixie, a publicly held corporation, provide, "The number of directors of the corporation is to be five." Insofar as pertinent, Dixie's Articles of Incorporation state that the number "constituting the initial board of directors" is five and provides for annual election of directors.

Since its incorporation five years ago, Dixie has been very profitable. Anticipating a hostile takeover attempt, the board voted to increase its size to nine and to stagger the terms of directors so that only three would stand for election each year.

Stan, owner of 29% of Dixie's voting stock, demanded that the board call a special meeting of shareholders, to disapprove the board's action and to remove the president from office. The board refused to call a meeting for those purposes. It filled the newly created board positions with persons who were experienced in business and were close friends of the original board members. The new board entered into transactions that resulted in financial loss to Dixie, but which made the corporation a less attractive target for takeover.

When Stan filed a derivative suit against Dixie and the directors challenging the board's conduct, the board appointed the new members as a "special litigation committee." Thereafter, the board moved to dismiss the suit because "based upon the recommendation of the special litigation committee, the board has concluded the suit is not in the best interests of Dixie."

1. Discuss whether the board acted lawfully:
   a. In increasing its size to nine members without a shareholder vote.
   b. In staggering the terms of board members without a shareholder vote.
   c. In refusing to call a special meeting of shareholders.
   d. In filling the newly created board positions without a shareholder vote.
2. Discuss whether the court should grant the board's motion to dismiss.

Do ***not*** discuss federal securities law issues.

Question 5

Corp., Inc. (Corp), has 200,000 authorized and outstanding shares of $1 par value stock. Andy, Barb, Carla and Dave each purchased at par, and each continues to hold, 50,000 shares of Corp. Corp's Articles of Incorporation prohibit incurring any single debt in excess of $75,000 and require a vote representing 80% of outstanding shares to amend the Articles. The Articles also provide for preemptive rights, cumulative voting, and a board of four directors. Each of the four shareholders has elected himself director at annual shareholders' meetings during each year of Corp's existence.

Corp's board unanimously decided to borrow $100,000 from Lender. Lender took Corp's ten-year note, bearing interest at 20% per annum, payable in monthly interest installments. Corp has the option to pay off the note at any time, without penalty. Later, Lender needed funds and approached Andy, Corp's treasurer. Lender offered to sell the note for $90,000. Andy, without consulting with Barb, Carla, or Dave, purchased the note for his own account.

The week following Andy's purchase of the note, Rich asked to subscribe to 100,000 shares of Corp stock at $1 per share. Barb, Carla and Dave approved of Rich's proposal. But, at the annual shareholders' meeting, Andy voted against, and thus defeated, a proposed amendment of the Articles of Incorporation which would have authorized additional shares free from preemptive rights. Because of the note's high interest, Andy did not want it paid off. The other directors, now aware that Andy had acquired the note, and hoping to use Rich's investment to pay the note, were angered and caused Corp to cease paying the monthly interest installments on the note.

Rich then caused the incorporation of Endrun, Inc. ("Endrun"), and subscribed to 100,000 of its shares for $100,000. Rich proposes that Corp be merged into Endrun, that each Corp share be converted into an Endrun share, and that Endrun pay the Lender note now held by Andy. Corp's board has approved the merger three to one, Andy dissenting.

Assume that the interest rate on the note is ***not*** usurious.

1. Discuss whether Andy breached any duty to Corp or fellow shareholders in voting against the proposal to issue 100,000 shares to Rich.
2. Discuss whether Andy can obtain an injunction to prevent the Corp-Endrun merger.
3. Discuss whether Andy can collect interest payments on Corp's note.

Question 6

Starco, stockbrokers, in attempting to market 1,000,000 common shares to be issued by Durmac, offered 500,000 shares to the Ennis Corp. at $50 per share. Already the owner of a substantial interest in Durmac, Ennis' financial condition was such as to make a large, immediate acquisition of additional shares of Durmac desirable.

Ennis' bylaws provided that a quorum consist of five out of its seven directors. After due notice to the four resident directors, but without notice to the three nonresident directors, a special emergency board of directors meeting was held. Resident directors Almon, Barnes, and Chester, armed with a proxy executed by director Grabe, the fourth resident director, attended the meeting. Also present was Webster, a nonresident director. The directors present voted unanimously (including the Grabe proxy) to purchase 400,000 additional Durmac shares. At the end of the meeting, Webster signed a waiver of notice.

Immediately following the meeting, Ennis purchased and paid for 400,000 shares of Durmac stock at $50 per share.

At their next regular meeting, attended by all the directors, the board voted unanimously to ratify the action taken at the special emergency meeting.

Before the actual offering of Durmac shares to Ennis, Starco had offered, for one day only, a few thousand shares of the new Durmac shares at $42 each, cash, to a few select persons. Among the offerees was director Almon, who purchased a total of 2,000 shares for her own account. Almon subsequently disposed of these shares at a substantial profit. By the time Ennis shareholders became aware of all these facts, the market price of Durmac shares had declined sharply.

1. Discuss whether the acquisition of Durmac shares by Ennis was a proper corporate action.
2. Discuss whether any of the Ennis directors are liable to their corporation for the decline in value of Durmac shares.
3. Discuss Almon's liability, if any, to Ennis for profits she made on her purchase and sale of Durmac shares.

Do ***not*** discuss federal statutory securities issues.

Question 7

Art has been president of Exco, a publicly held corporation with net assets of approximately $50 million, for the past six years. Exco manufactures computers. Two years ago, Art negotiated an agreement for the purchase by Exco of all of the outstanding shares of Yang, Inc. ("Yang"), a privately held maker of computer components, for $5 million cash. The purchase was completed about eighteen months ago. At the time, members of Art's immediate family held Yang's outstanding shares. This information was ***not*** known except to Art, Yang's management, and Bobbie, an Exco director.

Art negotiated Exco's purchase of Yang stock and executed the purchase agreement on behalf of Exco, relying on his authority as its president. Before the purchase documents were signed, Art discussed the proposed acquisition individually with Bobbie, Curt and Donna. Curt and Donna are Exco directors who, with Art and Bobbie, comprise a majority of Exco's seven-person board of directors. Bobbie, Curt and Donna each told Art that he or she approved of the transaction.

After Exco purchased the Yang stock, at the next regular meeting of the Exco board one month later, Art informed all of the directors of the acquisition. While some questions were asked, there was no vote taken on the acquisition at the meeting. Not counting Bobbie, no Exco director was informed of the ownership of Yang stock by Art's family members. Since Bobbie believed the acquisition was beneficial to Exco, she never mentioned her knowledge of the prior ownership of Yang stock by members of Art's family to any of the other Exco directors. The existence of the prior ownership could, however, have been discovered by a review of Yang's corporate records.

Since the stock purchase by Exco, Yang has been consistently and increasingly unprofitable. At the annual Exco shareholders' meeting two months ago, Art, Bobbie, Curt and Donna were ***not*** re-elected as directors. Last month, Exco's new board replaced Art as president.

1. Discuss whether Exco can rescind the purchase of Yang stock.
2. Discuss whether Exco can recover damages for Yang's unprofitability from any or all of the following:
    a. Art.
    b. Bobbie.
    c. Curt and Donna.

Question 8

Al, Bob, Carla and Dan own 20% each of the outstanding shares of the common stock of Etco, a profitable corporate retailer, and they are the corporation's four directors. Al and Bob are Etco's officers. The remaining 20% of the outstanding shares are divided among ten individuals, including Freda, who is a 5% shareholder. Etco has only one class of stock.

At a board meeting six months ago, Al announced that he had negotiated a contract to have all of Etco's stores cleaned nightly by XYZ, a partnership jointly owned by Al and Bob. Al disclosed XYZ's ownership at this Etco board meeting, but neither he nor Bob disclosed that the price for cleaning services to be charged Etco by XYZ under the contract was double the market rate. The board approved the contract with XYZ by unanimous vote of all four directors. XYZ immediately began its cleaning services and has been receiving payments under the contract with Etco.

At the same meeting, the Etco board unanimously voted in favor of Carla's proposal to have Etco redeem most of her shares at $25 per share, to provide funds to Carla for a sudden family emergency. At the time, Etco did not have retained earnings equal to the cost of redeeming Carla's stock, but Etco's earnings in the preceding fiscal year, which erased a prior earnings deficit, did exceed the cost of redeeming Carla's stock. Etco's Articles of Incorporation have no provisions regarding redemption of its stock.

1. Having recently found out about the XYZ contract, Freda has brought a shareholder derivative action against all four directors seeking a judgment rescinding the XYZ contract and for damages to Etco arising from the approval of the contract by the directors. Discuss what the result should be.
2. On her own behalf, Freda has sued Etco and its four directors for a judgment rescinding the redemption of Carla's stock or, in the alternative, to require redemption by Etco of Freda's stock at $25 per share, or for involuntary dissolution of Etco. Discuss what relief, if any, Freda is entitled to in the suit.

Question 9

Four years ago, Paula bought 10,000 shares of the common stock of Deco Corporation ("Deco"). Two years ago, Deco purchased four retail stores from Savco for $4 million, which was a fair price. Tom, president and a director of Deco, was also a director of Savco. He was absent from the meeting of the Deco board of directors at which the agreement for purchase of the Savco stores was considered. In Tom's absence, the proposed purchase was unanimously approved by the remaining four Deco directors, who constituted a quorum of the board.

About twenty months ago, the Deco directors resolved to issue 25,000 shares of authorized, but unissued, Deco common stock to Smith, in exchange for Greenacre, a store site owned by Smith. The directors did not offer any of the 25,000 shares for acquisition by Deco shareholders before consummating the deal with Smith.

At a special meeting of the Deco board three months ago, Tom advised the board that an audit had established that Deco had incurred a $25 million loss during the preceding fiscal year and that the loss would be publicly announced at the annual Deco shareholders' meeting in two weeks. Tom then tendered his resignation both as president and a director of Deco, effective immediately, which the board accepted.

Within the two-week period before the stockholders' meeting, Tom sold his 20,000 shares of Deco common stock for $25 per share. After the annual shareholders' meeting, Deco common stock dropped to $10 per share.

Paula died three weeks after the shareholders' meeting. Her daughter, Emma, inherited all of Paula's shares of Deco stock. Emma made three demands on the Deco board of directors, stating that if each of the demands was not met, she, as a shareholder, would bring appropriate legal action. The demands are:

a. That the purchase of the four stores from Savco be set aside.

b. That she be permitted to purchase a number of Deco shares in the same proportion as Paula's 10,000 shares bore to all Deco shares issued and outstanding at the time the shares were transferred to Smith.

c. That Deco bring suit against Tom to recover $300,000, based on the sale of his Deco stock in the two weeks before the annual shareholders' meeting.

Discuss how the Deco directors should respond to each of the demands by Emma.

Question 10

Three years ago, A and B decided to establish Z Corp to manufacture and sell electronic devices. They signed Articles of Incorporation and established themselves as a two-person board of directors. Each paid $10,000 in cash for 100 shares of the $100 par value common stock of the corporation. However, A and B inadvertently failed to file the Articles.

Two and a half years ago, A and B met C, a business consultant who advised them on Z Corp's business matters. One month later, C filed Z Corp's Articles of Incorporation with the Secretary of State. Immediately thereafter, C was issued 100 shares of Z Corp common stock: 10 shares in return for services rendered, 40 shares in return for services to be rendered in the future, and 50 shares in return for his personal note to the Z Corp for $5,000. C became the third member of the board of directors and was elected treasurer.

One month after filing the Articles, C discharged his $5,000 note obligation by transferring office equipment to Z Corp appraised at $6,500 by an independent appraiser. C had purchased this equipment at an auction three months earlier for $1,000.

Two years ago, Z Corp received $10,000 in cash from each of two investors, D, a local banker, and E. Each investor was issued 100 shares of common stock.

About six months ago, it became obvious that Z Corp was experiencing financial difficulty. C heard of a developmental opportunity in a field directly related to Z Corp's operations, but he did ***not*** advise the other directors because Z Corp lacked sufficient assets to exploit the opportunity. Instead, C, D and several friends formed a partnership which invested in, and made considerable profit on, the new business opportunity.

Recently, Z Corp's assets became insufficient to discharge its liabilities. Its creditors, many with claims dating back to three years ago, commenced an action against Z Corp and all five shareholders. E has cross-complained against the other four shareholders.

1. Discuss the liabilities, if any, of A, B, C, D and E to Z Corp's creditors.
2. Discuss the liabilities, if any, of A, B, C and D to E.

Question 11

Four years ago, Ida bought 50,000 shares of Martco. Three years ago, Martco contracted with Buildco for the construction of four new stores for $4 million. At the Martco board meeting at which the Buildco contract was considered, Chare, Martco's chair, revealed that she had been a director of Buildco for eight years, but said she had not participated as a member of the Buildco board in approving this particular contract. Chare, believing it to be a fair contract, joined the other four Martco directors in voting to approve the contract. In fact, however, subsequent investigation revealed that the price charged by Buildco was excessive and unfair to Martco.

Two years ago, Ida died, leaving her stock to her son Sol. Growing steadily more unhappy about Chare's leadership, two months ago Sol asked Chare for Martco's shareholder list to solicit proxies to unseat Chare at the annual stockholders' meeting. Chare, fearing that Sol would be successful, refused, and Sol was unable to gain a seat on the board. Later Sol learned that Waters, another shareholder, would have given Sol his proxy. Between the two, they owned sufficient shares to elect one director under Martco's cumulative voting rule.

At the annual stockholders' meeting three weeks ago, Chare announced that Martco had suffered a $10 million loss during the last fiscal year and that this information would be published within 10 days in Martco's annual report. She then tendered her resignation, which was accepted effective immediately.

Five days later, Chare sold 100,000 shares of Martco stock, her entire holdings, for $25 per share, the current market price. After the published announcement, Martco stock dropped to $10 per share. Sol recently asked the remaining directors to bring suit against Chare, but they refused.

Assume ***no*** federal securities laws are applicable.

1. Discuss Chare's personal liability, if any, to Sol.
2. Assuming Sol brings a derivative action against Chare, discuss the probable success of such a suit under the foregoing facts.

Question 12

Ajax Mfg. Corp. issued 250,000 shares of $50 par value common stock. 10,000 of the shares were reacquired and are currently held as treasury stock. After a board meeting in which a number of specific, possible Ajax plant expansion sites were discussed, Babb, one of Ajax's nine directors, paid $3,000 to obtain an option to purchase one of those sites, at a purchase price of $120,000. Ajax had allocated $250,000 for site acquisition. When the other directors learned that Babb had acquired the option, they demanded that she assign it to the corporation for the option price of $3,000.

At a subsequent board meeting, the directors voted to purchase Whiteacre for $50,000 from Carl, a director, who had acquired it for $10,000 before becoming a director.

The board also voted to sell the 10,000 treasury shares for $71 per share to Dale, who had been offered employment by Ajax as Vice President-Finance. Dale had insisted on becoming a shareholder as a condition to accepting the offered employment, and agreed to the price of the stock. Earl, an Ajax shareholder seeks to enjoin this sale, claiming that it violates his preemptive rights.

At the same meeting, the board approved the sale of Greenacre for $50,000. It had been purchased by Ajax five years ago for $70,000.

Fox, Vice President-Operations for Ajax, heard that Gert, an Ajax shareholder, was annoyed with management and was offering to sell her shares for $65 per share. The latest financial report for Ajax, distributed to all shareholders, indicated that Ajax stock had a book value of $70.50. Fox purchased Gert's shares at her price.

Discuss the following:

(a) the demand that Babb assign her option to purchase the expansion site to Ajax;

(b) the propriety of Ajax's purchase of Whiteacre from Carl for $50,000;

(c) Earl's right to enjoin the sale of 10,000 shares of treasury stock to Dale;

(d) the propriety of the sale of Greenacre for $50,000;

(e) Fox's liability, if any, by reason of his purchase of Gert's shares.

Question 13

The following actions were taken pursuant to unanimous vote of the directors of Ajax, a corporation:

1. To prevent a minority shareholder from acquiring control, Ajax purchased shares from three shareholders at their asking price of $80 per share. At the time, Ajax's shares had a book value of $92 and a market value of $75 per share.

2. After it was announced that Bob, the long-time treasurer for Ajax was retiring, Ajax agreed to pay Bob $5,000 annually during his lifetime.

3. Ajax agreed to pay the legal fees and costs of Curt, a vice-president, who was being sued in a shareholders' derivative action for making political contributions from corporate funds to candidates designated by other corporations with whom Ajax did business.

4. Ajax adopted a stock option plan for all officers and directors, and issued the first set of options.

Pat owns 100 Ajax shares which she acquired before the above events took place. She purchased 50 additional shares two months ago, but has been unable to have the shares transferred to her name because, according to the corporate secretary, the shares are subject to a restrictive shareholders' agreement preventing the transfer. No such restriction appears on the Ajax certificates, including those in Pat's name representing her earlier shareholdings.

Pat feels that all the above-described actions by Ajax and its directors have violated her rights as a shareholder and damaged her. She also wants to know if she is entitled to have the additional 50 shares of Ajax stock registered in her name.

(1) Discuss whether Pat has any claim for relief with respect to each of the above-described actions taken by Ajax.

(2) Discuss whether Pat has a right to have the 50 shares of Ajax stock registered in her name.

Question 14

Freightco is a State X corporation conducting a trucking business. On June 30 of last year, its board of directors voted to declare a cash dividend of $500,000 from earned surplus, and to borrow $1 million to finance an advertising campaign by issuing debentures to be purchased at face value by Landco, a State X corporation conducting a real estate business. Freightco owns 80% of the outstanding stock of Landco. Freightco's directors are also the directors of Landco.

An hour after the Freightco board meeting, the Landco board of directors met and voted not to declare any dividend, despite a staff recommendation that a dividend of $1 million be declared. Landco had a sufficient surplus from which such a dividend could be paid. At the same time, the Landco board voted to purchase the Freightco debentures at face value, even though previously issued Freightco debentures with the same terms were selling on the open market at 84% of face value. Both the Articles and bylaws of Landco expressly provide that the votes of "interested" directors may count toward a quorum and that "interested" directors may vote on contracts.

Six months after its dividend distribution, Freightco was adjudicated bankrupt. An investigation of Freightco's business affairs disclosed that: (1) a report by a specially hired management consulting firm, presented to each director of Freightco before the June 30 board meeting, predicted bankruptcy unless all available capital was allocated to the purchase of new trucks, and (2) only five of the fifteen Freightco directors actually read the report.

Agee owns 5% of the outstanding shares of Landco and also owns Freightco shares. Discuss each claim that Agee may assert either on his own behalf or on behalf of Freightco and Landco, and discuss the capacity in which he should assert each claim.

Question 15

Dynamics, Inc., was incorporated two years ago, with an initial authorized capitalization of 10,000 shares of $100 par value common stock. Ames subscribed to 100 shares prior to incorporation; later, still before Dynamics was incorporated, Ames threatened to withdraw her stock subscription unless she was issued an additional twenty shares at $50 a share. Because Ames' subscription was needed for initial operating capital, the promoters for Dynamics agreed to issue the bonus shares to her, and following incorporation, Ames paid $11,000 to Dynamics for which 120 shares marked "Fully Paid" were issued.

Soon after Dynamics was incorporated, Bates was issued 1,000 shares of stock for transferring to Dynamics his title to Blackacre, which Bates had purchased a year earlier for $55,000.

After issuing a total of 7,500 shares, including those issued to Ames and Bates, Dynamics could find no other purchasers for its stock.

Last year, its first fiscal year of operations, Dynamics had a net operating loss of $50,000. However, at the end of the year, the board of directors determined that Blackacre was worth $160,000, and by resolution directed that its book value be increased to that amount. The board then declared a $2 cash dividend on the 7,500 shares then outstanding.

Last month, without first offering the stock to any other shareholder, Dynamics issued 500 shares of stock to Carl in return for Carl's transfer of title to Greenacre, which the corporation wants for a future plant site.

Paula, a shareholder, gave Fox, vice-president of Dynamics, an "irrevocable" proxy to vote Paula's shares. When Paula later sought to revoke the proxy, Fox told her the proxy could not be revoked during Paula's lifetime, or so long as Paula owned the Dynamics stock.

1. Discuss whether Ames and Bates are liable to Dynamics for any additional money in connection with the issuance of shares to them.
2. Discuss whether the declaration of the $2 cash dividend was proper.
3. Discuss whether the transaction with Carl was valid.
4. Discuss whether Paula has the right to vote her Dynamics stock.

Question 16

A, B and C agreed to promote the formation of Z Corporation to engage in the manufacture of electronic equipment. A, without the knowledge of B and C, entered into a written agreement with X, whereby the Z Corporation would, upon its formation, hire X as Manager of Research at a salary of $20,000 per year for five years.

A, B and C executed Articles of Incorporation and their attorney forwarded these Articles to the Department of State. However, the attorney failed to include the required filing fee, and for that reason the Department of State refused to file the Articles. The Department of State sent notice of this failure to the attorney, but he had gone on vacation. This information was not brought to the attention of A, B, or C. A, B and C elected themselves as the first directors of Z Corporation, issued stock, and elected C as its President.

B, in possession of certain equipment reasonably worth $50,000, conveyed it to Z Corporation for $100,000 worth of common stock, at par value. C contracted with Q to supply the corporation with materials valued under the contract at $20,000, signing the contract, "Z Corporation, by C, President." These materials were shipped and received by Z Corporation.

Due to a number of difficulties, Z Corporation's business never got a proper start. B and C then refused to hire X. The business is now insolvent and has filed for bankruptcy. Q has not been paid for his materials.

Discuss the rights and liabilities of the various parties.

Question 17

Banco is a banking corporation with 50,000 shareholders. Its board of directors voted unanimously to organize "Combank," a corporation, to own and operate a bank in a low-income area. The resolution provided, among other things, that:

(1) Combank would have two classes of stock, Class A and Class B, the shares of each having a par value of $10, with equal rights in all respects, except that Class B stock would be nonvoting;

(2) Banco would purchase the entire issue of Class B stock of 100,000 shares for $1 million cash;

(3) The 100,000 shares of Class A stock would be issued only to persons becoming depositors, at $10 per share;

(4) For ten years, Banco would return its Class B dividends to Combank as a contribution to capital.

Before Combank's incorporation, O, an officer of Banco, negotiated a contract with Duc, a building contractor, to remodel a downtown building as offices for Combank. Work was to begin immediately and be completed within nine months. When Duc insisted that Banco's name be on the contract, O signed it, "Banco, by O, on behalf of Combank, a corporation to be formed."

One week later, Combank was duly incorporated. Banco purchased the entire authorized 100,000 shares of Class B stock and executed an assignment to Combank of all dividends on the Class B stock for a period of ten years. Three months after the Duc contract, Combank's officers and employees moved into the partially remodeled building. No action was taken by the Combank board of directors with respect to the Duc contract.

One month later, Combank's board voted 5 to 4, with director X voting with the majority, to hire Exco, a construction firm owned by X, to complete the remodeling in place of Duc. Pursuant to this action, Combank entered into a contract with Exco. At that time, Duc had performed satisfactorily and was on schedule.

(1) Z, a Banco shareholder, brings a derivative action against the Banco directors for wasting corporate assets. Discuss whether the action will succeed.

(2) Discuss whether Duc's contract is enforceable by Duc and, if so, against whom.

(3) Discuss whether Exco can enforce its contract with Combank.

Question 18

Gasco is a State X corporation involved in the petroleum industry. Its stock is traded on the New York Stock Exchange. Its Board of directors hired Media, a public relations firm, to campaign against the passage of a State X ballot proposition to use gasoline tax receipts for the development of a statewide public transit system. The contract provided that Gasco's financing of the campaign should not be made public by Gasco or Media.

A group of Gasco shareholders, calling themselves Citizens Against Pollution (CAP), learned of the contract. They submitted to Gasco management, for inclusion in the next proxy statement and for presentation to the Gasco shareholders at the next shareholders' meeting, proposals to:

(1) remove from the Gasco board those directors "who voted to authorize the Media contract or otherwise sought to prevent passage of the gasoline tax proposition";

(2) hire an independent auditor to review Gasco's books; and

(3) require the use of nonpolluting cleansing products in all company-owned gas stations.

CAP has complied with all SEC procedural requirements.

A State X statute requires public disclosure of all corporate expenditures "designed to influence the outcome of issues to be decided by public ballot."

Pursuant to a valid Gasco bylaw, only three of the nine Gasco directors are to be elected at the next shareholders' meeting. The Gasco charter provides that the board of directors may, by majority vote, remove a director for "sufficient cause."

Discuss and decide the following:

(1) Is management required to present the CAP proposals to the shareholders and include them in the proxy statement?

(2) If adopted at the shareholders' meeting, would the proposals be binding on the board of directors?

(3) If a new Gasco board repudiates the Media contract, may Media nevertheless have it enforced?

Question 19

Jetco, a corporation whose stock is traded on a national stock exchange, has 200,000 shares of $25 par value common stock outstanding. It has a seven-person board of directors.

Dan, who owns 100 shares of Jetco stock, is a director of Jetco. Five months ago, Dan learned of a secret new invention developed by Jetco to convert organic waste to commercial fuel and that a public announcement of the invention was soon to be made.

Dan immediately wrote to three of Jetco's shareholders who, Dan knew, had previously announced their willingness to sell their shares for $22 per share, a price that was $3 a share above book value. Dan offered them $25 per share. They accepted his offer and sold a total of 4,200 shares to Dan. At this time, Dan also exercised his stock option rights to purchase 1,000 authorized, but previously unissued, shares from Jetco, for which he paid the option price of $21 per share.

Two months ago, Jetco's board chair, Wood, learned of the 4,200 shares that Dan had acquired from the three dissatisfied shareholders. When Dan refused Wood's demand that he resign as a director, the board, at its meeting two weeks later, declared Dan's board seat vacant, although his term of office would not expire for another six months.

A week later, the invention was announced and the market value of Jetco stock rose substantially.

A few days ago, Dan sold, for $50 per share, the 4,200 shares he had acquired from the three dissatisfied shareholders.

1. Discuss whether Dan has the right to remain on the board for the balance of his unexpired term.
2. Discuss Dan's potential liabilities, and to whom, as a result of the above transactions.

Question 20

Art, Bob and Carla were the three shareholders of Getco, a State X corporation, each owning one-third of the shares issued. They were also the three directors of the corporation. In a written "Shareholder Agreement" executed by all of them, they each granted a right of first refusal to the other two, equally, "should such shareholder seek to sell his or her shares to anyone other" than to Getco itself. This agreement also required a "90% majority vote for all shareholder or director action, including the election of directors," and required each shareholder to cast his or her vote for the election of the other shareholders as directors of Getco.

A State X statute provides as follows:

> "Unless otherwise provided in the certificate of incorporation, if the directors of a corporation are equally divided respecting the management of its affairs, or if the votes of its shareholders are so divided that they cannot elect a board of directors, the holders of at least one-half of the shares of stock may present a verified petition for the involuntary dissolution of the corporation, as provided in this Chapter."

Carla died. Under the terms of her will, her shares of stock in Getco were bequeathed to Doris, her niece. Although Art and Bob claimed they had the right to purchase Carla's shares at her death, the probate court ruled that it had no jurisdiction to decide stockholder claims. The decree of distribution in the probate of Carla's estate distributed her shares in Getco to Doris.

Art and Bob have refused to elect Doris to the Getco board of directors, asserting that they are Getco's only valid shareholders. They have also held over in office as directors for two years since Carla's death, as no shareholder is able to muster a 90% vote to elect new directors. The board of directors has taken no action during the same period, and no dividends have been declared since Carla's death.

Doris seeks your advice as to how she can gain shareholder benefits and a voice in Getco's management, or, in the alternative, have Getco dissolved and its assets distributed.

Discuss what advice you would give her.

Question 21

Gil entered into a written contract in State X with Tanya in which it was agreed that Tanya would be paid $5,000 per month as a jewelry salesperson for six months, commencing three weeks later. Gil signed the contract, "by Gil, on behalf of Jelco, a corporation to be formed."

A week later Gil, Art, and Bob met and orally agreed to pay $3,000 each for all of the authorized stock of Jelco, a jewelry sales corporation to be formed by Gil. But before anything further was done, Art and Bob wrote to Gil, stating "we hereby revoke any agreement to subscribe to Jelco stock." Gil wrote back to Art and Bob, stating that it was "impossible to rescind."

Gil prepared Articles of Incorporation for Jelco naming himself, Carla and Dan as the initial incorporators. However, Gil failed to set forth the purposes of the corporation in the Articles as required by State X law. Despite this omission, Jelco's Articles of Incorporation were filed.

Gil, Carla and Dan then held the initial incorporators' meeting for Jelco in accordance with State X law, at which they were duly elected as Jelco's directors. By unanimous vote, the three directors then accepted the stock subscriptions of Gil, Art, and Bob. Neither Art nor Bob attended the meeting. Share certificates were issued to Gil, Art, and Bob. Gil paid $3,000 for his shares. Art and Bob refused to pay for any stock or to participate in Jelco's business.

Tanya worked in Jelco's jewelry business for three months without knowledge of any of the events occurring after her execution of the contract with Gil. When Tanya inquired about her compensation, she discovered that Gil had disappeared. Jelco has since refused to honor her contract.

Part of the Statute of Frauds of State X provides as follows:

"A contract for the sale of securities is not enforceable unless there is a writing signed by the party against whom enforcement is sought."

1. Discuss Tanya's rights against Jelco.
2. Discuss Tanya's rights against Gil.
3. Discuss Tanya's rights against Carla and Dan.
4. Discuss whether Art and Bob are bound by the agreement to each pay $3,000 to Jelco.

Question 22

Jax, Inc. ("Jax"), was incorporated almost seven years ago with authorization to issue 2,500 shares of common stock at a stated par value of $100 per share. Of these, 2,200 shares of Jax stock have been issued and are outstanding. For its initial five years, Jax incurred net operating losses totalling $80,000. Last year, however, the corporation had net earnings of $25,000. The Jax board of directors, consisting of A, B, and C met on February 16 of this year and unanimously voted to declare a cash dividend of $10 per share on outstanding stock.

Pursuant to a bylaw authorizing the board to appoint officers and committees, at the February meeting A, B and C also voted to create an Executive and Finance Committee composed of B, C and W. W is not a director or officer of Jax, but is a shareholder. The bylaw permitted, and the board resolution provided, that the Committee would have powers similar to those of the board of directors.

On June 15 of this year, the board authorized the purchase by Jax of 220 shares of its stock then held by D, at a price of $95 per share. D had indicated she was ready to sell the shares at that price to a competitor of Jax.

On July 18 of this year, the Executive and Finance Committee directed Jax to issue 100 shares of previously unissued stock to E as "fully paid" shares, in return for E's promissory note to Jax in the sum of $7,500. The stock was issued to E for her note as described.

On August 31 of this year, A, Jax's president, wrote to F, a superintendent employed by the company who was retiring in one week, as follows:

> "In light of your many years of faithful service to this company, Jax will pay you a monthly pension of $300 for the rest of your life."

S, a Jax shareholder, asks you to advise him on the legality of the following:

1. The declaration of the cash dividend.
2. The appointment of the Executive and Finance Committee.
3. The purchase of shares from D.
4. The issuance of the 100 shares to E.
5. The promise to pay F a monthly pension.

Discuss.

Question 23

Abby, chief executive officer of Oilco, was eating lunch with several Oilco executives when she saw her business school classmate, Barb, sit down at the next table. Abby was aware that Barb had become a prominent local stockbroker. In an unusually loud voice, Abby stated to her fellow executives, "I bet my former classmate would love to know that tomorrow we are going to announce a tender offer for ALT Corporation."

Barb overheard this remark, and when she returned to her office, bought 10,000 shares of ALT Corporation for her own account.

Barb also telephoned the Mutual Fund Complex (Mutual) and told its chief executive officer, "If you are smart, you will buy ALT Corporation stock this afternoon." Within one hour Mutual placed an order to buy 50,000 shares of ALT, using Barb as the broker.

That afternoon, Barb visited Cora, a neighbor whom she had come to dislike intensely. Cora, at Barb's recommendation, had previously purchased 100 shares of ALT stock. Barb told Cora that ALT shares were about to decrease in value and that she was willing to buy the ALT shares from Cora at the stock's current price because Cora had bought the stock on her advice in the first place. Cora immediately sold Barb all of her ALT stock.

The following morning, Oilco announced a tender offer for ALT Corporation shares at a price 50% above its current market price. Approximately one month later, the tender offer was completed, with Barb and Mutual receiving profits of approximately 50% on their shares. Abby has not purchased ALT shares for more than three years.

1. Discuss whether Abby, Barb, or Mutual have violated SEC Rule 10b-5.

2. Discuss whether Barb has incurred any potential nonstatutory civil liability.

Essay Exam Answers

Answer to Question 1

1. Space ("S") v. Conn ("C")

Special facts

Under the special facts doctrine, when a director, officer, or key employee, possessing knowledge of special facts (i.e., unusual or extraordinary nonpublic information) about her corporation by reason of the position she occupies, buys its stock from an existing shareholder without disclosing such facts, the seller can (1) rescind the transaction, or (2) recover the difference between the stock's market price when the special facts become known and the price actually paid.

C would contend that this doctrine does ***not*** apply because: (1) she learned of the Aerospace Act as a consequence of being Jones's friend, rather than as a result of her corporate position, (2) Jones merely made a prediction (rather than stating a fact), and (3) S didn't suffer any direct injury from C's actions.

S could argue in rebuttal, however, that (1) Jones advised C of the imminent legislation because C was S's lobbyist, so that C could marshal her resources to assure passage of the Act, (2) Jones's statement was actually true (as shown by the Act's passage into law shortly thereafter), and (3) a few jurisdictions permit a corporation to assert the special facts doctrine when the aggrieved seller fails to bring an action (*Diamond v. Oreamuno*, 248 N.E. 2d 910 (N.Y. 1969)). (*See* ELO Ch.8-II(C)(2).)

The foregoing issues would probably be resolved in favor of S. Thus, S should be able to recover C's profit from the purchase of S's stock.

(S would ***not*** appear to have an action against C under SEC Rule 16(b), since she was not a 10% shareholder when she acquired S's stock. Also, SEC Rule 10b-5 is not applicable, since that rule gives no right to a corporation to recover for insider trading if it was ***not*** directly involved, i.e., as a buyer or seller.)

2. S v. Adams ("A") /Banco ("B")

Duty of loyalty

S probably has no right of action against A for breach of the duty of loyalty, since S suffered no losses from A's disclosure to B.

SEC Rule 16(b)

Under SEC Rule 16(b), profits made by a director of a corporation listed on a national securities exchange, resulting from the purchase and sale (or sale and purchase) of that company's stock within a six-month period, may be recovered by the corporation. Since B, via its deputization of A to sit on S's board as a "representative" of B, was deemed a director when the shares were sold, S could recover B's $1-per-share profit under SEC Rule 16(b). (*See* ELO Ch.8-VI(C)(3).)

3. B v. C

SEC Rule 10b-5

Under SEC Rule 10b-5, the failure by a buyer to disclose nonpublic, material facts in connection with the purchase or sale of stock via an instrumentality of interstate commerce, gives rise to an action by the seller for rescission or damages (the difference between the sales price and the market price of the shares following disclosure of the material information). (*See* ELO Ch.8-III(D).)

C would contend that (1) again, a material "fact" is not involved, (2) as the facts indicate, no instrumentality of interstate commerce was used (although the mere use of a telephone in arranging the transactions would suffice), and (3) the doctrine of *pari delicto* is applicable against B, because B (based on the secret report) believed that S's stock would decrease in value.

The first issue has already been discussed. Second, the logistics of C's purchase (for example, by telephone) are absent from the facts and these could be significant. B should prevail on the last issue, since holding C liable promotes the federal policy of discouraging insider trading.

Special facts

B could assert a "special facts" claim against C. The issues discussed above with respect to S's lawsuit against C would be equally applicable to B's claim (except for the discussion of a corporation's right to recover from an insider when the aggrieved seller fails to bring an action). The *pari delicto* defense would also be raised to this claim. Based on the conclusions reached above, B should prevail.

4. B v. Jones ("J")

SEC Rule 10b-5

B may seek to recover from J under SEC Rule 10b-5 for tipping C. However, B will not prevail. Under Rule 10b-5, a party must be a ***corporate insider*** in order to incur liability as a tipper. In this case, Jones was not a corporate insider; he had no direct relationship with Space. Therefore, Jones didn't owe any fiduciary responsibilities to S or to B, and he will not be liable for the information he gave to C. (*See* ELO Ch.8-IV.)

(It's important to note that we raised this issue even though the answer was obvious. If you didn't put down this issue, you may have thought, "well, it's obvious that J wasn't a tipper, so I'll skip over that issue." That could be a costly mistake! Most often, you'll get points for spotting ***all*** possible or discernible issues, even if the issue can be resolved extremely quickly under settled law. Therefore, don't forget to raise ***any*** issue you see in any of these essay questions, even if the result is crystal clear.)

Answer to Question 2

1. What are Aco's liabilities under SEC Rule 16(b)?

Under SEC Rule 16(b), profits made within any six-month period by an owner of 10% or more of the beneficial interest of a corporation the stock of which is traded on a national exchange, from the purchase and sale (or sale and purchase) of stock, are recoverable by that corporation. However, the stockholder must *already* hold 10% or more of the shares at the measuring date. (*See* ELO Ch.8-VI(D)(2).)

Since Aco's purchase of Tco stock merely enabled it to become a 10% shareholder, only a subsequent transaction (the subsequent sale of Tco stock by Aco) is operative for purposes of SEC Rule 16(b). Thus, Aco has ***no*** liability to Tco under SEC Rule 16(b).

2. What are Dan's liabilities under SEC Rule 10b-5?

Under SEC Rule 10b-5, one who misuses inside information of a material nature (i.e., data that would cause a reasonable person to purchase or sell the stock) to acquire shares which subsequently appreciate in value, may be liable to (1) those persons who sold the stock in question, and (2) the SEC. Tippers also have potential liability under this provision. (*See* ELO Ch.8-IV.)

To determine whether Dan ("D") is liable under SEC Rule 10b-5, it is necessary to ascertain how he transmitted the information of Aco's impending tender offer to Sam and Leslie. SEC Rule 10b-5 does ***not*** apply unless an instrumentality of interstate commerce (i.e., the telephone, mail, etc.) is used in some manner. If D's comments to Sam and Leslie were made in face-to-face encounters (e.g., over lunch), D may have no liability.

Assuming that D's conversations with Sam and Leslie occurred over the telephone or via the mail, a tipper has liability for disclosing material, nonpublic information to someone who purchases or sells the stock after learning of these facts, ***if*** the disclosure was made to the tippee (1) to acquire some type of personal gain, or (2) to bestow a pecuniary gift on the tippee.

As to Leslie, D probably did not intend either of these results. However, it is unclear from the facts why D told Leslie, his personal lawyer, of the possible tender offer by Aco. Assuming D had sought Leslie's advice with regard to his rights in this situation, D presumably had no reason to assume that Leslie would act in an improper manner.

It is also unclear from the facts why D informed Sam about the possible tender offer by Aco. If this was simply idle conversation or D believed Sam was incapable of exploiting this data, D may have had no intention of bestowing a pecuniary benefit upon Sam. However, since Sam acted almost immediately after receiving the information and purchased $50,000 worth of Tco stock, a relatively high level of sophistication is manifest. Thus, D may have intended to bestow a financial benefit upon Sam, especially given their familial relationship.

Finally, D might also argue that the information was not "material," since Aco had indicated only that it was "considering" a tender offer. However, since (1) both Leslie and Sam acted promptly after receiving this information, and (2) Tco's stock almost doubled in price immediately after the stock purchase and proposed acquisition became public, the facts tend to show that the "materiality" element is satisfied. (*See* ELO Ch.8-III(F)(3).)

Assuming D loses on these issues, what is his potential liability?

Although it may be impossible to determine the actual sellers of the Tco stock Sam purchased (since the purchases were made over a national stock exchange), every person who sold Tco stock over the exchange on December 3 prior to Sam's purchases could probably recover $3.50 per share from D (the difference between the value of Tco stock once the tender offer was fully known and the actual sales price). In addition, the SEC could compel Sam to pay this amount to it.

3. What are Sam's liabilities under SEC Rule 10b-5?

Assuming Sam (1) did realize, or should have realized, that he was privy to inside information, and (2) used an instrumentality of interstate commerce in connection with his purchase of Tco stock, Sam could have tippee liability under SEC Rule 10(b)-5. If these two conditions are satisfied, the discussion above with respect to D's potential liability would also apply to Sam.

4. What are Leslie's liabilities under SEC Rule 10b-5?

Leslie would probably be deemed a constructive insider for the purposes of Rule 10b-5, because she was given confidential information by Dan (a corporate insider) in the course of performing services for him. (*See* ELO Ch.8-IV(D).) Assuming Leslie used an instrumentality of interstate commerce in connection with her purchase of Tco stock, she is probably liable to persons who sold Tco stock over the exchange on December 3 prior to the time her purchase was made. Again, the SEC could also oblige her to disgorge her profit.

Finally, it should be mentioned that punitive damages have ***not*** been permitted under an SEC Rule 10b-5 civil action. *Flaks v. Koegel*, 504 F.2d 702 (2d Cir. 1974).

Answer to Question 3

1. Motion for security for costs

Apparently, in State X security must be posted only for purposes of a derivative action.

A derivative action is one in which the harms complained about were done ***primarily*** to the corporation, rather than to the individual plaintiff. The defendants will contend that the refusal to distribute profits and the agreement to maintain Al ("A") as the managing director impact upon all of the shareholders, rather than personally upon Paul ("P"). Thus, they would argue, the action is derivative in nature.

However, since P's basic assertion is that A and the other shareholders (via their appointed directors) are attempting to freeze him (personally) out of the corporation by (1) withholding dividends, (2) maintaining A as managing director, and (3) denying P inspection rights, P's lawsuit would probably be viewed as being primarily personal in nature. (*See* ELO Ch.9-II.)

Thus, the defendants' motion for security should be denied.

2. P's requests for relief

a. That A be removed for misconduct

A director may ordinarily be removed by the shareholders for good cause (fraud, gross incompetence, breach of the duty of loyalty, etc.). (*See* ELO Ch.3-I(B)(2).) P could contend that A breached his duty of loyalty by putting his personal objective (i.e., the purchase of P's Durco stock) over his corporate duties (i.e., to pay dividends when there are funds in excess of those necessary for operating expenses). Furthermore, since a controlling shareholder has a fiduciary duty to refrain from exercising his position in a manner which oppresses minority shareholders, if P could prove that A orchestrated an effort to hold back dividends for the sole purpose of inducing P to sell his Durco stock, P's request for dismissal of A should be successful. (*See* ELO Ch.7-VI(B).)

Although A (as a 65% shareholder) could still presumably elect the new director who would be chosen to fill his vacancy, and therefore his removal might arguably be ineffectual, A's forced departure would nevertheless impress upon the other directors the importance of observing their fiduciary duties toward minority shareholders. Thus A should be removed on the facts stated above.

b. Invalidate the shareholders' agreement

While shareholders' agreements (i.e., contracts whereby shareholders have agreed to vote their shares in a particular way) are ordinarily valid, one controlling the management of a corporation is permissible only if: (1) the agreement was made with respect to a close corporation, and (2) the agreement involves only a minor encroachment upon the directors' managerial discretion.

The agreement in question was to retain A as "managing director." The primary issue is whether the shareholders' agreement substantially limits the discretion of the ***board***, not only the participants' discretion as shareholders. The discretion to choose who will run the business rests with the board of directors. Depending on the statutory law in State X, the shareholders' agreement to maintain A in office as the managing director could be considered interference with the board's ability to manage the business effectively, and P could argue that the board needs to be free to exercise its own business judgment without such limitations. (See ELO Ch.5-III(A)). In addition, there is the risk that A would try to instruct the other directors how to vote on matters pertaining to the management of the corporation. Allowing one director to dictate virtually all of management's decisions constitutes more than a "minor" encroachment upon the board. Decisions should be made only after a give-and-take discussion and majority vote of all of the directors present.

The cases indicate that if the shareholders' agreement can meet three basic tests, it will ordinarily be upheld. To be found valid, the agreement must: (1) not injure any minority shareholder, (2) not injure creditors or the public, and (3) not violate any express statutory provision. While it is not clear from the facts whether State X has an express statutory provision addressing this situation (or a statute dealing with the rights of creditors and the public), it appears that the shareholders' agreement here cannot satisfy the first test. P is a minority shareholder who is not a party to the shareholders' agreement, and he arguably would be injured by the agreement to maintain A as managing director indefinitely, without regard to A's performance. Thus, again P should prevail. (*See* ELO Ch.5-III.)

c. Compel directors to declare and pay a substantial cash dividend

While the defendants have asserted the business judgment rule (directors are not liable for corporate actions undertaken in good faith and with reasonable care) with respect to the nonpayment of dividends, this argument should fail. Their actions ***don't*** appear to have been undertaken in good faith (i.e., the objective seems to have been to "freeze out" P). (*See* ELO Ch.11-II(B)(1).) If P can show that Durco's reserves are greater than necessary to continue its business operations, the excess funds should be distributed to shareholders.

d. Confirm P's rights to inspect Durco's records

The State X statute unqualifiedly authorizes shareholders to examine the books and records of their corporation. The defendants appear to contend it should be an ***implied*** provision of the statute that inspection of corporate records cannot be compelled when the shareholder's objective is improper (a "strike suit" would be such an instance, because its purpose is simply to make a bad faith claim against the corporation). However, since P desires to review the documents for a legitimate purpose (i.e., to determine how much of the profits should be distributed as dividends), P should again prevail. (*See* ELO Ch.4-I(D).)

Answer to Question 4

1a. Legality of increasing the board's size to nine directors

Stan ("S") could contend that increasing the size of the board to nine members was illegal, in that this action contravened both the Articles of Incorporation and bylaws of Dixie. The directors of a corporation must ordinarily act in conformity with these documents.

The directors might argue in rebuttal that (1) the Articles don't expressly limit the number of directors to five (they state only that the "initial" board shall consist of five directors), and (2) corporate bylaws are often viewed as being implicitly amended by resolutions which have been properly approved by the directors (except as to actions that impact significantly upon the business operations of the corporation, such as a sale of its assets).

However, S could respond that (1) the Articles did intend the board to consist of only five members unless the document was amended (and this document can be altered only by shareholder action), and (2) in any event, enlarging the board is an action sufficiently significant to require shareholder approval (even if the directors could implicitly amend the bylaws).

S would conclude that increasing the number of directors unilaterally was illegal. (*See* ELO Ch.3-II(C)(2).)

1b. Legality of staggered terms

Since this action is contrary to the Articles of Incorporation (which provides for annual elections of directors), it is probably unlawful. While the board might contend that staggered terms still permit the annual election of ***some*** directors (probably three are elected each year), the ordinary meaning we would attach to the term "annual election" is that the ***entire*** board be elected at that time. Indeed, that is the meaning which ***this*** board attached to the phrase, as evidenced by their desire to change it.

1c. Refusing to call a special shareholders' meeting

Although directors, officers, and (usually) 10% or more of the shareholders may notice a special meeting of shareholders, there is ordinarily no obligation on the board to call such a meeting, unless the particular action sought to be accomplished must be approved by shareholders. Although S (as a 29% shareholder) is probably empowered to call a special meeting of shareholders, the board would not be obliged to undertake this action. In addition, the president can ordinarily be removed only by the board of directors (not shareholders). Thus, in this case the board did not act improperly.

1d. Filling the newly created positions without a shareholder vote

Whether this action was proper or not depends on Dixie's Articles of Incorporation and bylaws. Ordinarily, the bylaws of a corporation provide that interim vacancies in the board may be filled by majority vote of the directors. Thus, in the unlikely event that enlargement of the board was legal, the directors probably acted lawfully in filling the vacancies. (*See* ELO Ch.3-II.)

2. Should the court grant the board's motion to dismiss?

In some states, a derivative action cannot be maintained if a majority of the directors determines, in good faith, that the lawsuit is ***not*** in the corporation's best interests. However, where the derivative action asserts wrongdoing by a majority of the directors, director disapproval will ordinarily ***not*** preclude the lawsuit. (*See* ELO Ch.9-IV(B)(2).)

The facts are silent as to whether the entity seeking a takeover had a reputation for looting the corporations over which it gained control. If it did ***not***, the board's action in enlarging their number and staggering terms appears to have been undertaken (1) for their own self-interest (to protect their positions), and (2) to the detriment of the corporation (presumably, the additional directors are paid by Dixie). In any event, as discussed above, the board's actions appear to be unlawful.

In addition, while the new board members are experienced in business, their decisions have been highly questionable. The transactions approved by them were financially harmful to Dixie. The facts are insufficient to determine whether Dixie's financial setbacks resulted from unexpectedly changed economic conditions (in which case there would be no liability under the business judgment rule), or were due to faulty decision-making by the board. Of course, if it could be shown that the board deliberately entered into unprofitable transactions to make Dixie a less attractive takeover candidate, it would ***not*** have acted in good faith and would be liable for losses to Dixie from those actions.

While the board might contend that dismissal of the derivative action was made by a "disinterested" body (the four ***new*** members), this argument should fail. The new members are close friends of the original directors and would (presumably) lose their positions if the derivative action was successful. They are therefore ***not*** "disinterested." (*See* ELO Ch.9-IV(D)(5).)

Also, assuming S's derivative action alleges that ***either*** the business judgment rule ***or*** the directors' fiduciary duty to act in good faith was breached (as opposed to simply contending that increasing the number of directors and staggering their terms was unlawful), ***none*** of the directors is truly "disinterested." Thus, the court should ***not*** grant the board's motion to dismiss.

Answer to Question 5

1. Andy's vote against the proposal to issue 100,000 shares of stock to Rich free of preemptive rights

It is well established that majority shareholders cannot exercise control in a manner which is injurious to the minority. (*See* ELO Ch.7-VI(B).) Conversely, a minority shareholder is not permitted to act in a manner that promotes his or her interests to the detriment of other members of the corporation. Barb, Carla, and Dave could argue that by causing Corp to continue to pay an unusually high interest rate on the note, Andy has wrongfully exercised a "veto power" over Corp's attempt to preserve its assets.

Andy could contend in rebuttal, however, that he was not obliged to relinquish his preemptive rights, especially since Rich's acquisition of 100,000 shares would (under cumulative voting) cause Andy to lose the certainty of sitting on Corp's board of directors. Since an 80% vote is required to change the Articles (which provide for preemptive rights), this document could ***not*** be amended without Andy's vote. Because endeavoring to retain a specific equity position within a corporation is a legitimate concern, Andy may have acted properly in voting against the sale of shares to Rich. However, the facts also indicate clearly that Andy did not want the note paid off because of its high interest rate. If, in fact, ***this*** factor compelled Andy to vote against Rich's proposal, then Andy would not have acted properly.

The facts are silent as to whether (a) the other three were willing to permit Andy to purchase 25,000 of the additional shares, and (b) Andy had the financial ability to purchase an additional 25,000 shares (thereby retaining his 25% interest in Corp). Andy had a duty of loyalty to Corp pursuant to which he is not to place his personal interests before those of the corporation. If both of these conditions could be satisfied, so that Andy could retain his equity position in Corp, presumably he would have to vote to approve the modified proposal or else face accusations of violating this duty of loyalty.

2. Injunction to prevent the Corp-Endrun merger

Mergers ordinarily require approval by the board ***and*** a specified proportion of both companies' shareholders. Some jurisdictions require that only a majority of shareholders approve a merger, while other states impose a higher proportion (ordinarily two-thirds). (*See* ELO Ch.10-I(F)(1).) If the merger can be accomplished lawfully in accordance with Corp's presently existing Articles and bylaws, Andy could contend that the majority shareholders are breaching their fiduciary duty by diluting his 25% ownership interest. However, if the Other Shareholders can show that their motivation was to preserve Corp's assets by terminating an excessive financial obligation, they would probably prevail.

If a merger requires Andy's authorization, the resolution of this issue depends upon a consideration of the factors discussed above with respect to whether Andy breached his duty to place the Corp's interests before his personal concerns.

If Andy prevailed on the issues of breach of duty, a court could restrain Corp and Endrun from consummating the merger.

3. Collection of interest payments on Corp's note

Directors are obligated to refrain from gaining any personal advantage to the detriment of their corporations. The Other Shareholders could contend that, pursuant to this duty, Andy should have advised them of the chance to acquire Lender's note for 90% of its face value (thereby saving $10,000 of principal and subsequent interest payments). Assuming Lender approached Andy with the intent of asking Corp (as opposed to Andy, individually) to purchase the note, Andy has probably usurped a corporate opportunity. Even if Lender had approached Andy in his individual capacity (i.e., as his friend, rather than as Corp's treasurer), many jurisdictions would still require Andy to disclose Lender's offer to the other directors before taking advantage of it himself (*See* ELO Ch.7-IV(D)(3).)

Assuming Andy breached his duty of loyalty by not communicating Lender's offer to Corp's board, the Other Shareholders would be obliged to show that they could have raised the $90,000 demanded by Lender (i.e., obtained a loan, or authorized and sold additional stock). If Corp could have purchased the note, it can probably now acquire the instrument from Andy for $90,000.

Corp may also contend that the note is unenforceable under the *ultra vires* doctrine (the Articles of Incorporation prohibit incurring any single debt in excess of $75,000; the principal amount of the note was $100,000). However, since the entire board of directors (which also constituted all of the shareholders) approved the loan, the resolution can be characterized as an informal amendment to the Articles. Thus, it is unlikely that an *ultra vires* defense by Corp would be successful.

Answer to Question 6

1. Acquisition of Durmac ("D") shares by Ennis

It could be contended that the vote on the acquisition of D stock was improper because (1) not all of the directors were noticed (only four of the seven were sent notice), and (2) there was not a quorum (only four, rather than the required five, directors were present).

In support of this position, it could be argued that (1) Almon should not be counted, since she was interested (i.e., owned shares of D stock), although this was not known until much later, and (2) directors usually ***cannot*** give their proxies to other directors to vote at a board meeting (and so Grabe's vote should not be counted). If either argument is accepted, at most only three directors were present for purposes of a quorum.

Notwithstanding the foregoing, since the decision to purchase D's stock was unanimously ratified at the next regular board meeting, the corporate action was properly taken. While Almon should have disclosed her interest and refrained from voting on the D stock purchase, her failure to do so is probably ***not*** an adequate basis to avoid the purchase. The resolution would still have passed 6-0, even if she had abstained. (*See* ELO Ch.3-II(G)(2).)

2. Liability of the Ennis directors for the decline in D's shares

Under the duty of due care, a corporate director is required to exercise the same care with respect to corporate matters as she would with respect to her own assets. The facts are silent as to whether Almon or the other members of the Ennis board should have realized that the market price of D shares could decline sharply. It is also unclear whether Almon had any special basis to perceive the subsequent decline in D stock. If Almon was aware of the possibility of an imminent decline in D's shares, she probably had a fiduciary obligation to disclose that information to the Ennis board of directors. If she failed to do so, and that data could have dissuaded the board from making the acquisition, Almon would be liable to Ennis for the losses resulting from the decrease of D stock. (*See* ELO Ch.6-II.)

Assuming the decline in D stock was the result of market conditions which could ***not*** reasonably have been perceived by the Ennis board, the board has no liability to its shareholders. On the other hand, since Ennis was expending $2 million, the board of directors may not be protected by the business judgment rule if it authorized a major expenditure without a thorough investigation of D. (*See* ELO Ch.6-III(C)(2).)

Assuming the Ennis board violated the duty of due care, the two absent nonresident directors and Grabe could probably ***not*** successfully defend against liability. Nonresident directors are ordinarily held to the same standard as local directors, and Grabe waived notice of the meeting. Also, it should be noted that ***all*** of the directors later ratified the action taken at the emergency meeting.

3. Liability of Almon to Ennis for the purchase and sale of D's shares

Ennis could attempt to recover from Almon under the corporate opportunity and special facts doctrines.

Under the first theory, a director is obligated to refrain from gaining any personal advantage to the detriment of the company as a consequence of information derived through his corporate position. Thus, the Ennis board could contend that Almon should have (1) advised it of the possibility of purchasing D stock at $42 per share, and (2) permitted Ennis to purchase the shares at that rate.

However, the facts are silent as to whether (1) the offer to Almon was made as a consequence of her position at Ennis, (e.g., Almon may have simply been on a mailing list of wealthy individuals), and (2) Almon had reason to believe that D stock would subsequently be offered to Ennis at a higher rate. Assuming ***either*** inquiry is answered in the negative, Almon would have ***no*** liability under the corporate opportunity doctrine. (*See* ELO Ch.7-IV(D).)

Under the special facts doctrine, when a corporate insider with knowledge of extraordinary, nonpublic information buys stock from, or sells stock to, an existing shareholder without disclosing this data, he is liable for the profit made or the loss avoided. More recently, a few courts have permitted the insider's corporation to recover ***if*** the defrauded shareholders fail to bring an action (*Diamond v. Oreamuno, 248 N.E. 2d 910 (N.Y. 1969)*). (*See* ELO Ch.8-II(C)(2).)

Almon can make several arguments in rebuttal.

First, the special facts doctrine permits only the corporation whose shares were traded to recover. In this instance, Almon is not being sued by D, whose stocks were traded, but rather by Ennis.

Also, the facts are silent as to whether (1) Almon had reason to believe that D stock would decline sharply at the time she sold her shares, (2) she had inside information about the imminent decline of D stock, or (3) the purchasers of the shares were already stockholders of D. If ***any*** of these inquiries is answered in the negative, the special facts doctrine would probably ***not*** be a basis of recovery against Almon.

In summary, it appears that Almon probably has no liability to Ennis.

Answer to Question 7

1. Can Exco ("E") rescind the transaction?

There are three independent theories under which E could attempt to rescind the transaction with Art's family (the "Sellers").

a. Breach of fiduciary duty

When a director has a personal interest in a transaction the corporation is considering, he or she is ordinarily obliged to (1) disclose that interest to the entire board of directors, (2) refrain from voting on it, ***and*** (3) disclose any information indicating that the transaction may not be in the corporation's best interests. A transaction involving a director's immediate family would probably constitute a personal interest. While it is unclear from the facts whether Art believed the transaction was not in E's best interests, he clearly failed to meet the first two requirements. (*See* ELO Ch.7-II(D).)

Art ***cannot*** claim that the transaction was implicitly ratified by a majority of the board (i.e., when Bobbie, Curt, and Donna advised him that they approved of the transaction), since (1) there was never a formal vote upon it, (2) he and Bobbie never disclosed to the other members of the board that the Sellers were members of Art's immediate family, and (3) there is no clear majority in favor of the purchase if Art's vote is discounted.

b. Lack of authority

The president ordinarily oversees the day-to-day operations of a corporation. While this officer usually has the power to bind the corporation in routine transactions, a $5 million cash acquisition (constituting 10% of E's assets) would probably ***not*** be considered a routine or ordinary business transaction and, thus, would not be within this implied authority. (*See* ELO Ch.3-III(C)(4)(c)(i).)

c. SEC Rule 10b-5

Under SEC Rule 10b-5, it is unlawful to employ any scheme to defraud another in connection with the purchase or sale of a security. If it could be shown that (1) Art had reason to know that Yang stock was overvalued, or (2) Sellers knew (or should have known) that Art was effectuating the sale for the purpose of paying them an excessive amount for their Yang shares, the transaction is probably violative of SEC Rule 10b-5; *Superintendent of Insurance v. Banker's Life & Casualty Co.*, 404 U.S. 6 (1971). (This assumes that the interstate commerce element also exists.) (*See* ELO Ch.8-III(C).)

Can E obtain rescission?

Under rescission, (1) E would tender the Yang stock back to the Sellers, and (2) the Sellers would return the purchase price of the shares to E.

The Sellers could contend that rescission (an equitable remedy which is discretionary with the court) is ***not*** appropriate, since (1) laches is applicable (i.e., E's board was informed of the transaction eighteen months ago, and no action has yet been taken), and (2) Yang's decreased profitability may be due to either actions undertaken by E or to subsequent market conditions.

Unless E can show that (1) the decline in value of Yang stock was not due to market conditions, or (2) the Sellers knew that Art was deliberately paying them an excessive purchase price, rescission would probably ***not*** be granted.

2a. Can E recover for Yang's unprofitability from Art?

In addition to the theories described above, a derivative action against Art might also be sustained under the director's duty of due care (i.e., a director must exercise the same due care with respect to corporate matters as he would with regard to his or her own assets).

It is unclear from the facts whether Art investigated the transaction with the thoroughness a $5 million acquisition would require. If (1) he did not, and (2) the price paid by E was excessive, E could probably recover (under the duty of due care ***and*** the other theories described above) from Art the diminishment in the value of Yang stock between the (1) time of purchase, and (2) trial. In theory, this amount would be reduced to the extent, if any, that Art could show that Yang's decreased profitability was due to mismanagement by E. However, in practice this would be difficult if E's mismanagement of Yang also rested on Art's shoulders as E's president. (*See* ELO Ch.6-II.)

2b. Can E recover for Yang's unprofitability from Bobbie?

The discussions above with respect to the duty of due care and (for the most part) a director's fiduciary duties would be applicable to Bobbie. Although Bobbie did not conduct the transaction, she was probably under a fiduciary obligation to disclose Art's conflict of interest to the entire board (even though Bobbie, in good faith, believed the transaction to be beneficial to E). No action would lie under SEC Rule 10b-5 against Bobbie, since the scienter (desire or intent to deceive the corporation) element is lacking.

2c. Can E recover for Yang's unprofitability from Curt and Donna?

Curt and Donna are in a different position than Art or Bobbie since they never knew that the Yang shareholders were related to Art. As to the substance of the purchase agreement, without additional facts, it is difficult to establish that they did not use the requisite care in evaluating whether the purchase would be good for E. The facts do indicate that Art negotiated the purchase agreement and that he discussed the proposed acquisition with Curt, Donna, and Bobbie individually. It is not unlikely that Art described the transaction to Curt and Donna in a manner that persuaded them of its benefit to E.

One could argue that since the relationship between Art and the Yang shareholders could have been discovered by a review of Yang's corporate records, Curt and Donna had a duty to inquire into Yang's stockholder list. To evaluate this argument, we need to know whether, under these circumstances, a director has a duty to inquire into the stockholders of the other company. If this duty does not exist, or if Curt and Donna acted reasonably in relying on Art and the other directors, then their liability is tenuous, at best. (*See* ELO Ch.6-II(D).)

Answer to Question 8

1. Freda's derivative action against XYZ

Before he can bring a derivative suit, a shareholder must ordinarily make a demand on the directors to undo an improper action. However, this demand is excused when it is likely to be futile. Since all of the directors voted for the contract with XYZ, and would therefore be personally liable for damages (i.e., the difference between the contract price and the market rate for such services), Freda could assert that any demand would have been futile, and was therefore unnecessary. The directors could contend in rebuttal that the allegedly improper agreement was entered into only six months ago, and therefore they could have corrected their actions in a relatively inexpensive manner. However, Freda should prevail on this issue. (*See* ELO Ch.9-IV(B).)

Some jurisdictions require that a demand be made on disinterested shareholders prior to commencing a derivative action. If a majority of shareholders fails to ratify the lawsuit, it cannot be commenced. In addition, some states require that a security bond for expenses be posted. However, there is nothing to indicate that either requirement is present in this instance.

In summary, Freda's derivative action can probably proceed.

a. Duty of due care

Directors must make a reasonable effort to learn the facts necessary for proper decision. Freda would contend that Carla and Dan failed to undertake any such effort in approving a contract for services which was at double the market rate. While Carla and Dan could assert that they reasonably assumed Al and Bob would offer only a contract competitive with market conditions, this contention should fail. (*See* ELO Ch.6-III(C)(2).)

Thus, Freda should be successful in asserting that Carla and Dan breached their duty of care in approving the service agreement with XYZ.

b. Duty of loyalty

Directors owe a duty of utmost good faith to their corporations. If a director has a direct financial interest in a transaction, he is ordinarily obliged to make full disclosure and refrain from voting on that matter. While Al and Bob did disclose their ownership of XYZ, they failed to reveal that the contract with Etco was at double the normal market rate. They also should not have voted for the agreement (if Carla and Dan still approved it after knowing ***all*** of the relevant information, it would have passed, 2-0, even without their votes). (*See* ELO Ch.7-II(D).)

Presumably, had Al and Bob informed Carla and Dan that the cost of XYZ's services was twice the market rate, Carla and Dan would ***not*** have approved the contract. Thus, Al and Bob breached their duty of loyalty to Etco.

c. Remedies

Based on the foregoing, Freda's derivative suit should result in (1) rescission of the Etco-XYZ contract, and (2) a judgment that Etco's directors are jointly and severally liable for the overpayments. This sum would be paid to Etco, but Freda should be able to recover her attorneys' fees and legal expenses.

2. Etco's redemption of Carla's stock

The directors could initially contend that Freda cannot bring an individual lawsuit for their redemption of Carla's stock. A derivative action is appropriate when the conduct at issue ***primarily*** injures the corporation, not the individual shareholder. A depletion of corporate assets is ordinarily the subject of a derivative action. Thus, the directors could have Freda's suit dismissed. (*See* ELO Ch.9-II(A).) However, another potential issue must be discussed in the event that this conclusion is incorrect.

First, Freda could contend that redemption of shares must be provided for in the corporation's Articles of Incorporation. Since Etco had no such provision, this action would be invalid. The board's unanimous approval of this action would ***not*** constitute an amendment of the Articles, since changes to this document ordinarily require shareholder approval.

In the alternative, Etco could contend that the redemption is actually a repurchase of shares by Etco. Since corporations have an inherent right to repurchase shares from their shareholders, assuming the repurchase will not harm creditors or other shareholders, Freda's first contention would probably be rejected unless she could show harm to the corporation.

Assuming the redemption/repurchase question is decided against Freda, she could then argue that the directors breached their duty of care in approving the repurchase. Other than assisting Carla with a familial emergency, there appears to be ***no*** corporate purpose that benefits Etco. The fact that Etco's earnings in the previous year had erased a prior deficit and exceeded the cost of redeeming Carla's stock would not be persuasive. Even if assisting a director with familial financial needs constituted a legitimate purpose, Etco should probably pay its obligation only from its retained earnings. Otherwise, there is the possibility that Etco might be unable to perform its normal business activities due to a lack of available funds. (*See* ELO Ch.11-II.)

A court is likely to rescind the redemption of Carla's stock. However, an order requiring repurchase of Freda's shares would be unlikely. Finally, it would be foolish to dissolve Etco under these circumstances (it was apparently profitable in the preceding year).

Answer to Question 9

The first and third demands by Emma ("E") relate to claims primarily by Deco, rather than by herself, personally. Thus, in determining how the directors ("DIRS") should respond, it must initially be determined if she could successfully assert a ***derivative*** action.

The DIRS might contend that E was not a shareholder at the time of the alleged wrongs (she did not inherit the stock until later), and therefore ***cannot*** bring a derivative action. However, since E inherited stock from someone who ***was*** a shareholder (Paula) at the time of the alleged wrongs, E can be said to stand in Paula's shoes and she may prosecute a derivative action if Paula could. (*See* ELO Ch.9-III(C)(3).)

Since all the DIRS are alleged to have participated in the wrongful actions, any demand made upon them would presumably be futile (and probably therefore would be excused). (*See* ELO Ch.9-IV(B).) However, in some states, a majority of the disinterested shareholders must concur in bringing the derivative action (assuming the purported wrongs could be ratified by the shareholders). For purposes of this discussion, we'll assume no such rule exists in this jurisdiction, so no demand would be necessary.

Thus, a derivative action by E is possible.

1. Could the DIRS set aside the purchase of the Savco stores?

Since Tom was a director of Savco at the time of the purchase, he was "interested" with respect to Deco's purchase of the four Savco stores.

A transaction involving interested directors can ordinarily be set aside, unless: (1) there was a disinterested quorum, (2) the interested party disclosed his interest, (3) it was approved by a disinterested majority, and (4) the transaction was fair. The only point that could be put in issue is Tom's failure to disclose his interest (assuming it was not known by the other DIRS). However, since the purchase was fair at that time, nothing would have been gained from such a disclosure by Tom. (*See* ELO Ch.7-II(F).) In addition, two years have passed since the transaction, and it would be impractical to attempt to unwind it now.

Thus, the DIRS should reject E's first demand.

2. Will E be permitted to assert preemptive rights with respect to the 25,000 shares issued to Smith?

A shareholder often has the right to buy newly issued shares in a proportion equal to her existing stock ownership. However, this right ordinarily does ***not*** extend to previously authorized shares, even though they have never been sold. In addition, preemptive rights often do not apply to situations where, as here with Greenacre, stock is exchanged for assets, because it is a logistical nightmare for shareholders to participate proportionately in such transactions. (*See* ELO Ch.12-I(D)(4).)

Thus, this demand should also be rejected by the DIRS.

3. Can Deco recover the $300,000 saving by Tom?

There are three theories under which the DIRS could assert that Deco is entitled to recover the $300,000 loss avoided by Tom.

SEC Rule 10b-5

Under SEC Rule 10b-5, a corporate insider who fails to disclose a material fact with respect to the purchase or sale of stock may be liable to the buyer for the difference between the sales price and the value of the stock after the nondisclosed information becomes known. However, since Deco did not buy the shares, Deco would not have an SEC Rule 10b-5 cause of action in this instance. Thus, the DIRS should reject E's demand on this ground. (*See* ELO Ch.8-III(E).)

SEC Rule 16(b)

Under SEC Rule 16(b), the short-swing profit made through a sale and purchase, or purchase and sale, of stock by a corporate director or officer (or a shareholder who owns at least 10% of a class of stock) within a six-month period, can be recovered by the corporation. The corporation must be listed on a national securities exchange or have (1) assets of at least $5 million, and (2) at least 500 shareholders of one class of stock. (*See* ELO Ch.8-VI(B).)

Even assuming the latter requisite is satisfied, Deco would have ***no*** cause of action under SEC Rule 16(b) because the facts state only that Tom sold his Deco stock. There is no indication that Tom had purchased the shares within the prior six months. (The fact that Tom resigned prior to his sale of Deco stock would ***not*** be relevant, since he presumably purchased the stock while a director of Deco.) Thus, in the absence of additional facts, the DIRS should refuse E's demand to commence a lawsuit against Tom on this ground.

Special facts doctrine

Under the common law special facts doctrine, when a corporate insider fails to disclose special facts (i.e., those of unusual or extraordinary significance) with respect to a sale or purchase of stock to an existing shareholder, the latter can recover the difference between the price paid and the value of the stock when those special facts become known. A few courts (e.g., *Diamond v. Oreamuno*, 248 N.E.2d 910 (N.Y. 1969)) have held that the corporation involved can recover the gain made or loss avoided by the insider, if the aggrieved shareholder fails to seek recovery. In this instance, however, there is no indication that Tom sold his stock to persons who were Deco shareholders. And Tom had no duty of disclosure to a buyer who was not yet a shareholder. (*See* ELO Ch.8-II(B)(3)(a); II(B)(3)(c)(2).)

Thus, the DIRS should refuse E's demand to sue Tom under this doctrine, too.

Answer to Question 10

1. Liabilities of A, B, C, D, and E to Z Corp's creditors

a. Undercapitalization

Shareholders of a corporation are ordinarily ***not*** personally liable for its obligations (beyond their investment in the corporation). The corporate veil may be pierced, however, when the entity is originally organized without adequate capital to meet debts that can reasonably be expected to arise in its type of business. While the $40,000 in cash which Z Corp ("Z") raised from the sale of its stock seems to be a respectable amount of capital, if the electronic devices in question are ordinarily expensive to create and market and, in fact, the $40,000 would be insufficient, Z's shareholders could be personally liable to its creditors. Note, however, that in a majority of jurisdictions, inadequate capitalization is merely a factor to be considered along with affirmative fraud or wrongdoing, or a failure to follow formalities. (*See* ELO Ch.2-V(B)(4).)

It should be noted that some jurisdictions hold a shareholder liable only if he participated in the ***management*** of the corporation. In those states, D and E, being only investors, could probably avoid personal liability to Z's creditors despite undercapitalization.

b. Liabilities of A and B prior to the filing of Z's Articles of Incorporation

Assuming the undercapitalization argument described above is unsuccessful, creditors could assert that prior to filing the Articles, no corporation existed and, thus, A and B would be personally liable to them.

However, under the common law, a *de facto* corporation exists when there has been (1) a good faith attempt to comply with the applicable organizational requirements, and (2) some use of the corporate structure. Since A and B signed the Articles of Incorporation, held a shareholders' meeting (the facts indicate that they established themselves as a two-person board), and (apparently) conducted business under the "Z Corp" name, a *de facto* corporation would probably be found to have existed.

A and B could also contend that the corporation-by-estoppel doctrine should apply (i.e., since contract creditors presumably believed they were dealing with a corporation, they should not now be permitted to question its existence). Assuming it could be shown that creditors of Z believed, or reasonably should have believed, that they were transacting business with a corporate entity, they would be barred from recovering against A and B personally for debts incurred prior to the time the Articles were filed. (*See* ELO Ch.2-IV(B)-(D).)

In summary, assuming ***no*** undercapitalization, A and B probably have no personal liability.

c. C's possible liability for receiving watered stock

Usually, stock must be fully paid for at the time of issuance. Most states permit stock to be issued in payment for valuable services ***previously*** rendered to the corporation. Thus, the ten shares issued to C for his previous services are valid.

Since the $5,000 promissory note was exchanged for equipment independently appraised at $6,500, the stock received by C for the note is probably ***not*** watered. (The fact that C had obtained the office equipment for $1,000 is irrelevant, since he was not obliged to pass his bargain on to Z.)

Depending on the laws of the state in which Z incorporated, the 40 shares received by C for ***future*** services might, however, be deemed watered, since Z received no contemporaneous value for these shares. (*See* ELO Ch.12-I(B)(3).)

Assuming a portion of C's shares were watered, whether the difference between the par value and watered value can be recovered by Z's creditors would depend on the applicability of a theory based on misrepresentation, statutory obligation, or trust fund. In "misrepresentation" states, only unknowing creditors whose obligations accrued ***after*** the watered stock transaction can recover (i.e., they are presumed to have relied on the corporation's stated capital in deciding to transact business with the corporation). The "statutory obligation" states interpret the general corporation statute as implicitly providing creditors with the right to sue shareholders who have received watered stock. Those states have a statute giving the ***corporation*** the right to sue a shareholder for the unpaid portion of his shares. Courts have sometimes interpreted this to mean that, if the corporation is insolvent, creditors may sue the shareholder in the same manner as the corporation would be able to do. In a "trust fund" jurisdiction, any creditor (regardless of when the obligation was incurred) may recover up to the watered amount. (*See* ELO Ch.12-I(B)(2)(b).)

d. Corporate opportunity

If C learned of the developmental opportunity by reason of his corporate position, then the corporate opportunity doctrine would certainly be applied. Even if C learned of the opportunity in his individual capacity, many jurisdictions would still have required that he disclose the opportunity if it was in a field directly related to Z Corp's activities. (*See* ELO Ch.7-IV(D)(3).)

Assuming that this issue is resolved against C, D may still contend that he does not owe any fiduciary responsibilities to Z Corp, because he is not a director, officer, or controlling shareholder. Considering that D acted with C, a director, and that there are only five shareholders in the corporation, chances are that D would likely be held liable.

If an individual uses information gained from a corporate position for personal gain, the value of that opportunity can be recovered by the corporation (unless the corporation could ***not*** have exploited the opportunity). C and D will contend that, since Z was unable to take advantage of the developmental opportunity, no damage to the corporation occurred, but they would be obliged to show that a diligent effort to obtain the necessary funds for the corporation would ***not*** have been successful.

The underlying premise to this defense is not quite so simple, and it has caused the courts some difficulty. If accepted on its face, the person who has the high corporate position that enabled him to learn of the opportunity will not have any incentive to assist the corporation to overcome its difficulties. Furthermore, because of the person's inside position, the corporation's inability to take advantage of the opportunity is a fact that outsiders will have difficulty disproving because they are outsiders and not privy to knowledge about the corporation.

There are two types of corporate inability that are generally received well by the courts, and one that is not. The two theories that may pass judicial muster are (1) the corporation's ***legal*** inability (for example, because of antitrust restraints), and (2) the ***refusal*** by the person making the offering to deal with the corporation. The third theory, which is not always well-received by the courts, is the corporation's ***financial*** inability to take advantage of the opportunity. The courts reason that if the opportunity is a good one, there will be some way to persuade an entity or a person to lend the corporation money.

The courts are not in agreement about whether and when to accept the defense of corporate inability. Some courts have adopted a very strict position that the insider must make full disclosure to the corporation and offer it the opportunity. If the insider fails to do this, he will simply not be allowed to argue that the corporation could not have taken advantage of the opportunity in any event. Some courts have adopted more lenient views, such as inquiring whether the opportunity was one which the corporation could have undertaken financially, but the stricter position represents the general trend. (*See* ELO Ch.7-IV(D)(5).)

If this state is one in which the courts take a very strict view, C and D would not be allowed to defend themselves on the grounds of corporate inability, since the facts indicate they did ***not*** advise the other directors of the opportunity. If, however, this state has adopted a more lenient position, then C and D would probably not be liable, since the facts state clearly that Z's financial difficulties had become generally known.

Assuming a corporate opportunity was taken by C and D, only a few jurisdictions permit the corporation's creditors to recover the value of the lost opportunity. Some, however, permit creditors to assert any rights the corporation had against the culpable individuals ***if the corporation is bankrupt***.

Finally, the corporate opportunity must be valued. The damages in this instance would probably be the developmental opportunity's present fair market value, less the cost of exploiting that opportunity. While C and D would contend that this figure should be reduced by an amount equal to their proportionate interest in the corporation, the fair market value calculation is probably a more accurate indication of the harm suffered by Z.

2. Possible liabilities of A, B, C, and D to E

The possible grounds of recovery by E are (1) corporate mismanagement (against A, B, and C if their actions caused Z to fail, and their decisions were ***not*** within the business judgment rule), (2) the corporate opportunity taken by C and D, and (3) the watered stock issued to C.

However, these harms primarily affected the corporation (rather than E, individually). While E may be able to assert a derivative action against the culpable parties, there may be little incentive for her to do so, since any proceeds recovered would be paid to Z (which in turn would distribute the recovery to Z's creditors).

On the other hand, the most likely thrust of E's cross-complaint is to set herself apart from A, B, C, and D, and to relieve herself of any liability to the creditors (in effect saying, "***they*** committed these acts; I was merely a passive investor, and therefore I should not be held culpable"). (*See* ELO Ch.2-V(E)(2).) On this basis, E might still find enough incentive to continue the action.

The only individual action E could assert against A, B and C, personally, would be for misrepresenting the assets of the corporation (i.e., as a consequence of C's watered stock, E was fraudulently induced to purchase Z stock). However, it is unlikely that E could prove that Z would ***not*** have become insolvent if C had paid $10,000, rather than the $7,500 in value which C did deliver to Z ($1,000 in past services and $6,500 worth of office equipment).

It therefore appears that E could not, as a practical matter, successfully sue the other shareholders.

Answer to Question 11

1. Personal liability of Chare ("C") to Sol ("S")

When a director breaches a duty which runs primarily to the corporation, a shareholder's right of action is a derivative action on behalf of the corporation. The one possible basis for direct liability of C to S personally would be C's refusal to give S the shareholder list.

A shareholder ordinarily has a right to inspect corporate books and records for any reasonable purpose. C might contend that the request for the shareholder list in order to unseat her was ***not*** reasonable. However, S could probably successfully argue in rebuttal that, given the past dismal performance by Martco ("M"), his demand was proper. (*See* ELO Ch.4-I(D).)

S might, however, have difficulty in establishing damages. Since S and Waters could elect only one director (S), S could ostensibly claim loss of a director's compensation. However, it is doubtful that with only one seat on the board, S could have (1) avoided M's losses that year, or (2) prevented C from remaining on the board.

2. S's derivative action against C

S could conceivably bring a derivative action based on (1) M's contract with Buildco ("B"), (2) the $10-million loss suffered by M during the previous fiscal year, and (3) the losses avoided by C by the early sale of her stock.

While a derivative suit must usually be brought by one who was a shareholder at the time of the alleged wrong, an exception to this rule normally exists for persons acquiring their shares by inheritance (as S did from Ida, who was a shareholder at the relevant time). (*See* ELO Ch.9-III(C)(6).)

In some states, a further requirement for commencement of a derivative suit is that a majority of disinterested shareholders concur in the action. However, we may assume this condition is ***not*** operative or is waived in view of C's refusal to deliver a shareholder list to S.

a. The contract with B

Duty of loyalty

Directors owe their corporations a duty of loyalty to disclose and refrain from acting with respect to matters in which they have a conflict of interest.

While S would argue that C is liable for M's losses since she voted for the transaction with B, C could respond that (1) she disclosed the conflict, (2) the contract would have been approved even without her vote, and (3) she acted in good faith (actually believing the contract was fair). C should prevail, buttressed by the fact that the transaction is three years old and everyone acted honestly. (*See* ELO Ch.7-II(D).)

Duty of due care

Under the director's duty of due care, a corporate director must exercise the same degree of care with respect to corporate matters, as she would with regard to her own affairs. C (and the entire board) might be liable to M under this theory if they failed to exercise reasonable care in not thoroughly investigating whether the cost of the agreement with B (a $4-million transaction) was excessive. If C (and the other directors) are liable, M could recover the difference between the actual contract price and the price would have been fair under the circumstances. (*See* ELO Ch.6-II.)

b. M's loss during the previous fiscal year

The duty of due care would be applicable to the $10-million loss suffered by M during the previous fiscal year. If it could be demonstrated that this loss occurred by reason of the directors' negligence (rather than market conditions), C and the other directors would be liable to the extent the loss could have been avoided by the exercise of reasonable business judgment.

c. C's sale of M stock without disclosure

In some states, a corporate insider with knowledge of nonpublic, "special facts" (i.e., unusual or extraordinary information) must disclose this data to a seller or purchaser who is an existing shareholder of that corporation. C's knowledge of M's $10-million loss would be important to a prospective purchaser (as shown by the sharp drop in the stock's price after the information became public).

C would argue that (1) the information was known to the public, since the losses were disclosed at the annual shareholders' meeting, and (2) usually, only a purchaser or seller of the stock can sue for losses caused by the nondisclosure.

However, in *Diamond v. Oreamuno*, 248 N.E.2d 910 (N.Y. 1969), directors selling their shares without disclosing inside information were held to have breached a duty ***to the corporation*** and the corporation itself was allowed to sue. If this view is followed in this jurisdiction, ***and*** the number of shareholders at the annual meeting was relatively small, C is probably liable to M for the losses she avoided by the sale of her stock prior to publication of the annual report. (*See* ELO Ch.8-II(C)(2).)

Answer to Question 12

1. Babb's option

Under the "corporate opportunity" doctrine, a director or officer cannot use information acquired as a consequence of his corporate position for personal gain, unless (1) after full disclosure to the noninterested directors, the corporation declines to pursue the opportunity, or, depending on the jurisdiction, (2) is clearly unable to exploit it.

The underlying premise to the second of these defenses has caused the courts some concern. If carried to its limits, the director or officer will not have any incentive to assist the corporation to overcome its financial difficulties. Furthermore, because of the person's position as an insider, the corporation's alleged inability to take advantage of the opportunity is a fact that outsiders will have difficulty disproving simply because they are outsiders.

There are two types of corporate inability that are generally received well by the courts, and one that is not. The two theories that may pass judicial muster are (1) the corporation's ***legal*** inability (for example, because of antitrust restraints), and (2) a ***refusal*** to deal with the corporation by the person making the offer. The theory which is not always well-received by the courts, is the corporation's ***financial*** inability to take advantage of the opportunity. The courts reason that if the opportunity is a good one, there will be some way to persuade an entity or a person to lend the corporation money.

The courts are not in agreement about whether and when to accept the defense of corporate inability. Some courts have adopted a very strict position that the insider must not prejudge the corporation's ability, but must make full disclosure to the corporation and offer it the opportunity in any case. If the insider fails to do both of these things, he or she will simply not be allowed to argue that the corporation could not have taken advantage of the opportunity. Some courts have adopted more lenient views, such as inquiring whether the opportunity was one which the corporation could have undertaken financially, but the stricter position represents the general trend. (*See* ELO Ch.7-IV(D)(5).)

Since (1) Babb learned of Ajax's interest in the land at a board meeting, and (2) the property was one of the parcels Ajax had targeted for possible purchase, the corporate opportunity doctrine appears applicable. Although Babb might contend that Ajax's interest in the parcel was too remote, since no final decision to purchase the land had been made, the fact that Babb (presumably) acquired the option solely for the purpose of reselling the land to Ajax should result in Ajax's prevailing on this issue.

When a corporate opportunity has been usurped, the corporation can assert whatever equitable or legal remedy is available to make the culpable party disgorge his or her advantage. Since the best means of negating Babb's actions is to compel her to assign the option to Ajax, this remedy seems appropriate here.

2. Ajax's purchase of Whiteacre

A corporation is ***not*** precluded from conducting business with its directors. However, in most jurisdictions a director's duty of loyalty requires him to disclose his interest in the transaction and to refrain from voting on the matter. In addition, the transaction must be approved by a majority of disinterested board members.

The facts seem to indicate that the board knew it was buying Whiteacre from Carl. Even if Carl had not explicitly disclosed this, the other directors may have been aware that Carl was the owner of Whiteacre via the title records. In addition, the purchase would have been authorized even without his vote. Assuming (1) the other directors of Ajax knew that Carl owned Whiteacre, and (2) the purchase was approved by a disinterested majority of the board, the transaction could ***not*** be rescinded by Ajax. (*See* ELO Ch.7-II(D).)

Possibly, it could be asserted that the directors violated the director's duty of due care by paying $50,000 for land originally acquired by the seller for $10,000. Under the doctrine of due care, directors must exercise the same degree of care and skill with respect to corporate matters as would a reasonably prudent person with respect to his own affairs. However, there is nothing in the facts to indicate how long Carl had owned Whiteacre or whether Whiteacre had appreciated in value to the purchase price. Assuming the $50,000 purchase price represented the approximate present fair market value of Whiteacre, the transaction could ***not*** be avoided under the business judgment rule. (*See* ELO Ch.6-II, III.)

Finally, it might be asserted that Carl breached his duty of loyalty if he failed to disclose the price for which he had purchased Whiteacre. Perhaps this information might have indicated that the price being paid by Ajax was too high. Nevertheless, if Whiteacre is presently worth $50,000, lack of this disclosure would probably ***not*** be an adequate basis for avoiding the purchase.

3. The sale of treasury stock to Dale

A shareholder ordinarily has preemptive rights to acquire shares authorized subsequent to the shares he initially purchased, in proportion to his original interest in the corporation. However, this right usually does ***not*** extend to treasury stock. The resale of treasury shares does ***not*** constitute a dilution of the shareholder's interest in the corporation.

In addition, stock issued for services is frequently not subject to preemptive rights. Since Dale insisted upon purchasing the shares as a condition to employment, the stock was arguably an inducement for her services to the corporation. (*See* ELO Ch.12-I(D)(4).)

Thus, Earl will probably ***not*** be able to enjoin the sale of treasury stock to Dale.

Finally, the sales price charged to Dale for the shares is probably ***not*** subject to attack, since $71 per share exceeds the par value ($50) and book value ($70.50) of the stock. If, however, it could be shown that the fair market value of Ajax stock clearly exceeded $71 per share, a breach of the duty of due care may have occurred, and watered stock liability may have been incurred.

4. The sale of Greenacre

Although Greenacre is being sold at a $20,000 loss, the sales price alone is ***not*** sufficient to demonstrate breach of the duty of due care by Ajax's directors, and the facts are silent as to why the land depreciated over the five years. Assuming the fair market value of Greenacre is presently about $50,000 and the directors believed in good faith that overall corporate purposes were best served by disposing of this land, the directors would be protected by the business judgment rule, and the sale could not be successfully attacked. (*See* ELO Ch.6-III(C).)

5. Fox's purchase of Gert's shares

Under the "special facts" doctrine, a corporate insider who obtains nonpublic information about material facts affecting the value of stock has a duty to disclose such information to an existing shareholder in connection with a purchase or sale of the corporation's shares. Where this duty is breached, the aggrieved party can recover any damages resulting from the defendant's fraudulent conduct.

If a sufficient period of time had elapsed between the time the financial report was distributed to Gert and Fox's purchase of Gert's shares, the fact that Ajax's stock had a book value of $70.50 would be considered ***public*** information. Therefore, no disclosure would be necessary and there would be no breach of a duty to disclose. (*See* ELO Ch.8-II(B)(2)(b)(ii).)

Under SEC Rule 10b-5, it is unlawful for an insider, via an instrumentality of interstate commerce, to withhold nonpublic, material information in the context of a purchase or sale of his corporation's stock. Again, however, assuming Gert received the financial report from Ajax with sufficient time to have read it, the information was "public." Thus, Fox would have no SEC Rule 10b-5 liability. (*See* ELO Ch.8-III(B).)

Finally, Fox has no liability to Ajax under SEC Rule 16(b), since there is nothing to indicate that he sold the stock for a profit within six months of its purchase from Gert. (*See* ELO Ch.8-VI(B).)

Answer to Question 13

1. Derivative action

When an alleged harm is done primarily to the corporation, rather than to an individual shareholder, a derivative action is the exclusive remedy. While the directors' actions in events (1)-(3) stated in the facts arguably diminished the value of Pat's stock, thereby causing her a personal loss, their conduct would probably be viewed as impacting ***primarily*** on the corporation. Therefore, Pat ("P") must commence a derivative action, and any recovery would accrue to Ajax (although P can recover her attorneys' fees and court costs if the lawsuit is successful).

The directors' vote approving all the actions was unanimous, making a demand on the board futile; therefore, it would probably not be required as a prerequisite to bringing a derivative suit. In some states, it is also necessary to give disinterested shareholders an opportunity to approve the directors' actions (provided the board's conduct was not illegal or *ultra vires*). Assume that this is not one of those states. (*See* ELO Ch.9-III,IV.)

a. Ajax's repurchase of its shares at $80 per share

Directors owe a duty of loyalty to act for the corporate good, rather than to further their personal interests. The facts are silent as to why the directors sought to prevent the minority shareholder from acquiring control of Ajax. However, if there was reason to believe that this shareholder would loot or otherwise have a detrimental effect upon Ajax, no breach of the duty of loyalty would have occurred. On the other hand, if the board's motivation was to protect their directorships, using corporate funds to repurchase stock for this purpose would be improper.

Under the director's duty of due care, directors must exercise the same degree of skill and care with respect to corporate matters as would a reasonably prudent person with respect to his or her own affairs. Arguably, paying $80 per share for stock that has a market value of $75 per share would constitute a breach of this standard. However, given the fact that Ajax's shares had a book value of $92 per share and the sellers demanded $80 per share, the price paid by the directors probably would be considered reasonable, and thus they would be protected by the business judgment rule.

Thus, assuming (1) an adequate justification for preventing the minority shareholder from acquiring control of Ajax, and (2) the availability of sufficient surplus to acquire the shares in question, an action against the directors for paying shareholders $80 per share would probably fail. (*See* ELO Ch.6-II,III(C).)

b. The agreement with Bob

Traditionally, retirement benefits for ***past*** services have been invalid. These benefits have often been viewed as a "waste" of corporate assets, since no value accrues to the corporation from such an arrangement.

However, recent statutes and case law permit this type of compensation as a reasonable exercise of the business judgment rule (e.g., the morale of other employees is enhanced by the recognition that loyal employees are treated appropriately). The Revised Model Business Corporations Act ("RMBCA"), § 3.02(12), permits such payments to former employees. (*See* ELO Ch.2-II(D)(2)(b).)

Since Bob was Ajax's "long-time" treasurer, a $5,000 per year lifetime retirement bonus is probably reasonable. Thus, whether Ajax's agreement with Bob can be annulled depends upon the applicable rule in this jurisdiction.

c. Indemnification payments to Curt

Most jurisdictions permit indemnification for an officer when she reasonably believed her actions were in the corporation's best interests and the conduct was ***not*** illegal. However, when the indemnity is given in connection with a derivative action, there is a division of authority. While some states permit ***no*** indemnity in this situation, most jurisdictions (and the RMBCA) permit indemnification of legal fees and costs if the action is dismissed or settled ***prior to*** the director's being adjudged liable to the corporation. (*See* ELO Ch.9-IX(D)(4).)

The facts are unclear as to whether Curt reasonably believed that the contributions were proper and as to the legality of the contributions. Assuming there is no question of legality, an agreement by Ajax to indemnify Curt regardless of whether he is adjudged liable is, as described above, invalid in most jurisdictions.

d. The stock option plan

Directors and officers are entitled to reasonable compensation for the services they render to their corporation. Stock options are a form of compensation which is ordinarily acceptable, since it gives the recipients an inducement to remain with the corporation and operate it in a profitable manner. (*See* ELO Ch.7-III.)

The facts are silent as to the present value of the stock options and the extent of the responsibilities assumed by the recipients. Assuming the options do ***not*** result in clearly excessive compensation, taking these factors into account, the stock option plan is probably valid.

2. P's right to have the Ajax shares registered in her name

Since this action affects P individually (as opposed to the corporation), she could bring a personal claim in this instance.

A transferee of corporate stock is ordinarily ***not*** bound by restrictions which are absent from the face of the certificate, unless she otherwise had actual notice of them. (*See* ELO Ch.5-V(E).) Therefore, unless P was somehow aware of the restriction, it would ***not*** be binding upon her. Thus, P can probably compel Ajax's secretary to transfer the shares to her. It should also be noted that, if the restriction is unreasonable, it is invalid (even if P had knowledge of it).

Answer to Question 14

1. Agee's claims against Freightco ("F")

Agee arguably has two claims against F's directors: (1) improperly declaring a dividend, and (2) breach of the duty of due care by (a) failing to allocate available capital to the purchase of new trucks, and (b) investing $1 million in an advertising campaign.

a. Type of action

Since the alleged harms were done primarily to the corporation (rather than to Agee, individually), Agee is obliged to bring a ***derivative*** action against F's board of directors.

It is assumed that Agee was a shareholder at the time the described events occurred. If he wasn't, a derivative action could not be asserted. The directors are the alleged wrongdoers. Therefore, a demand on the board would be futile and would probably not be required as a prerequisite to bringing a derivative suit. (*See* ELO Ch.9-IV(B)(2).)

b. Improperly declaring a dividend

A decision to declare dividends from earned surplus ordinarily rests with the good faith business judgment of the directors. However, dividends are ***never*** proper where these payments would result in the corporation's becoming insolvent. (*See* ELO Ch.11-I(C)(8).)

The facts are unclear as to whether the $500,000 in dividends paid by F so depleted the corporation as to cause its bankruptcy. Since F raised $1 million from the sale of debentures, it will probably be difficult for Agee to prove that the dividend caused F's insolvency.

c. Failing to repair the trucks

Under the director's duty of due care, directors are required to exercise the same degree of skill and care with respect to corporate matters as they would with regard to their own affairs. If they do, they are protected by the business judgment rule, which means that the fact that their decisions subsequently result in losses to their corporation is not a basis for attack. (*See* ELO Ch.6-III(B).)

Agee could argue that the failure (1) by ten directors to even read the report of the management consulting firm, and (2) of the entire board to implement the corrective action (i.e., the purchase of new trucks) necessary to avoid bankruptcy, constituted a breach of their duty of care.

The directors could possibly argue in rebuttal that (1) the report of a consulting firm need not be accepted by the board, and (2) in their reasonable judgment,

F's overall financial interests were best served by a large scale advertising campaign (which, in fact, was undertaken).

Nevertheless, if Agee can show that F's bankruptcy was primarily due to its failure to purchase new trucks, the business judgment rule would probably not afford protection. The directors should have at least read and seriously discussed a specially prepared report which predicted bankruptcy unless a ***particular*** course of action was undertaken promptly.

d. Advertising campaign

Lastly, Agee could assert that undertaking a $1-million advertising campaign (which was obviously unsuccessful) breached the duty of due care. He would contend that by incurring such a large, speculative indebtedness, F's ability to pay its ordinary corporate obligations was undermined. However, the directors might have reasonably believed that the advertising campaign would generate sufficient revenues to satisfy F's present and subsequent obligations.

Assuming F's directors could show some basis for believing the advertising campaign would be successful, they probably have ***no*** liability to their shareholders on this basis.

Summary

Assuming Agee can show that F's bankruptcy is attributable to its failure to acquire new trucks (rather than general market conditions), the directors would be liable for the corporation's losses. The five directors who did read the report are ***not*** absolved from liability, since they apparently failed to (1) insist on consideration of the report, or (2) argue for the purchase of new trucks.

2. Agee's claims against Landco ("L")

a. Failure to declare dividends

Since dividends are paid directly to stockholders, a shareholder must bring an action in his individual capacity to compel directors to undertake this type of action.

As noted above, the payment of dividends is ordinarily within the good faith business discretion of the board. However, dividends cannot be withheld arbitrarily or in bad faith. If L's directors repudiated the staff recommendation to declare a $1-million dividend for the purpose of supporting the parent corporation (via purchase of the debentures), the bad faith element would probably be satisfied. (*See* ELO Ch.11-II(B)(1).)

b. Purchase of F's debentures above market price

Agee could alternatively assert a derivative action against L's directors for (1) breach of the duty of loyalty, and (2) breach of the duty of due care in purchasing F's debentures.

(1) Breach of the duty of loyalty

Directors are ordinarily obliged to disclose any personal interest in a corporate transaction and refrain from voting on these matters. However, L's directors could argue that (1) given the close relationship between F and L, each of them was already aware that the others were also members of F's board, and (2) L's Articles and bylaws explicitly permitted them to vote in these instances.

Nevertheless, directors must still exercise good faith (i.e., act in a manner that is fair to all of the shareholders). There appears to be no reason for the purchase of debentures at a price in excess of their open market value, other than to bestow a "gift" on that entity. Here, L's directors voted to purchase F's debentures for much more than their market value. Thus, the L directors should at least be liable for this aspect of the transaction. (*See* ELO Ch.7-II(F).)

(2) Breach of the duty of due care

Agee could also assert that the debenture purchase violated the director's duty of due care, since L's directors were aware of the relatively speculative manner in which the proceeds from the debenture sale were to be used by F. As a consequence, L's directors should have realized that F might become bankrupt, and therefore be unable to repay the debentures. Thus, Agee can probably recover the $1-million purchase price, plus interest (which L presumably lost as a result of F's bankruptcy), from L's directors in a derivative action.

Also, it seems from the facts that L's directors almost assuredly breached the duty of due care by (apparently) failing to ascertain the price of F's debentures on the open market prior to purchasing those securities. (*See* ELO Ch.6-II.)

Answer to Question 15

1. Liability of Ames and Bates to Dynamics

a. Liability of Ames

Shares issued ***for cash*** less than the stated par value are called "discount shares." (*See* ELO Ch.12-I(B)(2).) Some states hold that if shares are marked "fully paid" by a corporation, no action can be taken against the person who receives the stock. If this is such a jurisdiction, Dynamics ***cannot*** recover the discounted amount from Ames.

Another view, however, holds that a corporation may recover the discounted amount, or at least rescind the transaction to the extent of the discounted shares. However, in these states, a corporation can contend that its directors may sell stated par value stock for a discounted amount if there is a good faith, business justification for such action. This appears to be the case here, since (1) Ames could have repudiated her stock subscription agreement prior to the time Dynamics was formed, and (2) her contribution was (apparently) needed for operating capital.

Finally, it should be noted that, since the discounted shares have a par value of only one thousand dollars (20 shares x $50), it may be impractical to pursue this relatively small amount from Ames.

b. Liability of Bates

A share issued for services or property representing a value which is less than the stated par value is called "watered stock." The facts are silent as to the value of Blackacre at the time Bates was issued shares with a par value of $100,000.

While Bates had purchased Blackacre one year earlier for $55,000, it is possible that its fair market value had increased to $100,000. Since only one year later the board of Dynamics valued Blackacre at $160,000, there appears to have been a pattern of appreciation in real estate in that area. If Blackacre was worth approximately $100,000 when Bates received his shares, the stock was ***not*** watered. If, however, Blackacre was not worth exactly $100,000 when Bates transferred title to this property to Dynamics, Bates could alternatively argue that, in most states, if the board in its good faith business judgment determines that certain property is important to the corporation, it may issue watered stock in exchange for that asset. If Blackacre was worth less than $100,000, but in the good faith business judgment of Dynamics' board, Blackacre was important to the corporation's future success, the transaction would be valid. (*See* ELO Ch.12-I(B)(4).)

In summary, it appears that Bates probably has ***no*** liability to Dynamics.

2. Declaration of $2 dividend

While the determination to declare dividends ordinarily is subject to the good faith discretion of the directors, there must be an adequate surplus from which these distributions will be made. (*See* ELO Ch.12-I(C).)

Since Dynamics experienced a net operating loss of $50,000 during its first fiscal year of operation, no dividend could be paid from earned surplus (the usual source of corporate dividends). In addition, there is no indication in the facts of a paid-in surplus (e.g., value received by a corporation for its stock in excess of the par value of those shares).

The only possible source of paying dividends in this situation is revaluation surplus (i.e., when assets of a corporation are revalued upward to reflect their current fair market value). However, only a few jurisdictions permit dividends to be paid from revaluation surplus. In addition, even if this jurisdiction did permit revaluation surplus, Dynamics' surplus would only be $10,000 (revaluation surplus of $60,000, less the $50,000 of operating losses). Since the dividend would require Dynamics to pay out $15,000 (7,500 x $2 per share), there is still a $5,000 shortfall.

In summary, the dividend appears to be improper. The directors could be restrained from paying the dividend or, if it has already been made, the directors are liable to Dynamics for the $15,000 paid out, along with any other losses suffered by the corporation as a result of the dividend payments.

3. Transaction with Carl

While existing shareholders may have preemptive rights to maintain their proportionate interests in the corporation when new shares are issued, this doctrine is ordinarily inapplicable to shares that have already been authorized. Since Dynamics was authorized to issue 10,000 shares and only 7,500 were outstanding at the time of the transaction with Carl, preemptive rights of existing shareholders would ***not*** attach to this transaction. (*See* ELO Ch.12-I(D)(4)(a).)

It should also be noted that in many jurisdictions, preemptive rights do not apply where shares are issued as consideration for assets or services. Finally, the modern trend is to recognize preemptive rights only if the Articles of Incorporation expressly provide for them.

Determining whether Carl's stock was watered depends on whether Greenacre was worth approximately $50,000 when the shares were issued to him. Since the board apparently had a good faith business rationale for obtaining Greenacre (i.e., the site of a future plant), the transaction could probably ***not*** be successfully attacked, unless the price for Greenacre was clearly excessive. (*See* ELO Ch.12-I(B)(4).)

4. Paula's right to vote her Dynamics stock

Unless coupled with an interest, a proxy is ordinarily revocable. There is no indication in the facts that Paula's proxy was coupled with an interest. Assuming Paula gave her proxy to Fox because it was too inconvenient for her to attend the annual shareholders' meetings, Paula could revoke her proxy. This is the rule even if the proxy was in writing and purported to be effective for Paula's lifetime.

Paula may revoke the proxy either by notifying the corporate secretary that the proxy given to Fox has been revoked, or by her attending the shareholders' meeting and personally voting her shares.

Answer to Question 16

1. X's rights

a. Against Z Corporation

A corporation ordinarily has no liability under a pre-incorporation contract, unless the agreement is approved or otherwise adopted after the corporation is formed. First, there is a question as to whether Z Corporation ever attained a corporate status (discussed below).

However, even if Z Corporation did attain corporate status, the agreement between X and A was never expressly or implicitly adopted by Z Corporation. In fact, B and C, two-thirds of the board, did not know of the original agreement and later refused to hire X. This refusal is probably tantamount to a rejection by the board of Z Corporation. (*See* ELO Ch.2-III(C).)

Thus, X has no rights against Z Corporation.

b. Against A

Unless he has explicitly disclaimed liability, a promoter ordinarily has liability for his pre-incorporation contracts. Although the agreement provided that Z Corporation would, upon its formation, hire X, X arguably assumed that someone would be bound by the contract. Thus, while it was obvious to X that A was acting on behalf of a ***prospective*** corporate entity (rather than in his personal capacity), A is probably personally liable to X. (*See* ELO Ch.2-III(B)(4).)

2. Personal liability of A, B, and C to Q

Ordinarily, shareholders are not personally liable for corporate debts. However, if the corporate status is ***not*** established, the business relationship of A, B, and C may be deemed a partnership. As such, each of them would be jointly and severally liable for the debts of the entity.

Since the Articles of Incorporation were never filed with the Department of State, it is unlikely that the shareholders could claim that a *de jure* corporation existed.

However, under the common law, a *de facto* corporation exists when (1) there has been a good faith attempt to comply with the requisites for corporate formation, and (2) the persons involved have made use of the corporate form. A, B, and C made a good faith effort to comply with corporate formalities by executing Articles of Incorporation and retaining an attorney to make the appropriate filings. They also acted in accordance with a corporate form by issuing stock, electing directors and a president, and entering into transactions on behalf of the corporation (e.g., the contract with Q was signed, "Z

Corporation, by C, President"). It is therefore likely that a *de facto* corporation existed, and A, B, and C probably are not personally liable to Q. (*See* ELO Ch.2-IV.)

The facts are silent as to whether the initial capitalization of Z Corporation was adequate. If it was not, the corporate veil could be pierced, and A, B, and C would each be personally liable for Z Corporation's debts. Note, however, that in a majority of jurisdictions, inadequate capitalization is merely a factor to be considered along with affirmative fraud or wrongdoing or a failure to follow formalities. (*See* ELO Ch.2-V(B)(4).)

Finally, under the common-law doctrine of corporation-by-estoppel, a plaintiff who deals with a party under the belief that it is a corporation is estopped from disputing the corporation's status for purposes of that transaction. Since Q was aware that C signed the agreement, "Z Corporation, by C, President," the corporation-by-estoppel doctrine is applicable with regard to the transaction with Q. Therefore, A, B, and C probably have no personal liability to Q. (*See* ELO Ch.2-IV(D).)

3. Liability to other creditors of Z Corporation

As discussed above, if a *de facto* corporation exists and Z Corporation was adequately capitalized, the shareholders have no personal liability to ***any*** of the corporation's creditors. The corporation-by-estoppel doctrine might also apply depending on the facts surrounding each creditor's transaction.

4. Liability of B

Once a corporation marks shares "fully paid," it is usually estopped from claiming that the shares have not been paid. However, its creditors may be able to recover any "watered" portion of that stock from the recipients of the shares. Shares issued for services or assets the value of which is less than the par value constitute "watered stock." (*See* ELO Ch.12-I(B)(2).)

Since the equipment conveyed by B to Z Corporation was worth $50,000 less than the par value of the stock received in exchange, B may be liable to creditors of Z Corporation to the extent of $50,000. Recovery by these creditors may depend on which of three theories — the "trust fund," "misrepresentation," or "statutory obligation" theory — is applicable.

Under the trust fund theory, a corporation's capital is considered to be a trust fund for ***all*** creditors. Thus, a shareholder who receives watered stock is liable to corporate creditors, whether or not (1) acquisition of the shares occurred before the debt to the creditor was incurred, or (2) the creditor relied on financial information provided by the corporation.

Under the misrepresentation theory (which is the majority view), the issuance of stock is an implied representation to creditors that the corporation has received consideration at least equal to the par value of its outstanding shares. A shareholder who receives watered shares has participated in a misrepresentation to persons who ***subsequently*** extend credit to the corporation. Under this theory, only persons who became creditors of Z Corporation ***after*** the transaction with B could recover the watered amount from him.

Under the statutory obligation theory, the general corporation statute has been interpreted by some states as implicitly providing creditors the right to sue shareholders who have received watered stock. This is based on the corporation's right to sue a shareholder for the difference due on those shares. If the corporation is insolvent, the courts in essence have allowed the creditors to bring the action that the corporation might have brought.

It should be mentioned that for a creditor to recover for watered stock, it must first obtain a judgment against the corporation. After an attempt to satisfy the judgment from corporate assets fails, the creditor may proceed against the shareholder.

The trustee-in-bankruptcy of Z Corporation might also attempt to recover the watered amount of B's stock under a breach of fiduciary obligation theory. Where a potential conflict of interest exists, a director is ordinarily obliged to (1) disclose his interests and any material information pertaining to the transaction, and (2) refrain from voting on the matter. (*See* ELO Ch.7-II(D).)

If it could be shown that B was aware that (1) the equipment was worth only one-half of the par value of the stock, and (2) A and C thought the equipment was approximately equal in value to the par value of the stock B received, B breached his fiduciary obligation to Z Corporation by not disclosing this disparity. If B voted in favor of the transaction and his vote was necessary for its approval, an additional breach of his fiduciary obligations would have occurred.

If B violated his fiduciary responsibilities, Z Corporation's trustee-in-bankruptcy could either rescind the transaction or recover the losses Z incurred as a result of B's conduct.

Answer to Question 17

1. Z's derivative action

We will assume that Z was a shareholder when Banco formed Combank (the plaintiff must ordinarily be a stockholder at the time of the alleged wrong to commence a derivative action).

Ordinarily, a plaintiff must make a demand on the directors of a corporation prior to commencing a derivative action. However, this demand is excused where it would obviously be futile. Since (1) Z's action would demand return of $1 million (the amount Banco paid for the Class B stock), plus interest, from the directors, and (2) the directors ***unanimously*** voted to organize Combank, it is highly unlikely that a demand upon the directors would be successful. (*See* ELO Ch.9-IV(B).)

Thus, Z's failure to make a demand upon Banco's directors would probably ***not*** prevent him from commencing a derivative action.

Z is apparently contending that the board of Banco wasted corporate assets by expending $1 million to create a competitor (i.e., Combank is also a bank), without any immediate possibility of realizing a return on this investment (i.e., dividends are to be returned to Combank as additional capital for ten years). In addition, since Banco's Class B stock is nonvoting, Banco would have no input in matters involving Combank's operations. Under these circumstances, Banco's directors have arguably made a"gift" of their corporation's assets to Combank.

Under the director's duty of due care, directors must exercise the same degree of care with respect to corporate matters as they would with regard to their own affairs. (*See* ELO Ch.6-II.) Since Banco is apparently a substantial corporation (e.g., it has 50,000 shareholders and the ability to commit $1 million to Combank), its directors might argue that this action is justified by the goodwill and attendant favorable publicity which will accrue to it by the creation of Combank. They could contend that the investments in Combank might induce new customers to deposit their funds in Banco.

In addition, they could contend that the original $1 million investment remains an asset of Banco, and the agreement to return dividends for a period of ten years was necessary to assure adequate capitalization of Combank during its initial phase of operations.

Although a close question, the investment in Combank can arguably be expected to benefit Banco. Depending on how thoroughly Banco's board examined the potential benefits and disadvantages, Z's derivative action might fail.

It should also be mentioned that an argument can be made that the resolution providing for return of all dividends to Combank for ten years can be repudiated by Banco, since there is no consideration for this promise.

2. Duc's contract

a. Banco's liability

If Duc attempts to enforce the contract entered into with O, Banco could assert that O did not have authority to bind it. While the facts state that O was an officer of Banco, there's no indication whether (1) O was expressly authorized to enter into the contract with Duc, or (2) O held an office which would normally have the authority to commit Banco to such a costly contract.

If, however, O did have the implied authority of office to bind Banco, Banco would be liable under the agreement regardless of whether it was subsequently approved by Combank.

Without additional information about O's status, it is not clear whether or not Banco has liability to Duc. (*See* ELO Ch.3-III(C).)

b. Combank's liability

While it is not clear from the facts at what point in time Combank's board knew of the Duc contract, Duc could argue that Combank implicitly approved the contract by failing to object to it for at least one month after Combank's officers and employees moved into the building while remodeling was in progress. Combank could contend in rebuttal that it took them a month to recognize that Duc's work had not been authorized by Combank's board and that the resolution to retain Exco constituted a rejection of the O-Duc contract.

It is possible that Combank should have inquired more promptly into Duc's authorization to perform the remodeling, and thus it may have implicitly adopted the O-Duc agreement. (*See* ELO Ch.2-III(C)(2).)

In any event, Duc could probably recover the reasonable value of the benefit bestowed upon Combank under a *quantum meruit* theory. The work done by Duc prior to retention of Exco presumably reduced the work required of Exco.

c. Personal liability of O

O would probably be deemed a corporate promoter. Although she specifically indicated that the contract was for a corporation "to be formed," in most states O would be personally liable to Duc if the contract was not performed. (*See* ELO Ch.2-III(B)(4).)

3. The contract with Exco

If directors have a personal interest in a transaction, they are ordinarily obliged to (1) disclose that interest to the other directors, and (2) refrain from voting on the matter. Here, Combank director X owned Exco, but there is no indication in the facts that director X disclosed this information. Further, he did vote on the Exco matter.

Since (1) director X voted in favor of the contract, and (2) his vote was necessary for its passage, the contract with Exco can probably be rescinded. This course of action is arguably supported by the possibility, discussed above, that Combank had implicitly ratified the agreement with Duc. Thus, ordering Duc to discontinue the remodeling of Combank's premises might be a material breach of this agreement and needlessly expose Combank to an action by Duc for contractual damages.

Finally, while Exco might have an action for breach of contract if Combank repudiates their agreement, since director X (1) was (or should have been) aware of the preexisting relationship with Duc, and (2) nevertheless voted for the agreement, Exco would probably be ***estopped*** from bringing an action against Combank.

Answer to Question 18

1. Management's obligation to present the CAP proposals to shareholders and include them in the proxy statement

Since Gasco's stock is traded on a national exchange (the NYSE), it is subject to the proxy rules promulgated under Section 14 of the Securities Exchange Act of 1934. Under SEC Rule 14a-8(a), a shareholder is ordinarily entitled to submit, for inclusion in management's proxy solicitation, proposals she intends to present at the upcoming shareholders' meeting. However, there are many exceptions to management's obligation to include such materials, some of which may apply to these facts.

a. Proposal to remove those directors who authorized the Media contract and sought to impede the gas tax proposition

Management may refuse to include a proposal if, under the laws of the corporation's domicile, it is ***not*** a proper subject for shareholder action. (*See* ELO Ch.4-V(C)(5).) It is unclear from the facts whether stockholders can remove a director in this state. We are advised only that Gasco's charter provides that the ***board*** may remove a director for sufficient cause.

In addition, it is important to examine the language used in the proposal. A shareholder proposal stating that management be required or ordered to do something will always be excludable under this theory (that it is not a proper subject for shareholders) if the action proposed is something shareholders do not have the right to vote on under the corporation's state law. However, the majority of states do permit shareholders to make recommendations or requests and, therefore, the proposal would then not be excludable if it used this type of language.

Consequently, even if the language proposing removal of the directors who voted to authorize the Media contract could be considered an improper subject for shareholders under this state's laws, the shareholder group could rephrase the proposal as a recommendation or request rather than a demand, and the proposal would not then be excludable.

In most jurisdictions there is a common-law right of shareholders to remove directors for cause. Furthermore, the majority of modern statutes have expanded the rights of shareholders to remove directors. These statutes most often permit directors to be removed with or without cause, unless the Articles of Incorporation provide differently. Here, there is no indication in the facts that Gasco's Articles contain language addressing this issue. (*See* ELO Ch.3-I(B)(2)(c).)

"Cause" typically exists if a director has committed fraud or waste, or otherwise overtly misused her position. This standard is arguably satisfied by the directors'

deliberate effort to circumvent the State X statute requiring disclosure of corporate expenditures made for the purpose of influencing public ballot measures.

However, the directors could contend in rebuttal that, unless this law provides for significant criminal penalties in the event it is violated, removal is ***not*** proper. They were only attempting to promote corporate objectives by preventing action which would presumably make Gasco's business less profitable.

While a close question, unless the directors' actions were criminal in nature, their removal is probably ***not*** a proper subject for shareholder action.

b. Proposal to hire an auditor to review Gasco's books

The directors could assert that retaining auditors to review the corporation's books is a matter within management's discretion, and therefore ***not*** a proper subject for shareholder action.

However, given the board's deliberate effort to avoid the State X statute, the request for an independent party to determine whether there was other misconduct by Gasco seems appropriate.

Thus, the directors can probably be compelled to include this proposal in their proxy materials.

c. Proposal to require only nonpolluting products in company-owned gas stations

Directors may refuse to include a proposal if it appears clearly to have been submitted primarily to redress a personal grievance or for the purpose of promoting general economic, political, racial, religious, social, or similar causes. It could be argued that this proposal is a general grievance stirred by the pro-environmental lobby, reflecting the personal views of the complaining shareholders.

The stockholders could respond that, even if the proposal emanates from the desire to have an environment free of pollutants, it nevertheless relates to an aspect of Gasco's general business policy. The use of nonpollutants in company-owned gas stations would place Gasco on the cutting edge of environmentally conscious energy companies, which would arguably constitute a unique advertising appeal to its consumers.

Nevertheless, this proposal would probably be characterized as a personal grievance, and so the directors may omit it.

2. Binding effect of proposals

As already discussed, unless there has been a serious criminal violation, involvement of the directors in the Media contract is probably ***not*** sufficient "cause for dismissal." Thus, the proposal is not binding upon the directors. In addition, a director must ordinarily have an opportunity to defend her actions and obtain judicial review of an unfavorable decision.

It might also be argued that, since only three of the nine directors are to be elected at the shareholders' meeting, removing all of the directors (assuming the decision to enter into the contract with Media was approved unanimously) would result in there being no management of Gasco. However, Articles of Incorporation ordinarily provide for interim appointments or elections if a director is removed. Thus, the six vacancies could be filled by the three newly elected directors soon after the meeting.

The proposal to have an auditor review Gasco's books relates to verifying past conduct of the directors, and should be binding upon the board.

The third proposal, if pertaining to the operation of Gasco's business, would ***not*** be binding upon the board. Management decisions are the exclusive province of the directors.

3. The contract with Media

Two arguments can be made that this agreement is unenforceable.

First, it might be asserted that the contract is *ultra vires*, since it requires Gasco to do something that is contrary to State X's law (i.e., refrain from disclosing corporate spending designed to influence public ballot issues).

However, a court could simply strike the illegal provision and permit the balance of the contract to stand. This remedy seems more appropriate since the provision, having become known, has ceased to have any effectiveness.

Second, Gasco might argue that it and Media are in *pari delicto* with regard to an illegal provision, and therefore the contract is unenforceable. However, since the provision was presumably inserted at Gasco's insistence, a court would probably not permit Gasco to evade its contractual responsibilities under these circumstances.

Thus, Media can probably enforce the contract.

Answer to Question 19

1. Dan's right to remain on the board of directors

Unless expressly authorized to do so by the Articles of Incorporation or bylaws, directors cannot ordinarily remove another board member. Even when the directors are authorized to remove another board member, it can only be for cause (e.g., fraud upon the corporation, gross incompetency, misuse of corporate assets, etc.) Making a profit by using inside information to acquire shares, which results in no diminution of corporate assets, arguably would not satisfy this standard. However, given recent case law and legislation aimed at discouraging such conduct, as well as the negative publicity to a corporation which results from insider trading, Dan's actions might constitute sufficient cause for dismissal.

2. Dan's potential liabilities

a. Liability to shareholders

There are several theories under which Dan could be liable to the three shareholders from whom he purchased stock.

(1) *Special facts doctrine*

Under the special facts doctrine, a corporate insider is obliged to disclose unusual or extraordinary nonpublic information to an existing shareholder from whom he or she is buying stock. (*See* ELO Ch.8-II(B)(2)(b)(ii).)

The secret invention in this instance is certainly extraordinary, as evidenced by the fact that the market value of the Jetco stock more than doubled after news of the invention became public.

The shareholders can either (1) rescind their transactions with Dan (i.e., tender to Dan the purchase price of their stock and receive in return the shares sold to him), or (2) recover the difference between the present market value of Jetco stock and the purchase price to Dan.

(2) *SEC Rule 10b-5*

Under SEC Rule 10b-5, deceitful practices involving the purchase or sale of securities are prohibited. These include the failure of corporate insiders to disclose nonpublic, material information. (*See* ELO Ch.8-III.)

While an instrumentality of interstate commerce must be used in connection with the purchase or sale of securities to activate this provision, this element would be satisfied by Dan's use of the mail (i.e., Dan wrote to the shareholders).

The remedies available to aggrieved shareholders under the special facts doctrine are also applicable pursuant to SEC Rule 10b-5.

b. Liability to Jetco

(1) ***SEC Rule 10b-5***

Dan's exercise of his stock option would also constitute a "purchase" of Jetco shares using inside information; *SEC v. Texas Gulf Sulphur Co., 401 F. 2d 833 (2d Cir.* 1968). Thus, with regard to the 1,000 shares Dan purchased from Jetco, the corporation can either recover the profit made by Dan or rescind the transaction.

(2) ***SEC Rule 16(b)***

Under SEC Rule 16(b), a corporation such as Jetco, which is traded on a national exchange, can recover short-swing trading profits made, or losses avoided, by a director with respect to the purchase and sale, or sale and purchase, of securities within any six-month period. If the culpable party is a director, he would need to have occupied that position only at ***either*** the purchase ***or*** sale date.

Since Dan purchased and sold the shares obtained from the former stockholders within a six-month period, Jetco can recover Dan's profit.

When calculating the profit earned for purposes of SEC Rule 16(b), the lowest purchase price is matched against the highest sale in order to maximize the profits. Stock certificate numbers are not matched to determine the profits produced by the sale of particular shares. Dan sold 4,200 shares for $50 per share. Since Dan had purchased 1,000 shares at $21 per share within the previous six months, he realized a $29 per share profit on 1,000 of the 4,200 shares (1,000 shares x $29 per share = $2,900). His profit on the remaining 3,200 shares was $25 per share because he had, within the previous six months, purchased 4,200 shares for $25 per share (3,200 shares x $25 per share = $80,000). Therefore, Dan's total profit under SEC Rule 16(b) was ***$109,000.*** (Note that if profits had been calculated by matching the particular shares sold and bought, it would have amounted to $105,000 (4,200 shares x $25 per share), because the 1,000 shares acquired for $21 per share would not have entered into the calculation. (*See* ELO Ch.8-VI(D), (F).)

(3) ***Special facts doctrine***

In jurisdictions that recognize *Diamond v. Oreamuno*, 248 N.E. 2d 910 (N.Y. 1969), Jetco also has an action against Dan under the special facts doctrine for the 4,200 shares which he acquired from the former stockholders (assuming the aggrieved parties failed to commence suit against Dan). Under the holding of this case, when former shareholders who have an action under the special facts doctrine refrain from asserting their rights, ***the corporation*** can recover the profit made or loss avoided by the insider.

It is also conceivable that an action for the profit made by Dan from his purchase of the 1,000 shares of Jetco stock could be recovered by the corporation under this theory. However, if Jetco was legally obliged to sell the shares to Dan despite his disclosure of the inside information, this theory would probably fail.

c. Liability to the SEC

Under the Insiders Trading Sanctions Act of 1984, an insider may be obliged to disgorge his or her profits to the SEC and is subject to treble damages for any profits gained or losses avoided. In addition, there is a potential criminal penalty of $100,000 for each violation of SEC Rule 10b-5.

Answer to Question 20

1. Doris's right to obtain shareholder benefits

a. Right to receive stock

Courts ordinarily construe provisions that restrict the transfer of shares in a narrow manner. The language in the Shareholder Agreement addresses the situation in which a shareholder "seeks to sell" his or her shares. Here, however, Carla did not "sell" her Getco stock; she devised the shares under her will. Under these circumstances, no right of first refusal could exist, since no offer involving the shares in question was made. (*See* ELO Ch.5-V(C)(1)(b).)

In addition, if Art, Bob, and Carla had intended the provision to be operative on death, their contract could have easily provided that upon the death of any shareholder, the remaining stockholders were entitled to purchase the decedent's shares for their fair market or book value.

Thus, a court would probably determine that the Shareholder Agreement does ***not*** apply to testamentary transfers. Therefore, upon surrender of Carla's shares, Doris would be entitled to a decree of specific performance, requiring Getco's secretary to issue an equal amount of stock in her name.

b. Right to dividends

The payment of dividends ordinarily rests within the discretion of the board of directors. However, when the directors' refusal to make dividend distributions constitutes bad faith or an abuse of their discretion, they can be compelled to make the payments to the shareholders. (*See* ELO Ch.11-II(B).)

If it can be shown that Art and Bob have withheld dividends for the purpose of "freezing out" Doris (i.e., persuading her to terminate her ownership interest in Getco), Doris can compel them to make a reasonable distribution of the available corporate surplus.

2. Voice in Getco's management

Doris could first contend that, as Carla's successor-in-interest, she steps into Carla's position under the Shareholder Agreement. Under that contract, each shareholder is required to vote for the election of the other stockholders as directors of Getco. Thus, Doris could probably obtain a court order compelling Art and Bob to comply with the Shareholder Agreement.

In the alternative, assuming Doris could vote Carla's stock, she could make two arguments.

Doris could assert that the provision requiring shareholders to vote for the other stockholders is not binding upon her, since she did not sign the Shareholder Agreement. However, it would be difficult for Doris to assert both that she stands in Carla's shoes under the Shareholder Agreement and that the provision in question does not bind her because she never signed the agreement.

In addition, Doris could assert that the provision is invalid, since application of this clause might preclude election of the most capable individuals available. However, it should be noted that not all shareholders' agreements are invalid; on the contrary, most shareholders' voting agreements are valid. But a distinction is made where the shareholders' agreement attempts to control matters that are appropriately left to the discretion of the board of directors. (*See* ELO Ch.5-II(B)(2).)

Assuming either argument is successful, Doris could elect herself (or another person of her choosing) as a director, if cumulative voting is in effect. Under "straight" voting, each shareholder casts her votes for ***each*** potential director. Under cumulative voting, which is often required by the Articles of Incorporation, bylaws, or applicable state corporate law, each shareholder has votes equal to the number of directors to be elected, multiplied by the number of his shares, but these votes can be cast ***only once.*** Thus, under cumulative voting, Doris could elect one of the three directors.

3. Dissolution of Getco

a. Pursuant to the statute

The statute provides for two situations under which a corporation may be dissolved:

(1) there is an equal division among directors with respect to management of the corporation, or

(2) the votes of shareholders are so divided that a board of directors cannot be elected.

The first situation does not apply, since two-thirds of the directors are in agreement about Getco's management.

The second reason is arguably operative, since a full board (presumably three persons) has not been elected for two years. However, the failure to elect a board emanates from Art and Bob's insistence that Doris does not qualify as a shareholder, rather than because of fractionalized shareholder voting.

However, in either event, Doris possesses only one-third, not the requisite one-half, of Getco shares needed to act. Thus, Doris probably ***cannot*** dissolve Getco under the State X statute.

b. Pursuant to common law

Since there is no indication that the statute in question was meant to supplant common-law principles, Doris could assert any grounds for dissolution that exist under general corporate law.

There are four typical grounds for dissolution: (1) the directors are deadlocked in the management of the corporation, (2) the directors or those in control have acted in an illegal, oppressive, or fraudulent manner, (3) the shareholders are deadlocked in voting and have failed to elect successor directors for at least the last two consecutive annual meetings, or (4) the corporation's assets are being wasted or misapplied. (*See* ELO Ch.5-VI(B).)

If Doris can show that (1) Art and Bob have acted, and are likely to continue to act, for the purpose of suppressing her legal rights with respect to Getco, and (2) there is no other reasonable means of safeguarding her position, some states will permit the court to dissolve a corporation (i.e., sell off the corporate assets and distribute the proceeds to shareholders). Because Art and Bob (1) have continuously refused to recognize Doris' ownership interest in Getco, and (2) have failed to declare dividends, Doris' can argue for dissolution.

Further, Doris can assert that Getco should be dissolved due to Art and Bob's incompetency. As shareholder/directors they have (presumably) breached the Articles of Incorporation by failing to hold shareholders' and directors' meetings. In addition, their failure to take ***any*** action during a two-year period arguably demonstrates a lack of corporate responsibility.

Confronted with the probability of an adverse court determination, Art and Bob would presumably recognize Doris' ownership and dividend rights. If Doris receives the shares previously owned by Carla and is permitted to vote this stock, it is unlikely that Getco would be dissolved at this point. Assuming the corporation has operated profitably, there is probably an insufficient basis for dissolution. However, if Art and Bob continue to exploit their majority position to oppress Doris, dissolution of Getco could be ordered.

Answer to Question 21

1. Tanya's rights against Jelco

A corporation is usually not liable under pre-incorporation agreements, unless it expressly or implicitly adopts the contracts after it is formed. Since the Tanya-Gil agreement was never approved by Jelco's board, the corporation will assert that it has ***no*** liability to Tanya.

Tanya could make two arguments in rebuttal.

First, she could argue that Jelco implicitly adopted the agreement by failing to object to it for the three-month period during which Tanya worked for the corporation prior to its repudiation of the contract. Gil, as a director of the corporation, was cognizant of the agreement and never objected to it. (*See* ELO Ch.2-III(C).)

The facts are unclear as to whether Carla and Dan were aware of Tanya's activities on behalf of Jelco and therefore should have made inquiry as to her status with the corporation. However, to the extent that Carla and Dan had, or should have had, knowledge of Tanya's efforts to promote Jelco's business, her argument for implied adoption by the board would be strengthened.

In the alternative, Tanya could assert a right to recover at least the reasonable value of her services in *quasi* contract. Under this theory, Tanya would receive the reasonable value of the benefit she bestowed on Jelco.

In summary, the Gil-Tanya agreement was probably adopted by Jelco, or, alternatively, Tanya can recover the reasonable value of her efforts in *quasi* contract.

2. Tanya's rights against Gil

A promoter is ordinarily liable under a pre-incorporation agreement, unless the other party had reason to believe the promoter would not be bound if the corporation was never formed or the corporation rejected the contract. Even when a promoter specifies that he is signing on behalf of "a corporation to be formed," it is usually presumed that the other party intends the promoter to be personally liable if the corporation fails to perform the agreement. Thus, Gil would be liable to Tanya under the contract. (*See* ELO Ch.2-III(B)(4).)

3. Tanya's rights against Carla and Dan

Tanya could contend that Jelco was never properly formed because its Articles of Incorporation were incomplete, and that as a consequence, the incorporator-directors were actually partners. Each of them would then be jointly and severally liable if the contract was implicitly accepted by the partnership. The facts do not indicate whether an implicit acceptance took place.

Carla and Dan could assert several theories in rebuttal.

First, a *de jure* corporation exists, despite noncompliance with all of the express formalities, if the Articles of Incorporation have been filed and there is compliance with all ***mandatory*** steps for formation. It is unclear from the facts whether the provision requiring a statement of corporate purposes was mandatory (i.e., it "shall" or "must" be filed) or merely permissive (i.e., it "should" or "may" be filed).

Second, under the common law, a *de facto* corporation exists when (1) there has been a good faith effort to comply with the requisites for corporate formation, and (2) there has been some use of the corporate form. These conditions are arguably satisfied by (1) the filing of the Articles of Incorporation, (2) the election of directors, (3) the issuance of stock, and (4) the carrying on of at least some business under Jelco's name. Thus, Jelco was probably a *de facto* corporation.

Finally, under the corporation-by-estoppel doctrine, when a party transacts business with an entity believing that the entity is a corporation, that party is barred from asserting that the entity has not attained corporate status. In light of the pre-incorporation agreement, Tanya presumably believed that a corporation had been formed and that she was working for a corporation.

Since Carla and Dan are likely to prevail on at least one of these theories, they would have ***no*** liability to Tanya. (*See* ELO Ch.2-IV.)

4. Art and Bob's liability under the subscription agreement

First, Art and Bob could argue that their promise is unenforceable by reason of the quoted Statute of Frauds provision that applies to sales of securities, since their agreement to purchase the shares was made orally. However, their repudiation letter to Gil (which Art and Bob presumably signed) might satisfy the State X writing requirement.

Traditionally, subscribers could revoke their promises to purchase stock at any time prior to acceptance of the contract by the corporation. More recently, however, subscription agreements have been upheld under two independent views.

First, some states have enacted legislation that precludes revocation of a subscription agreement for a prescribed period of time. If (1) this jurisdiction has such a statute, and (2) the applicable time period has ***not*** expired, Art and Bob could be compelled to perform their promises.

Second, some states take the view that each subscriber's promise is consideration for those of the other subscribers. Thus, unless ***all*** of the subscribers agree to cancel the agreement, it cannot be revoked. If this theory is applicable, Art and Bob cannot avoid their obligations under the subscription agreement, since Gil would presumably refuse to consent to its cancellation. (*See* ELO Ch.12-I(A).)

Answer to Question 22

1. Declaration of cash dividend

Ordinarily, dividends are paid from earned surplus (assets in excess of stated capital and liabilities). Since Jax has a deficit of $55,000 ($80,000 in losses over its initial five years, less the $25,000 in net earnings for the prior year), no dividends should be forthcoming.

In some states, however, nimble dividends may be paid. Under this theory, dividends may be paid from the prior or current year's operating profits. Assuming that the applicable law recognizes this view, an aggregate dividend of $22,000 ($10 x 2,200 outstanding shares) is proper, in view of Jax's $25,000 operating surplus for the prior year.

In addition, some states permit dividends to the extent that total assets exceed liabilities by a prescribed financial ratio (e.g., assets must be 1.5 x the liabilities). Since Jax's capitalization was $220,000, dividends are probably permissible under this theory. (*See* ELO Ch.11-I(C)(7), I(D).)

2. Appointment of Executive and Finance Committee

Corporations are ordinarily permitted to create committees and delegate powers to these bodies. One such committee is the Executive Committee. An Executive Committee, because it has powers equal to the powers of the board, must ordinarily consist only of insiders and quasi-insiders (which would ***exclude*** W, a shareholder). These committees are sometimes prohibited from performing certain acts, such as authorizing the issuance of shares. RMBCA § 8.25(e). Even if the Executive Committee was properly created, its action of issuing stock was probably illegal. (*See* ELO Ch.3-II(J)(2), (J)(6).)

Thus, it is likely that the Committee will be invalidated.

3. Purchase of shares from D

A corporation may ordinarily repurchase its shares, provided (1) there are adequate funds available, (2) the price is reasonable, and (3) the motivation of the directors is proper.

In many jurisdictions, the right to repurchase outstanding shares is subject to the same conditions applicable to declaring dividends. If this is the rule in this state, the discussion contained under item **1.** above would also be relevant. (*See* ELO Ch.11-III.)

The price of $95 — $5 under the par value — appears to be reasonable, unless there is some reason to believe that the fair market value of Jax shares is below this figure.

Finally, if a 10% shareholder (which the competitor would become by reason of acquiring 220 shares) is able to obtain information about Jax that could be used to the corporation's detriment, the board's motivation probably would be proper.

In summary, the repurchase of 220 Jax shares by the board to preclude their sale to a competitor appears to be valid.

4. Issuance of 100 shares to E

In virtually all states, there is legislation which requires that shares be issued only for money paid, services rendered, or property actually transferred to the corporation. A promissory note (unless adequately secured) is usually ***not*** sufficient value for the original issuance of shares. If E's promissory note was ***not*** secured, the sale to E would have been improper and can be rescinded by Jax.

If E's note ***was*** adequately secured, a corporation ***cannot*** ordinarily issue stated par value shares for an amount below the prescribed figure. However, if (1) the board in its good faith judgment believes the purchase price is fair in light of the current market value of the shares, and (2) there is an immediate need for cash, many states permit the sale of stock for a price below the stated par value. Here, more facts are needed to determine whether these two preconditions are satisfied.

Finally, it should be noted that, in a few states, when discounted shares have been marked "fully paid," the corporation is estopped from rescinding the transaction or requiring the purchaser to pay the difference between the amount paid and the par value. (*See* ELO Ch.12-I(B).)

5. Promise to pay a pension to F

The promise by A to pay F a pension could be unenforceable for two reasons.

First, the determination to authorize a lifelong pension is arguably something that requires board action. Thus, while A is the president of Jax and may determine the salary of day-to-day employees, he probably ***cannot*** bestow lengthy pensions. (*See* ELO Ch.3-III(C)(4).)

Second, bonuses gratuitously given at the termination of an employee's career are sometimes viewed as a "waste" of corporate assets, and therefore unenforceable.

Nevertheless, some jurisdictions (and the RMCBA) permit pensions to be bestowed at the conclusion of an employee's career. These states view these payments as a reasonable exercise of the business judgment rule, since pensions arguably enhance loyalty to the corporation and make it a more attractive place to work. (*See* ELO Ch.2-II(D)(2)(b).)

However, since (1) A probably lacked authority to bestow pensions upon Jax's employees, and (2) pensions can be viewed as gratuitous and, thus, as waste, the pension is probably unenforceable.

Answer to Question 23

1a. Did Abby violate SEC Rule 10b-5?

A tipper is liable under SEC Rule 10b-5 when (1) she is an insider of the corporation ***whose shares have been traded,*** (2) she receives a benefit from disclosing the information or intends to make a pecuniary gift to the tippee, and (3) the tippee knew (or should have known) that the tipper was breaching a fiduciary duty to the corporation whose shares were traded. (*See* ELO Ch.8-IV.)

The first condition for tipper liability is absent here. Abby was not an "insider" of ALT. Rather, she was the chief executive officer of an entity that intended to make a public tender offer for ALT stock. Thus, assuming Abby did not receive confidential information from ALT executives regarding Oilco's tender offer, Abby probably has ***no*** liability under SEC Rule 10b-5.

Assuming, however, that liability under SEC Rule 10b-5 may extend to a person who, though not an insider of the company, possessed nonpublic information about the company, other potential issues must also be discussed.

A "tip" probably occurred by reason of Abby's recognition of Barb as a prominent stockbroker and her mention of the impending tender offer in an unusually loud voice. The lack of a direct statement to Barb is not likely to be significant.

As to the second condition, it does ***not*** appear that Abby obtained any direct personal gain from disclosing the impending tender offer to Barb. Possibly, she merely wanted to impress Barb with her special knowledge of an imminent, large-scale transaction.

It is difficult to determine from the facts whether Abby intended to bestow a pecuniary benefit upon Barb. Since they were business school classmates and Abby was aware that Barb was a stockbroker, Abby arguably should have known that Barb would use this information for financial gain. On the other hand, if they were mere classmates (rather than close friends), intent by Abby to bestow a gift upon Barb is less likely.

The third condition appears to be satisfied because Barb, as a business school graduate and prominent stockbroker, presumably realized that the information was nonpublic and, therefore, that Abby was breaching a fiduciary duty.

Considering all these factors, it does ***not*** appear that Abby has incurred "tipper" liability.

1b. Did Barb violate SEC Rule 10b-5?

Barb has potential liability under SEC Rule 10b-5 as a tippee (by purchasing ALT shares for her own account); as a tipper (for advising Mutual to purchase ALT stock); and for her misrepresentation to Cora in connection with her purchase of Cora's shares.

Tippee liability (information from Abby)

A tippee violates SEC Rule 10b-5 if (1) the information is received in breach of the tipper's obligation to refrain from disclosing the information, (2) the tippee recognizes that a breach of that relationship has occurred, and (3) the tipper (Abby) receives some benefit from the disclosure or intends to bestow a pecuniary gift upon the tippee. These requirements were discussed *supra* under **1a.**

In light of the conclusions reached above regarding the probability that Abby would not incur liability as a tipper, Barb would not be liable as Abby's tippee.

Tipper liability (information to Mutual)

The standard for tipper liability is described above under **1a.** (first paragraph).

First, Barb is not an insider of ALT. Second, if Barb was obliged to refrain from disclosing the tender offer, there is nothing to suggest that Mutual knew, or had reason to know, that Barb received her information improperly. It might be contended that (1) the pointedness of Barb's statement ("If you are smart"), and (2) the urgency which she imparted to Mutual (that afternoon), should have suggested to Mutual that Barb was using improperly obtained information. On the other hand, Barb's urging could be viewed as merely vigorous business advice. Since the three conditions for tipper liability are not all present, Barb would ***not*** be liable under SEC Rule 10b-5 for Mutual's purchase.

Liability for transaction with Cora

SEC Rule 10b-5 requires that the defendant have used an instrumentality of interstate commerce. Since Barb personally visited Cora and apparently purchased the shares from her at that time, Barb's possible fraud upon Cora would ***not*** be within the jurisdictional purview of SEC Rule 10b-5.

1c. Did Mutual violate SEC Rule 10b-5?

As discussed above, since Barb probably did not violate SEC Rule 10b-5 by tipping Mutual and Mutual had no reason to suspect that Barb obtained her information improperly, Mutual would have no SEC Rule 10b-5 culpability (despite the fact that it acted upon Barb's information).

2. Has Barb incurred any nonstatutory civil liability?

Under the special facts doctrine, when a corporate ***insider*** enters into a stock transaction with an existing shareholder, the insider has a fiduciary duty to disclose any unusual or extraordinary nonpublic, material facts to the shareholder. (*See* ELO Ch.8-II(B)(2)(b)(ii).)

Although Barb deliberately misled Cora, she was ***not*** an insider of ALT Corporation and therefore arguably owed no special duty of disclosure to Cora.

If, however, the court found that Barb, as Cora's stockbroker, had a common-law fiduciary duty of disclosure to Cora, Barb would be liable under common-law fraud principles. If so, Cora could either (1) rescind the transaction (i.e., cause Barb to re-convey the stock to her for the purchase price), or (2) recover the enhanced value of the stock.

Multiple-Choice Questions

1. In return for an unsecured promissory note in the amount of $5,000, ABC Corp. issued 500 shares of $100 par value stock to Bill. Upon receipt of Bill's note, ABC's Secretary marked the shares as "fully paid" on its books. A short time later, the board of ABC seeks to repudiate the transaction and, after tendering the $5,000 note back to Bill, requests return of its shares. However, Bill refuses to give up his shares. (You may assume that ABC is solvent.)

   Based on the foregoing, which of the following statements is most likely to be correct?

   (A) ABC may rescind the transaction.
   (B) Judgment creditors of ABC can enforce the note.
   (C) The shareholders of ABC can demand payment of the note from Bill.
   (D) None of the above statements is correct.

2. One year ago, in exchange for her property, the board of ABC Corp. issued stock to Jackie with a stated par value of $12,000. The board reasonably believed, in good faith, that the property was worth $12,000. However, shareholders of ABC now have an expert who is willing to testify that the property's fair market value is presently only $10,000. The shares are designated as "fully paid" on the corporation's books.

   Based on the foregoing, which of the following statements is most likely correct?

   (A) ABC Corp. can rescind the transaction or recover $2,000 from Jackie.
   (B) Persons who became judgment creditors of ABC Corp. after the transaction with Jackie can recover $2,000 from her.
   (C) The shareholders of ABC Corp. at the time of the transaction can recover $2,000 from Jackie.
   (D) The transaction cannot be rescinded, nor can any sum be recovered from Jackie.

3. In exchange for property worth $10,000, ABC Corp. issues stock to Jackie with a stated par value of $12,000. (You may assume the directors were aware that the stock was issued for property worth less than the par value of the shares.) The shares are designated as "fully paid" on the books of the corporation. Subsequently, Jackie transfers the shares to Moe for $15,000. ABC has recently become insolvent.

   Based on the foregoing, which of the following statements is most likely correct?

(A) Judgment creditors of ABC Corp. can recover $2,000 from Jackie.
(B) Shareholders of ABC Corp. at the time of the transaction can recover $2,000 from Jackie.
(C) Shareholders of ABC Corp. at the time of the transaction can recover $5,000 from Jackie.
(D) No sum can be recovered from Jackie by creditors and/or shareholders.

4. A and B sign an agreement with Carl, a promoter for X Corporation, whereby A and B each agrees to purchase 500 shares of $10 per share par value stock. This contract is made prior to the time X Corporation is formed. After X Corporation is formed, but before the subscription agreement is affirmed by the board, A advises X's directors that she is repudiating the subscription agreement.

Assuming there is no legislation that makes subscription agreements irrevocable for a prescribed period of time, which of the following answers is most likely correct?

(A) A is not liable, since she revoked prior to acceptance of the contract by the corporation.
(B) A is liable, because the corporation was formed prior to her attempted repudiation.
(C) A is liable, because B failed to join her in repudiating the subscription agreement.
(D) A is liable, ***if*** she failed to notify Carl of her repudiation.

5. A and B sign a subscription agreement. Subsequently, the corporation is formed and accepts the contract via a properly adopted board resolution. However, prior to tender of the shares A promised to buy, the corporation goes bankrupt. Creditors of the corporation (via the trustee-in-bankruptcy) now seek to enforce the subscription agreement against A and B.

Based on the foregoing, which of the following answers is most likely correct?

(A) A is not liable, since the stock was not delivered to her prior to the corporation's bankruptcy.
(B) A is not liable, since the corporation is bankrupt and therefore the shares she would receive are worthless.
(C) A is liable, since the corporation was formed and had accepted the contract.
(D) A is liable only to the corporation, but ***not*** to its judgment creditors.

6. Zeek, a promoter for Amco Corporation, entered into a contract with Paula, to purchase widgets. Zeek signed the agreement "Zeek, on behalf of Amco, a corporation to be formed." Amco is subsequently formed, but refuses to ratify the contract.

Based on the foregoing, which of the following statements is most likely correct?

(A) Zeek is personally liable under the agreement.
(B) Zeek is not personally liable under the agreement.
(C) Zeek and Amco are jointly and severally liable.
(D) None of the above.

7. Zeek enters into a contract with Paula to purchase widgets. Zeek signs the agreement, "Zeek, on behalf of Amco, a corporation to be formed." Subsequently, Amco is formed and the contract is ratified unanimously at a properly called board of directors meeting.

Based on the foregoing, which of the following statements is most likely correct?

(A) Only Zeek is liable under the agreement.
(B) Only Amco is liable under the agreement.
(C) Both Zeek and Amco are liable under the agreement.
(D) None of the above.

8. John, a promoter, enters into a contract with Alice, whereby Alice will serve as a consultant to Exco Corporation for $2,000 per month for one year. John signs the agreement as follows, "John, on behalf of Exco, a corporation to be formed, but not for himself personally." Subsequently, Exco is formed and a board of directors of seven persons is appointed. Although John does not initially advise the Exco board about the contract with Alice, most of the board's members observe Alice working at Exco's premises on behalf of the corporation. However, when the contract is considered at the monthly board meeting five months after incorporation, it is unanimously rejected.

Based on the foregoing, which of the following statements is most likely correct?

(A) John is liable under the contract with Alice.
(B) Exco is liable to Alice.
(C) Neither John nor Exco is liable to Alice.
(D) None of the above.

Questions 9-11 are based on the following facts:

A, B, and C decide to form Exco Corporation, which will manufacture and sell widgets. They agree that A will be the President and that all three will be directors. They communicate this information to Len, a lawyer, and request that Len perform the necessary requisites for corporate formation. Len agrees to perform this function, but advises A, B, and C that it normally takes several weeks to incorporate. Len sends the Articles to the Secretary of State. However, he inadvertently omits the necessary filing fee. Due to a backlog at the Secretary of State's office, the rejected Articles are not returned to Len for almost two months.

Three weeks after deciding to form Exco, A contracts with Billie to purchase $20,000 worth of widget components, to be delivered in four months. A, assuming the Articles would be filed, stock issued, and officers elected within four months, signs the agreement: "A, future President of Exco Corporation."

One week after this transaction, B accidentally collides with Chuck while driving her personal vehicle to pick up office materials for Exco's future operations.

9. Based on the foregoing, which of the following statements is most likely correct as of the time of B's accident with Chuck?

(A) Exco is a *de jure* corporation.
(B) Exco is a *de facto* corporation.
(C) No corporate structure exists.
(D) Exco is a corporation by estoppel for purposes of the accident with Chuck.

10. Exco is subsequently properly formed. If Billie commences an action against A, personally, for the $20,000 owed under the contract, A's strongest argument to avoid or minimize personal liability would be that:

(A) Exco was a *de jure* corporation.
(B) Exco was a *de facto* corporation.
(C) The corporation by estoppel doctrine is applicable.
(D) He is only liable for one-third of the debts incurred on behalf of Exco.

11. Exco is subsequently properly formed. (You may assume that in the collision between B and Chuck, B was at fault.) If Chuck sues A, personally, for the injuries sustained in his accident with B, it is most likely that A:

(A) Has no liability for the accident.
(B) Is personally liable for Chuck's damages.

(C) Is liable for only one-half of Chuck's damages.
(D) Is liable for only one-third of Chuck's damages.

12. X works in the mail room at ABC Corporation. One day, while delivering mail to the corporation's executives, X overhears a company geologist advise the President of ABC that the corporation has just discovered oil. That day, June 1, X purchased, via a telephone call to his broker, 200 shares of ABC stock at $25 per share. On June 15, the oil discovery was made public, and ABC stock increased to $50 per share. X sold his 200 shares on June 16, at $50 per share. ABC shares are traded on the American Stock Exchange. Prior to overhearing the conversation, X had ***not*** owned any ABC shares.

Based on the foregoing, which of the following statements is most likely correct?

(A) X is liable to the corporation under SEC Rule 16(b).
(B) X is liable to the corporation under SEC Rule 10b-5.
(C) X is liable to the sellers of the shares under SEC Rule 10b-5.
(D) X has ***no*** liability to the persons from whom he purchased the ABC stock.

13. X is the Treasurer at ABC Corporation, which is traded on the American Stock Exchange. On June 1, X purchases 200 shares of the corporation's stock over the American Stock Exchange. Two weeks later, on June 15, ABC discovers oil. X had no idea this event would occur when she purchased the ABC stock. On June 30, the oil discovery becomes publicly known, and ABC's stock increases to $50 per share. On September 20, X sells her ABC stock for $48 per share.

Based on the foregoing, which of the following statements is most likely correct?

(A) X is liable to the corporation under SEC Rule 16(b).
(B) X is liable to the corporation under SEC Rule 10b-5.
(C) X is liable to persons who sold her the ABC shares under SEC Rule 10b-5.
(D) X is likely to be liable to the corporation under common-law principles.

14. X is the Vice-President of ABC Corporation, which is traded on the American Stock Exchange. X learns, via a conversation with Obie, the President of ABC, that the corporation has recently made an unexpected discovery of a large oil field on property it owns. That night X visited Bob, a friend of hers who owned 200 shares of ABC stock. X offered to purchase these shares from Bob for $25 each, their then fair market value. The transaction was concluded in Bob's apartment. X gave Bob a check for $5,000 and Bob delivered the stock certificate pertaining to the shares with an appropriate endorsement to change the name of the stockholder on ABC's records. Two weeks later, the oil find becomes publicly known and ABC's stock dramatically appreciates in value.

Based on the foregoing, which of the following statements is most likely correct?

(A) X is liable to ABC under SEC Rule 16(b).
(B) X is liable to ABC under SEC Rule 10b-5.
(C) X is liable to Bob under SEC Rule 10b-5.
(D) X may be liable to ABC under the "special facts" doctrine.

15. ABC Corporation's shares are traded on the American Stock Exchange. Ossie purchased 100 shares of ABC's common stock on January 4, for $60 per share. These shares represented less than 1% of ABC's outstanding common shares. Three months later, Ossie became a director and, the next day, sold these shares for $50 per share. One month after his sale of the ABC stock, Ossie bought 100 additional shares for $10 per share.

Based on these facts, which of the following statements is most likely correct?

(A) Ossie has no liability under SEC Rule 16(b).
(B) Ossie has liability of $1,000 under SEC Rule 16(b).
(C) Ossie has liability of $4,000 under SEC Rule 16(b).
(D) Ossie has liability of $5,000 under SEC Rule 16(b).

16. ABC Corp. stock is traded on the American Stock Exchange. Ossie, who was ***not*** an officer or director, purchased 100 shares of ABC's common stock on January 8, paying $40 per share. These shares represented 3% of ABC's outstanding common shares. Three months later, Ossie became a director and, two months after this event, sold the 100 shares for $70 per share.

Based on the foregoing, which of the following statements is most likely correct?

(A) Ossie has no liability under SEC Rule 16(b).
(B) Ossie has liability to the purchaser(s) of his shares under SEC Rule 10b-5.
(C) Ossie is liable to ABC for $3,000.
(D) Ossie is liable to the seller of the ABC shares for $3,000.

17. ABC Corp. retained Smith & Smith, a prominent, established accounting firm, to prepare its financial statement for presentation to the shareholders at the annual meeting. In preparing the statement, the accountants negligently omitted a material item of negative financial information. This resulted in ABC's financial statement appearing much more positive than warranted. No one at ABC was aware of this error. Joan purchased 100 shares of ABC stock on the basis of the accountants' financial information. Immediately after the true facts became public, ABC stock fell in value by $10 per share.

Based on the foregoing, which of the following statements is most likely correct?

(A) Smith & Smith is liable to Joan under SEC Rule 10b-5.
(B) ABC is liable to Joan under SEC Rule 10b-5.
(C) Smith & Smith and/or ABC are liable to Joan under the special facts doctrine.
(D) Neither Smith & Smith nor ABC has liability to Joan under SEC Rule 10b-5 or the "special facts" doctrine.

18. Amy was about to sell her shares of ABC Corporation stock. Paul, who had once met Amy at a party and disliked her, told Amy that ABC shares would soon increase in value because the company had discovered a new process for extracting nicotine from cigarettes. In fact, Paul had heard from a friend who worked at ABC that the company was laying off employees. On the basis of Paul's statement, Amy kept her ABC stock. However, it soon decreased in value by $5 per share after ABC's true financial condition became known. (You may assume that Paul does ***not*** work for ABC.)

Based on the foregoing, which of the following statements is most likely correct?

(A) Amy could successfully sue Paul under SEC Rule 10b-5.
(B) Amy could successfully sue Paul under SEC Rule 16(b).
(C) Amy could successfully sue Paul under the special facts doctrine.
(D) Amy cannot successfully sue Paul under any of the foregoing doctrines.

Questions 19-21 are based on the following facts:

Arlo, a director of ABC Corporation (a publicly traded entity), is informed that the annual financial statement, soon to be made public, will show that the corporation has suffered losses during the previous fiscal year. While purchasing some food in the corporation's cafeteria, Arlo mentions to Mark, the head food processor, that the corporation "has lost a lot of money" during the year. Arlo did this because Mark had asked her why she looked so "down." Gale, who was visiting a business school friend at ABC and was on the food line behind Arlo, overheard this information.

19. The next day, Arlo sold her ABC shares for $20 per share. When ABC's losses became known three months later, its stock slipped to $12 per share. Based on the foregoing, which of the following statements is most likely correct?

(A) Arlo is liable under SEC Rule 16(b), ***if*** she purchased her shares for an amount less than $20 within the six months preceding her sale of ABC stock.
(B) Arlo has no liability under SEC Rule 10b-5, ***if*** she made no express statement in connection with her sale of the ABC shares.
(C) Arlo has no liability under SEC Rule 10b-5, ***if*** she originally purchased the stock for less than $20 per share.
(D) Arlo is liable under SEC Rule 10b-5, but under no circumstances is she liable under SEC Rule 16(b).

20. The next day, Gale sells her ABC stock, which she purchased one year ago for $18 per share, for $20 per share. Based on the foregoing, which of the following statements is most likely correct?

(A) Gale has liability under SEC Rule 16(b).
(B) Gale has liability under SEC Rule 10b-5.
(C) Gale has liability under the special facts doctrine.
(D) Gale has no liability.

21. The next day, Mark sells his ABC stock (all of which he purchased one month ago) to avoid any losses. Prior to this sale, Mark held an 11% interest in ABC. Based on the foregoing, which of the following statements is most likely correct?

(A) Mark is liable under SEC Rule 16(b).
(B) Mark is liable under SEC Rule 10b-5.
(C) Mark is liable under the special facts doctrine.
(D) Mark has no liability.

22. M owns 20% of Zeta Corporation's common stock. There are 10,000 shares outstanding. Zeta Corporation is traded on a national stock exchange. M is ***not*** an officer or director of Zeta. M engages in the following transactions, all during the last calendar year:

Date	Transaction	Sale price
1/1	buys 500 shares of Zeta common stock	$7
4/5	buys 200 shares of Zeta common stock	$6
5/5	sells 600 shares of Zeta common stock	$8

Which of the following represents M's liability, if any, to Zeta Corporation under SEC Rule 16(b)?

(A) no liability.
(B) $400.
(C) $600.
(D) $800.

23. Jackson, a famous and wealthy singer, has patented a portable recording device, which he wants to manufacture and sell. If Jackson chooses to do business under a sole proprietorship structure, which of the following statements best describes Jackson's personal liability to contract creditors of the proprietorship?

(A) Jackson has no personal liability to proprietorship contract creditors.
(B) Jackson is personally liable to the proprietorship's contract creditors.
(C) Jackson is liable to the proprietorship's contract creditors, ***if*** he had personally guaranteed their obligations.
(D) None of the above.

24. Cook formed a general partnership with two other individuals. Which of the following best describes Cook's liability to partnership creditors?

(A) Cook is personally liable to partnership creditors, but only up to the amount of her contribution to the partnership.
(B) Cook is personally liable in tort, but ***not*** contract, to creditors of the partnership.
(C) Cook is personally liable in contract, but ***not*** tort, to creditors of the partnership.
(D) None of the above.

25. Martin, the President and a director of Ardvark Inc., owns 60% of Ardvark's common stock. The remaining 40% is owned by 125 other shareholders. On April 1, Martin, as a consequence of his control of the Ardvark board, persuaded a majority of the directors to reject an offer by Ant Corporation to merge Ardvark into Ant Corporation. The vote to accept Ant's offer lost,

5-4. Ant Corporation had offered consideration worth $35 per share of Ardvark stock. The fair market value of Ardvark stock is approximately $30 per share. On April 15, Martin sold his controlling interest in Ardvark to Zoo Company, which was previously a competitor of Ardvark, for $50 per share. Martin and Zoo had been negotiating the price for his stock for about one month.

Based on the foregoing, which of the following statements is most likely ***not*** correct?

(A) Ardvark may have a cause of action against Martin for breach of his duty of loyalty.
(B) The minority shareholders of Ardvark may have individual actions against Martin for breach of the majority shareholder's duty to minority shareholders.
(C) The minority shareholders may bring a derivative action against Martin for breach of his duty of loyalty.
(D) The minority shareholders may have individual actions for damages against Martin under SEC Rule 10b-5.

Questions 26-34 are based on the following facts.

Fox Corp. issued and has outstanding 1,000 shares of common stock which are owned by a husband, wife, their son (Jr. Fox), and an employee (Jones), as follows:

Mr. Fox .... 250 shares (25%)
Mrs. Fox .... 250 shares (25%)
Jr. Fox .... 250 shares (25%)
Jones .... 250 shares (25%)

For the past two years, Fox Corp. has had the following balance sheets:

FIRST YEAR

ASSETS	
Cash	$ 50,000
Accounts receivable	125,000
Inventory	55,000
Nevada real estate	400,000
Equipment	80,000
TOTAL ASSETS	$ 710,000

LIABILITIES

Accounts payable	$ 250,000
Note payable to Bank X	115,000
Note payable to Bank	250,000
TOTAL LIABILITIES	$ 615,000

SHAREHOLDERS' EQUITY

1,000 Shares of $1 par value common stock	$ 1,000
Capital in excess of par	104,000
Negative retained earnings	(10,000)
TOTAL SHAREHOLDERS' EQUITY	$ 95,000

SECOND YEAR

ASSETS

Cash	$ 75,000
Accounts receivable	50,000
Inventory	100,000
Nevada real estate	200,000
Equipment	75,000
TOTAL ASSETS	$ 500,000

LIABILITIES

Accounts payable	$ 95,000
Note payable to Bank X	105,000
Note payable to Bank	100,000
TOTAL LIABILITIES	$ 300,000

SHAREHOLDERS' EQUITY

1,000 Shares of $1 par value common stock	$ 1,000
Capital in excess of par	149,000
Negative retained earnings	50,000
TOTAL SHAREHOLDERS' EQUITY	$ 200,000

You may assume that Fox Corp. is solvent and that none of the transactions described ***below*** would impair Fox's ability to operate.

26. Which of the following numbers represents the net worth of Fox Corp. at the end of the Second Year?

(A) $50,000.
(B) $100,000.
(C) $200,000.
(D) $350,000.

27. The book value of one share of stock in Fox Corp. at the end of the Second Year is:

(A) $100.
(B) $200.
(C) $500.
(D) $1,000.

28. Assume for this question only that after the Second Year, Fox Corp. purchased Jr. Fox's 250 shares in exchange for a five-year, $100,000 promissory note made by Fox Corp. in favor of Jr. Fox. Would Jones's voting rights be ***adversely*** affected as a result of this transaction?

(A) Yes.
(B) No.
(C) Cannot tell without knowing the number of directors at Fox Corp.
(D) Cannot tell without knowing whether Fox Corp. has cumulative voting.

29. In a retained earnings jurisdiction, on the first day after the First Year, Fox Corp. may:

(A) Pay each shareholder a dividend not exceeding $35,000.
(B) Pay each shareholder a dividend not exceeding $2,500.
(C) Pay each shareholder a dividend not exceeding $37,500.
(D) Not pay any of its shareholders a dividend.

30. For purposes of this question only, assume that Fox Corp. sold its Nevada real estate on the first business day after the First Year to Mr. and Mrs. Fox for $175,000. Would this transaction dilute the present fair market value of Jones's shares?

(A) Yes.
(B) No.
(C) Cannot tell without additional facts pertaining to the Nevada real estate.
(D) Cannot tell without additional facts pertaining to whether Fox has straight or cumulative voting.

31. For purposes of this question only, assume that Fox Corp. has a board of five directors who are elected each year. Would Fox Corp.'s payment of a 10% common stock dividend ADVERSELY affect Jones's voting rights?

(A) Yes, regardless of whether Fox Corp. has straight or cumulative voting.
(B) No.
(C) Yes, but only if Fox Corp. has cumulative voting.
(D) Yes, but only if Fox Corp. has straight voting.

32. If Fox Corp. is incorporated in a typical nimble dividend state, immediately after the First Year it may:

(A) Issue no dividends.
(B) Issue dividends in an amount not exceeding $250 per shareholder.
(C) Issue dividends in an amount not exceeding $2,500 per shareholder.
(D) Issue dividends in an amount not exceeding $140,000 per shareholder.

33. If Fox Corp. is incorporated in a state that permits dividends to be paid only from retained earnings or earned surplus, could Fox Corp., on the first business day immediately after The Second Year, repurchase Jr. Fox's shares in exchange for its $100,000, five-year promissory note?

(A) Yes.
(B) No, because the purchase price exceeds $50,000.
(C) No, because Fox Corp. would become insolvent as a result of this transaction.
(D) Cannot tell without additional facts.

34. If Fox Corp. is incorporated in a state that permits distributions to be paid out of retained earnings or earned surplus, on the first business day after the Second Year it could:

(A) Pay a dividend of $10,000 to each shareholder.
(B) Pay a dividend of $13,000 to each shareholder.
(C) Pay a dividend of $37,500 to each shareholder.
(D) Pay a dividend of $50,000 to each shareholder.

35. Bob Barbell is the principal shareholder and president of CG Corporation. The corporation incurred a large unsecured obligation to Barbell as a result of consultation and management services he rendered to CG. (You may assume that these transactions were ***not*** fraudulent in nature, and that CG's board approved them. You may also assume that the transactions were not *ultra vires*.) As a result of partial payments to Barbell and several high risk transactions undertaken by him on behalf of CG, CG became insolvent and filed for bankruptcy. The other unsecured creditors of CG want Barbell's claim disallowed entirely, or at least subordinated to their claims.

Based on the foregoing, which of the following statements is most likely correct?

(A) The indebtedness of CG to Barbell will be unenforceable because a corporation cannot validly transact business with its officers.
(B) The indebtedness of CG to Barbell may be subordinated to the claims of other unsecured creditors under the Deep Rock doctrine.
(C) The indebtedness of CG to Barbell will be subordinated to the claims of CG's other unsecured creditors because Barbell is a shareholder of CG.
(D) Barbell will be able to enforce his claim against CG on par with all of CG's other unsecured creditors.

36. At the liquidation of a corporation, which of the following describes the priority of claims as between shareholders and creditors of a corporation?

(A) Secured creditors are paid first to the extent of their security. The remainder, if any, is split between the shareholders and unsecured creditors.
(B) First, preferred shareholders are paid any dividend arrearages. Next, the creditors are paid their debts. The remainder, if any, is distributed to the shareholders according to their rights and preferences.
(C) First, secured creditors are paid to the extent of their security. They then become unsecured creditors for any remaining deficiency. Next, the unsecured creditors are paid. Finally, the remainder, if any, is distributed to the shareholders according to their rights and preferences.
(D) First, creditors are paid in full. The remainder, if any, is distributed to the shareholders according to their respective rights and preferences.

Questions 37-38 are based on the following fact pattern:

On January 2, XYZ Corporation entered into a contract with Paula to purchase her bowling alley. XYZ's Articles of Incorporation expressly empower it only to operate a restaurant. The purchase price of the bowling alley is $200,000, which is to be paid at the change of possession of the premises. The date established for this to occur is April 4.

37. Assume that XYZ repudiates the contract on April 2. In a suit brought by Paula for breach of contract, XYZ asserts the *ultra vires* doctrine as a defense. Assuming this is a common-law jurisdiction, which of the following choices best describes the most likely result?

(A) XYZ will prevail, since the *ultra vires* defense is available to it under these circumstances.
(B) XYZ will prevail, ***if*** Paula had not reviewed its Articles of Incorporation prior to entering into the contract.
(C) Paula will prevail because only XYZ's shareholders can assert the *ultra vires* defense under these circumstances.
(D) Paula will prevail, ***if*** XYZ's shareholders had ratified the transaction prior to the board's attempted repudiation of the contract.

38. For purposes of this question, assume that the contract required a prepayment of $25,000 by XYZ to Paula on February 1, and that this payment was made. On February 20, XYZ entered into a two-year contract with Oliver to operate the bowling alley. If Paula tenders the $25,000 back to XYZ and repudiates the contract on March 30, which of the following is the most likely result in a common-law jurisdiction?

(A) Paula will prevail because the contract constitutes an *ultra vires* transaction.
(B) Paula will prevail because she gave notice of repudiation and returned the down payment prior to the April 4 closing date.
(C) XYZ will prevail because it made the prepayment and relied on consummation of the agreement to a substantial degree.
(D) XYZ will prevail, ***unless*** its shareholders had approved the transaction prior to Paula's repudiation.

39. Simone, the Treasurer of Fruitco, Inc., was given authority by a properly passed resolution to purchase fruits and vegetables from local growers. After Simone performed this function for one year, another resolution was validly passed limiting the dollar amount of the transactions into which she could enter. During the next year, Simone entered into agreements on behalf of Fruitco with several growers who had not sold to Fruitco in the past. However, these transactions exceeded Simone's monetary limitation. Fruitco recently learned of these contracts and seeks to repudiate them. (You may assume the agreements are ***not*** *ultra vires* transactions.)

Based on the foregoing, which of the following statements is most likely correct?

(A) Fruitco can rescind the transactions, since they exceeded the express monetary limitation set forth in the applicable resolution.
(B) Fruitco can rescind the transactions, since the growers are deemed to be on constructive notice of all Fruitco resolutions.

(C) Fruitco cannot rescind the transactions, since Simone had apparent authority to enter into these agreements.
(D) Fruitco cannot rescind the transactions, since Simone had the implied authority of her office to enter into these agreements.

40. Matt is the Secretary of ABC Corporation, a corporation formed for the purpose of manufacturing and selling bedroom furniture. Matt enters into a contract with Elmer to purchase the land on which ABC's factory is to be built. Subsequently, Matt enters into a contract with Joanne to acquire the steel needed to produce bed frames. When ABC's board learns of these transactions, it seeks to rescind the one with Joanne (but ***not*** the one with Elmer).

Based on the foregoing, which of the following statements is most likely correct?

(A) ABC cannot rescind the transaction because Matt had the implied authority of office to enter into it.
(B) ABC cannot rescind the transaction because Matt had apparent (or ostensible) authority to enter into it, based upon his agreement on behalf of ABC with Elmer.
(C) ABC can rescind the transaction because Matt lacked authority to enter into such an agreement.
(D) ABC can rescind the transaction, ***if*** it also repudiates the agreement with Elmer.

41. Charles, the Secretary of XYZ Corporation, signed a contract to lease commercial premises, at which XYZ's products would be sold. (You may assume that the contract did ***not*** pertain to an *ultra vires* matter.) When the board was apprised of the lease at its next meeting, it neither ratified nor rejected the contract. It did, however, approve a resolution instructing XYZ's President to obtain at least three bids for remodeling the premises. A short time later, however, the board determined that it would be unwise to market XYZ's products through retail premises, and passed a resolution which expressly rejected the lease.

Based on the foregoing, which of the following statements is most likely to be correct?

(A) The corporation can rescind the lease, since Charles lacked authority to enter into the transaction.
(B) The corporation can rescind the lease, since it was expressly rejected by the board.

(C) The corporation cannot rescind the lease, since it was within Charles' apparent authority.
(D) The corporation cannot rescind the lease because, although Charles lacked authority to enter into the transaction, the contract was implicitly ratified by the board.

42. Joan, the President of Bilko Corporation, entered into an agreement to merge Bilko into Apex Corporation. In return for conveying all of Bilko's assets to Apex, Bilko shareholders would receive Apex stock with a fair market value which was slightly higher than their Bilko shares. The boards of Apex and Bilko, at properly called meetings, approved the transaction.

Based on the foregoing, which of the following statements is most likely correct?

(A) The transaction is invalid because it involves the sale of all of Bilko's assets.
(B) The transaction is invalid because Joan is not a proper officer to sign the applicable documents for Bilko.
(C) The transaction is valid, since it was approved by the Apex and Bilko boards.
(D) The transaction is valid, since Joan had authority to enter into it, regardless of whether the board approved of it.

43. The Articles of Incorporation of Buildco require the corporation to have five directors, and that resolutions be passed by a "majority vote" of the directors at a properly called meeting. Buildco Corporation was formed to "acquire land for the purpose of subdividing it and constructing tract homes for sale to the public." For this purpose, the corporation validly acquired a large parcel of farm land.

However, when the permits necessary to develop the land were delayed due to lawsuits commenced by environmental groups, a board meeting was properly called to decide whether farming operations should be commenced on the land until the development permits could be obtained. Only three of the five directors attended this meeting, and two of them voted to undertake farming operations until the land could be subdivided. When the two nonattending directors were told of this resolution by the dissenting director, they indicated that, had they been at the meeting, they would have voted ***against*** the resolution.

Based on the foregoing facts, which of the following statements is most likely correct?

(A) The resolution is invalid because it authorizes an *ultra vires* activity.
(B) The resolution is invalid because less than a majority of the entire board voted for it.
(C) The resolution is invalid because a majority of the entire board actually disapproved of it.
(D) The resolution is valid because the activity authorized is reasonably necessary to the accomplishment of Buildco's express purposes.

44. The bylaws of Ajax Corporation state that, on the first Monday of each month (or the next business day thereafter, if that Monday is a legal holiday), the board of directors shall meet. Soon after Carson was elected to be a director on Ajax's five-member board, she missed a Monday meeting. At that gathering, the board approved, by a 3-1 vote, a management contract with Paul. Carson now contends that the resolution approving this contract was invalid, since she failed to receive written notice of the meeting. (You may assume the agreement would otherwise be valid.)

Based on the foregoing facts, which of the following statements is most likely correct?

(A) The resolution is invalid because Carson did not receive written notice of the meeting.
(B) The resolution is invalid, ***if*** the board failed to inform Carson that their meeting was held each month.
(C) The resolution is valid because it would have passed even if Carson had received proper notice.
(D) The resolution is valid because the meeting was properly held.

45. Oilco Corporation was interested in purchasing an extensive oil field from Nancy. (You may assume Oilco is empowered by its Articles of Incorporation to enter into all legal transactions.) At a special meeting of the board, six of the nine directors were present. The purchase was approved by a vote of 5-1. The other three directors failed to receive the written notice required by the bylaws for a special meeting, nor did they execute written waivers of notice.

Arthur, the President of Oilco, when requested by Nancy, showed her the resolution approving the transaction. Upon presentation of this resolution by Arthur, Nancy executed the purchase and sale documents.

Based on the foregoing, which of the following statements is most likely correct?

(A) Oilco can rescind the transaction, since the meeting at which the resolution was approved was not properly noticed.
(B) Oilco can rescind the transaction because a corporate president lacks actual or apparent authority to enter into a transaction of this magnitude.
(C) Oilco cannot rescind the transaction because Nancy had a right to rely on the resolution presented to her by Arthur.
(D) Oilco cannot rescind the transaction because the resolution would have passed even if the three absent directors had attended the special meeting.

46. Ajax Corporation recently acquired Greenacre from Mary Nelson for $300,000. Greenacre consisted of land with a pen manufacturing facility upon it. (You may assume that this transaction was ***not*** *ultra vires*.) However, the board of directors of Ajax, after consideration at a properly noticed board meeting, voted to decline to acquire fire insurance for the building. This 4-3 decision was made because Ajax had not declared a dividend in over two years and a majority of the directors wanted to have funds available for a dividend. Subsequently, a fire occurred causing damage to the premises in the amount of $100,000.

Based on the foregoing, which of the following statements is most likely correct?

(A) The directors have no liability under the business judgment rule.
(B) The directors who voted against the insurance are jointly and severally liable for the $100,000 loss, plus any consequential damages (e.g., lost business profits).
(C) The directors who voted against the insurance are liable only for their proportionate share of the $100,000 loss, plus any consequential damages (e.g., lost business profits).
(D) The directors who voted in favor of purchasing fire insurance are liable to the same extent as those voting against the insurance.

47. At a properly called meeting, the directors of Beta Corporation approved a resolution to purchase, for cash, many of the assets of Alpha, Inc., another corporation, including a leasehold Alpha possessed. This leasehold had almost three more years to run prior to its expiration. Since the lease payments required of Alpha were less than present market value, acquisition of the lease was an important aspect of the transaction.

An officer of Alpha informed Beta's directors that there was an outstanding dispute in the amount of approximately $10,000 resulting from the landlord's claim that Alpha was responsible for certain improvements which had been made to the premises by the lessor. Alpha agreed that funds in this amount should be left in an escrow account, which Beta could access if the matter was not successfully resolved by Alpha.

Soon after the transaction was consummated, the lessor informed Beta that Alpha was in arrears in rental payments in the amount of $50,000, and that eviction proceedings would commence immediately if Beta (as assignee of the leasehold) did not pay the full amount of this delinquency.

Based on the foregoing facts, which of the following statements is most likely correct?

(A) The directors who approved the transaction have no liability to the corporation because they relied on the statements of Alpha's officer.
(B) The directors who approved the transaction have no liability to Beta under the business judgment rule.
(C) The directors who approved the transaction are liable to Beta because they failed to obtain shareholder approval prior to entering into the agreement with Alpha.
(D) The directors who approved the transaction are liable to Beta because they should have ascertained Beta's complete liability to the lessor.

48. The Articles of Incorporation and bylaws of Acme, Inc. provide for three directors and that a director can be removed without cause by majority vote of its shareholders. The bylaws also provide that directors shall serve for three-year terms. At the annual shareholders' meeting, a proposal was put forth to remove Mitchell, one of the directors, two years prior to expiration of his term, because of his anti-abortion stance. The resolution was approved by the shareholders, 600-400 (there are 1,000 shares of Acme stock issued and outstanding).

Based on the foregoing facts, which of the following statements is most likely correct?

(A) Mitchell cannot be removed because the shareholders lack the authority to do so.
(B) Mitchell cannot be removed because no gross abuse of his corporate position has been alleged.
(C) Mitchell can be removed by the shareholders because the Articles and bylaws of Acme permit such action to be undertaken.
(D) Additional facts are necessary to determine whether Mitchell may be removed under these circumstances.

49. At the annual shareholders' meeting of Apex, Inc., the shareholders undertook the following actions:

(1) elected Joan as a director in place of Paul, who had resigned during the previous year, even though the board had appointed Edward to fill this position only six weeks prior to the shareholders' meeting,
(2) elected Adolpho president,
(3) ratified a contract to acquire Blackacre, which is jointly owned by three of Apex's five directors, and
(4) elected Tina as a director in place of Allen, who had been properly removed for cause as a director during the prior year.

Based on the foregoing facts, which of the following statements is most likely correct?

(A) All of the actions undertaken by the shareholders are valid.
(B) Actions (1), (2), and (4) are valid, but not (3).
(C) Actions (1), (3), and (4) are valid, but not (2).
(D) Actions (1), (2), and (3) are valid, but not (4).

50. The three directors of XYZ Corporation are elected each year. The annual meeting at which the new board is to be elected is usually held on January 15th. However, since this date was inconvenient for most of the seven shareholders, the annual shareholders' meeting was rescheduled for March 1. On January 11, the board entered into a two-year employment agreement with Kent, whereby Kent was to make all corporate decisions with regard to the selection and termination of officers, the determination of their salaries, and all expenditures to be incurred by XYZ. The agreement with Kent provided that he could be dismissed for incompetence and failure to satisfy specifically described performance standards.

Based on the foregoing, which of the following statements is most likely correct?

(A) The contract with Kent is invalid because it exceeds one year (the term of each directorship).
(B) The contract with Kent is invalid because it encroaches upon the management decisions of the corporation.
(C) The contract with Kent is invalid because the directors had no authority to bind the corporation after January 15, when a new board was to be elected by the shareholders.
(D) The contract with Kent is valid.

51. The directors of ABC Corporation learned that one of their employees had embezzled corporate funds in the amount of approximately $12,000. At the next board meeting, which was properly noticed and conducted, the board decided 5-4 to decline to seek recovery of the embezzled funds from the employee. This decision was premised on the directors' good faith belief that (1) the corporation would be adversely affected by the publicity that litigation would cause, and (2) any judgment which might be obtained would be difficult to collect.

Shawn, a dissenting director and shareholder who believed that an action against the employee was warranted, wanted to commence a derivative action against the directors who voted ***against*** commencing the lawsuit. However, an independent attorney, appointed by the entire board, advised against commencing a derivative action.

Based on the foregoing, which of the following statements is most likely ***correct***?

(A) A derivative action can be commenced, since directors cannot condone criminal conduct.
(B) A derivative action can be commenced, ***if*** a majority of ABC shareholders vote to pursue it.
(C) A derivative action cannot be commenced by Shawn, since an independent attorney appointed by the board advised against it.
(D) A derivative action cannot be commenced by Shawn, since she was present and voted at the board meeting which declined to seek recovery from the employee.

52. Alice is a shareholder of ABC Corporation. She seeks to bring a derivative lawsuit in ***federal*** court (based upon diversity jurisdiction) against two of the directors, Ted and Michael, claiming they had usurped a corporate opportunity, resulting in lost income to ABC of $500,000. ABC has three directors.

Based on the foregoing, which of the following statements is most likely ***incorrect***?

(A) Alice cannot personally commence an action directly against Ted and Michael.
(B) Alice is probably excused from making a demand on the directors.
(C) Alice need not (1) make a demand on the directors, or (2) show adequate reason for failing to make a demand (assuming she is not required to do so by applicable state law).
(D) Alice must post a bond if required to do so under applicable state law.

53. Mike, a shareholder of ABC Corporation, alleges that certain directors engaged in the following actions:

(1) deliberately sold off corporate assets at less than fair market value to induce Mike to sell his shares for a sum below their actual worth,
(2) refused to permit him to vote at a recent shareholders' meeting, on the pretext that he had previously given another person a proxy for his shares,
(3) issued additional shares without honoring Mike's preemptive rights, and
(4) negligently entered into various contracts which resulted in financial loss to ABC.

Which of the foregoing assertions would most likely be the subject of a derivative action?

(A) (1), (2), and (3).
(B) (1), (2), and (4).
(C) (1) and (4).
(D) (4) only.

54. Alex, a shareholder of XYZ Corporation, asserts that the directors have breached their duty of loyalty by entering into a certain contract with an entity in which they had a personal interest. The contract occurred one year prior to the time Alex inherited her XYZ shares from her deceased father. Alex also contends that following her acquisition of the stock, the directors acted negligently by allowing XYZ to enter into particular transactions which resulted in significant financial loss to the corporation.

Based on the foregoing, which of the following statements is most likely correct?

(A) Alex can bring a derivative suit ***only for*** breach of loyalty.
(B) Alex can bring a derivative suit ***only for*** negligence.
(C) Alex can bring a derivative suit for both breach of loyalty and negligence.
(D) Additional facts are needed to determine which of the three preceding answers is correct.

55. Moe, a shareholder of XYZ Corporation, commences a derivative action in federal court against three of the five directors, alleging that the three directors are liable to the corporation under SEC Rule 16(b). The transactions complained of occurred five weeks prior to the time that Moe purchased his shares in XYZ.

Based on the foregoing, which of the following statements is most likely correct?

(A) The action is barred because Moe was not a shareholder when the alleged wrongs occurred.
(B) The action is barred, unless Moe has made a demand on the three directors to reimburse XYZ for the profits they made from the transactions in question.
(C) State law requiring a bond or other security is superseded in this instance.
(D) Any recovery by Moe will be distributed, on a *pro rata* basis, to XYZ's shareholders.

56. Chris, a shareholder of Boynton Corporation, alleges that the directors unanimously approved a dividend distribution which was contrary to the applicable state law (e.g., the dividend was not made from Boynton's retained earnings). If Chris commences a derivative action in federal court, based upon diversity jurisdiction, asserting that an illegal distribution was made, which of the following statements is most likely correct?

(A) Chris can dispense with the requirement, if any exists in this jurisdiction, of obtaining shareholder approval.
(B) Chris must make demand upon the directors prior to commencing a derivative action against Boynton.
(C) Any bond or security requirements of the state are inapplicable because the action was commenced in federal court.
(D) Chris is barred from commencing a derivative action because, as a shareholder, she accepted and benefited from the distribution.

57. Alpha Corporation has seven directors, four of whom are members of a single family (a father and three adult children). The corporation decides to purchase land owned by the father. At a properly noticed meeting, the father/director discloses his interest prior to the vote on the purchase. The purchase is then approved by a 5-1 vote (the father/owner and his children voting in favor of the sale). At the annual shareholders' meeting held soon afterward, the purchase is ratified by a 42-18 vote of Alpha's disinterested stockholders.

Based on the foregoing, which of the following statements is most likely correct?

(A) The transaction is invalid because it was not approved by a majority of disinterested directors.
(B) The transaction is invalid because shareholders cannot become involved in the management of a corporation by ratifying board action.

(C) The transaction is valid because it was approved by a majority of the disinterested directors.

(D) The transaction may be challenged in a derivative lawsuit by a disinterested shareholder who did ***not*** vote for the purchase, if the transaction is patently unfair to Alpha.

58. Charles is one of the five directors of Tilden Corporation. He is also a general partner of Unger Enterprises, a fact that is not known to the other four Tilden directors. Knowing that Tilden is considering the acquisition of another plant, Charles persuades Unger Enterprises to purchase a nearby plant suitable for Tilden's market needs. Unger buys the plant for $300,000. Charles then recommends to the Tilden board that the plant be acquired by the corporation, but he does not reveal his interest in Unger.

One month after Unger buys the plant, the Tilden board, by a 4-0 vote, approves the purchase of the facility for $450,000. Charles does not attend the meeting at which the purchase is approved; he advises the board that he is too ill to attend. An agreement to purchase the facility is then entered into between Tilden and Unger. Prior to the closing of title, the other board members discover Charles' interest in Unger.

Based on the foregoing, which of the following statements is most likely correct?

(A) Tilden cannot rescind the purchase because Charles did not vote upon the matter.

(B) Tilden cannot rescind the purchase if the board, in good faith, concludes that the transaction was fair to the corporation.

(C) Tilden cannot rescind the purchase, because rescission would be unfair to the other general partners of Unger.

(D) Tilden may either rescind the transaction or recover $150,000 from Charles.

Questions 59-60 are based upon the following facts:

Prior to becoming President of Drugco, Inc. Green entered into an employment agreement which, among other things, contained the following provision:

> "Drugco, Inc. agrees to indemnify Green against all liabilities, costs, and expenses, including attorneys' fees and any amounts paid in settlement of threatened or pending claims or lawsuits, incurred by Green in connection with her duties as President of this corporation."

Two years later, while Green is President of Drugco, a chemist employed by the company advises Green that he has just discovered a cure for the common cold.

Before anyone else knows about the discovery, Green purchases 10,000 shares of the company's stock at $5 per share, the closing price of Drugco shares on the American Stock Exchange on the day the stock is purchased.

Green is sued in ***state*** court. The action seeks rescission of the stock purchase by Green.

59. If the complaint alleges a cause of action against Green under SEC Rule 10b-5, will a motion by Green to dismiss the action be granted?

(A) Yes.
(B) No, assuming it is alleged that no instrumentality of interstate commerce was used in Green's purchase.
(C) No, assuming a state law claim was also made in the pleading.
(D) Additional facts are necessary to determine whether Green's motion will be successful.

60. Assume that Green settles the action against her for $15,000, without any admission of liability, after expending $10,000 on legal fees and court costs.

Based on the foregoing, which of the following statements is most likely correct?

(A) Drugco should indemnify Green for the entire $25,000.
(B) Drugco should indemnify Green for only $10,000.
(C) Drugco should indemnify Green for only $15,000.
(D) Drugco should refuse to indemnify Green for any amount.

61. Hannah, a shareholder of Island Corporation, properly commenced a derivative action against Joe and Todd, directors, alleging that they failed to exercise adequate diligence in selecting an officer who subsequently embezzled a substantial sum of money from the corporation. The case proceeded to trial. Judgment was rendered, resulting in findings (1) that Joe was not liable, but (2) that Todd was negligent and thereby liable to the corporation for its losses due to the embezzlement. (You may assume there was no specific finding that Joe and Todd were"fairly and reasonably" entitled to reimbursement for their expenses.)

Based on the foregoing, which of the following statements is most likely correct?

(A) Both Joe and Todd may validly be indemnified for their litigation expenses and attorneys' fees from Island.
(B) Neither Joe nor Todd may validly be indemnified by Island for his litigation expenses and attorneys' fees.

(C) Joe (but not Todd) may validly be indemnified by Island for his attorneys' fees and litigation expenses.
(D) Todd may validly be indemnified by Island for his attorneys' fees and litigation expenses, but not for the amount of the judgment rendered against him.

62. Karl is the President of Acro Corporation. Jill, a Vice-President of Acro, commenced an action against Acro and against Karl, personally, contending that, due to sexual harassment by Karl, it had become necessary for her to cease employment with the corporation. In his answer, Karl denied Jill's assertions and contended that she failed to perform her functions in a competent manner requiring criticism of her performance, which in turn brought about Jill's decision to leave Acro.

Subsequently, the action was settled for $10,000 (20% of the amount demanded in Jill's complaint), part of which was paid by Karl. The board approved a resolution stating that Karl had acted in good faith and for purposes which he reasonably believed to be in the best interests of the corporation. (You may assume that Karl is not a director, and that he did not influence the board's determination with regard to his conduct.)

Based on the foregoing, which of the following statements is most likely correct?

(A) Karl cannot be validly indemnified by Acro because he was named personally in Jill's action.
(B) Karl may be validly indemnified by Acro for his attorneys' fees, litigation expenses, and the $10,000 settlement.
(C) Karl cannot be validly indemnified by Acro because he was not successful "on the merits."
(D) Karl may be validly indemnified by Acro for the sum of money paid to Jill in settlement of her action, but ***not*** for his attorneys' fees and litigation expenses.

63. The board of directors of Beta Corporation approved a resolution to make a $50,000 payment to the Ministry of Ashwan. (You may assume that Ashwan is a foreign country with which many U.S. corporations have previously had business dealings.) The board was advised by its agent in Ashwan that a payment of this type was a necessary prerequisite to consummation of all transactions with that government.

Subsequently, the U.S. Justice Department charged Beta Corporation, its directors, and the agent, with violation of a federal criminal statute which prohibits bribing foreign officials. After advice from counsel that a successful criminal prosecution was a "realistic possibility," Beta's board settled the proceeding by authorizing payment of a $150,000 fine.

Based on the foregoing, which of the following statements is most likely correct?

(A) The board members cannot validly be indemnified for their attorneys' fees and litigation costs, since they were charged with a criminal offense.
(B) The board members cannot validly be indemnified for their attorneys' fees and litigation costs, since they did not prevail on the merits.
(C) The board members can validly be indemnified for their attorneys' fees and legal costs, provided a majority of the disinterested shareholders approves a resolution finding that the board acted in good faith and reasonably believed their actions were in Beta's best interests.
(D) The board members can validly be indemnified for their attorneys' fees and legal costs, if a majority of disinterested shareholders determines that the board acted in good faith, reasonably believed their actions were in Beta's best interests, ***and*** had no reason to believe that their actions were unlawful.

64. The Articles of Incorporation of Tool Corporation authorized the issuance of 1,000 shares of common stock. All of the shares were purchased by Underhill (300 shares), Barnes (400 shares), and Whitson (300 shares). Subsequently, Tool properly amends its Articles of Incorporation so that the authorized number of shares is increased by 1,500 shares. The board undertakes this action, in part, so that it can acquire a unique patent from Smith in exchange for 500 of the newly authorized shares. The board believes this patent will revolutionize its industry. (You may assume that no state law or provision in the Articles of Incorporation or bylaws precludes the assertion of preemptive rights.)

Based on the foregoing, which of the following statements is most likely correct?

(A) Underhill may assert preemptive rights for up to 300 of the newly authorized shares.
(B) Underhill may assert preemptive rights for up to 450 of the newly issued shares.
(C) Underhill may not assert preemptive rights in the newly issued shares because they had not been authorized at the time she acquired her original stock in Tool.
(D) Underhill may not assert preemptive rights to any of the newly issued shares because some of this stock is being exchanged for property rights.

65. Ajax Corporation originally authorized the issuance of 1,000 shares of $100 par value common stock. It sold these shares at $100 per share. Arthur purchased 50 of these shares. Subsequently, Ajax redeemed 500 shares (none of which belonged to Arthur), which it held as treasury stock. Ajax now wishes to sell 1,000 common shares of $100 par value stock for $150 per share (the stock's present fair market value). It has properly amended its Articles of Incorporation to authorize issuance of 500 more shares. (You may assume that no state law or provision in the Articles of Incorporation or bylaws precludes the assertion of preemptive rights.)

Based on the foregoing, which of the following statements is most likely correct?

(A) Arthur may exercise preemptive rights to purchase 25 of the newly authorized shares at $150 per share.
(B) Arthur may exercise preemptive rights to purchase 50 of the newly issued shares at $100 per share.
(C) Arthur may exercise preemptive rights to purchase 50 of the newly issued shares at $150 per share.
(D) Arthur may exercise preemptive rights to purchase 50 shares at $100 per share, and another 50 shares at $150 per share.

66. Vernon Corporation originally authorized and sold 1,000 shares of its common stock for $100 per share. Williams purchased 400 of these shares. After a management dispute arose between Williams and the other two stockholders who owned the balance of Vernon's outstanding shares, the Articles of Incorporation were properly amended to authorize issuance of another 1,000 shares. The other two shareholders each purchased 500 of these shares for $200 per share (the stock's fair market value), without offering Williams an opportunity to acquire any of the newly authorized stock.

There is ***no*** indication that the additional capital raised by the sale of the newly authorized stock was necessary for any of Vernon's business purposes. (You may assume that no state law or provision in the Articles of Incorporation or bylaws precludes the assertion of preemptive rights. You may also assume that there is nothing in Vernon's Articles of Incorporation which specifically allows preemptive rights.)

Based on the foregoing, which of the following statements is most likely correct?

(A) Williams has no preemptive rights, since the additional 1,000 shares had not been authorized when she originally purchased her stock.
(B) Williams has preemptive rights, but her exclusive remedy is to purchase 40% of the newly authorized shares at $200 per share.
(C) Williams has no preemptive rights because, at common law, such rights did not exist unless specifically provided for in the Articles of Incorporation.
(D) Williams has preemptive rights, and may be able to obtain a court order rescinding the issuance of the newly authorized shares.

67. Joan and Mervin are two stockholders of Delta Corporation. Mervin gave Joan a proxy to vote his shares at the upcoming annual shareholders' meeting. He did this because he planned to be on vacation when this meeting was scheduled to occur. However, Mervin had to cancel his vacation because of an illness in his immediate family, and he was present at the meeting.

Based on the foregoing, which of the following statements is most likely correct?

(A) Joan cannot vote Mervin's shares **if** Mervin attends the meeting.
(B) Joan cannot vote Mervin's shares because the purpose for which the proxy was given has ceased to be applicable.
(C) Joan can vote Mervin's shares, unless Mervin objects to this action by Joan.
(D) Joan can vote Mervin's shares, provided the Articles of Incorporation expressly authorize voting by proxy.

68. Mindy sold her shares of Zebco stock to Sally. Since the annual shareholders' meeting was to occur in two weeks and the record date for voting at that event had passed one week prior to the transaction, Mindy delivered a written proxy to Sally relating to the purchased shares.

Based on the foregoing, which of the following statements is most likely correct?

(A) If Mindy attends the shareholders' meeting and expressly revokes her proxy, Sally cannot vote the shares.
(B) Sally cannot vote the shares since, despite the proxy, Mindy is the stockholder of record for that meeting.
(C) Sally can vote the shares, even if Mindy personally appears at the shareholders' meeting and insists upon voting the shares herself.

(D) Since there was an outright sale of shares to Sally, the corporation must allow Sally to vote her shares, regardless of whether she obtained a written proxy from Mindy.

69. Elmer is a shareholder of Fairway Corporation. (You may assume this corporation is subject to Section 14 of the Securities Exchange Act of 1934.) He owns approximately 2% of the corporation's outstanding common stock.

Elmer has learned that the management of Fairway intends to send out proxy solicitations to its shareholders for the purpose of obtaining their votes to re-elect the present board of directors. Elmer makes a written demand on the board to include the following proposals in their solicitation materials: (1) that Jones be appointed Chief Financial Officer (basically, the equivalent of Treasurer), and (2) that a coffee room for employees be installed in Fairway's manufacturing facility.

Based on the foregoing, which of the following statements is most likely correct?

(A) Management is ***not*** required to include either proposal in its solicitation materials.
(B) Management must include the first proposal (pertaining to Jones), but not the second one (pertaining to the coffee room), in its solicitation materials.
(C) Management must include both proposals in its solicitation materials, if Elmer has owned his shares for at least one year.
(D) Management must include the second proposal in its solicitation materials, but not the first one.

70. Emma is a shareholder of Belton Corporation. (You may assume this corporation is subject to Section 14 of the Securities Exchange Act of 1934.) She owns stock of the corporation which has a value of $6,000 and she has been a shareholder for fourteen months.

Emma wants to submit an advisory proposal to the stockholders of Belton, urging the corporation to expand its operations into the nuclear energy field via the purchase of a now defunct reactor in a nearby town. Belton was formed for the purpose of developing energy sources, but has not previously been involved in nuclear power. (You may assume that this proposal does ***not*** relate to Belton's ordinary business operations, and that the directors intend to make a proxy solicitation.)

Based on the foregoing, which of the following statements is most likely correct?

(A) Management must include Emma's proposal in its proxy solicitation materials because of its significance, regardless of its length.
(B) Management must include Emma's proposal in its proxy solicitation materials, ***if*** it does not exceed 500 words.
(C) Management must include Emma's statement in its proxy solicitation materials, but may charge Emma for the reasonable costs associated with mailing her proposal to Belton's shareholders.
(D) Management is ***not*** required to include Emma's proposal in its solicitation materials, but must provide her with a mailing list of Belton's shareholders, or else independently mail her proposal to the shareholders at the corporation's expense.

71. Ralph is a director of Zeta Corporation. (You may assume this corporation is subject to Section 14 of the Securities Exchange Act of 1934.) The board of Zeta solicited proxies for their re-election. While other members of the board had, from time-to-time, heard rumors of Ralph's ties with organized crime, no conclusive proof of this status had ever been brought to their attention. However, a reasonably thorough investigation would have disclosed that Ralph had been charged with gambling violations on two occasions and once with extortion. The first gambling charge was dismissed for lack of evidence. Ralph pleaded guilty to the second charge, resulting in three years' probation (but ***no*** actual imprisonment). The extortion trial ended in a hung jury, and Ralph was not re-tried on this charge.

The proxy solicitation failed to make mention of Ralph's prior contacts with the criminal justice system and Ralph was elected. Following the election, Mary, a shareholder with ***less*** than 1% of Zeta's stock who did not want Ralph to sit on Zeta's board, commenced an action to rescind the proxy votes obtained by Ralph before the election. (You may assume Mary gave her proxy to re-elect the board and that Ralph would ***not*** have been elected but for the proxies obtained via the solicitation.)

Based on the foregoing, which of the following statements is most likely correct?

(A) Mary should be successful and will probably be awarded her reasonable attorney's fees and litigation expenses.
(B) Mary's suit will not be successful, since she lacks standing (i.e., she owned less than 1% of Zeta's stock).
(C) Mary is not likely to be successful, since she did not commence her action until ***after*** Ralph's election.
(D) Since Ralph has never been convicted of a felony, the omission of his past criminal background was probably not material.

72. Jim and Phillip together own 65% of the outstanding stock of Acorn Corporation, but they are not directors or officers of the company. After meeting Cindy at a class reunion, Jim and Phillip signed an agreement with her whereby it was agreed that she would serve for one year as Secretary of Acorn. The previous Secretary of Acorn had recently resigned.

When Jim and Phillip advised the three Acorn directors by telephone of the contract with Cindy, two of the directors signed a typewritten resolution to appoint Cindy as the Secretary of Acorn. The third director refused to sign the resolution, asserting that he wanted to do more research into Cindy's qualifications for this office.

Based on the foregoing, which of the following statements is most likely correct?

(A) Cindy is the Secretary, based on her written agreement with Jim and Phillip.
(B) Cindy is the Secretary, based on the resolution signed by a majority of the directors.
(C) Cindy is ***not*** the Secretary because she has not been properly appointed by the directors.
(D) Cindy is ***not*** the Secretary because shareholder appointment of officers must be unanimously ratified by the board to be valid.

73. Paula is a shareholder of Weldon Corporation. She is unhappy with management because, although the corporation was profitable last year, it lagged behind the growth of similar companies. Paula advises management that, during regular business hours, she intends to review the corporate books of account and all agreements entered into by Weldon throughout the most recent fiscal year, for the purpose of determining why its profits have been relatively low.

Based on the foregoing, which of the following statements is most likely correct?

(A) Paula may view the books of account, but not the contracts entered into by Weldon.
(B) Paula may view the books of account and contracts entered into by Weldon.
(C) Paula may ***not*** view the items she seeks because the corporation has been profitable and no wrongdoing by management is evident.
(D) Paula may ***not*** view the items she seeks because she has an absolute right only to inspect basic corporate documents, such as the Articles of Incorporation, bylaws, and resolutions.

74. John, a shareholder of Boolon Corporation, has heard rumors that the corporation has entered into a number of "sweetheart deals" with firms owned by friends of the directors. As a consequence, John advises the board that, during regular business hours, he wants to review the corporate books of account and shareholder lists. The shareholder lists are sought for the purpose of obtaining their proxies to elect John as a director at the upcoming annual shareholders' meeting.

An applicable state statute provides that shareholders may inspect corporate ***books of account*** only after they have owned the company's stock for not less than twelve consecutive months. John has owned his shares for only seven months.

Based on the foregoing, which one of the following statements is most correct?

(A) John may inspect the shareholder list, but not the corporate books of account.

(B) John may inspect the shareholder list and the corporate books of account.

(C) John may inspect neither set of documents, since the an intent to unseat management in the absence of evidence of wrongdoing is an improper purpose for the solicitation of proxies.

(D) John may inspect neither set of documents, since the inspection of corporate documents is limited to books of account and John has not been a shareholder for the required period of time.

75. The directors of Bota Corporation unanimously passed a resolution which required compensation for the President (Josephine) of the corporation in the sum of about $2 million. James, a shareholder of Bota, immediately complained to the directors that Josephine's compensation was excessive. Nevertheless, the Bota directors unanimously approved an employment contract with Josephine that included compensation close to that fixed in the resolution. The disinterested shareholders of Bota ratified the contract, although by an extremely close vote (252 for approval of the resolution, 238 against ratification).

Assuming James has a viable assertion that Josephine's compensation is excessive in view of salaries received by presidents of similarly situated corporations, which of the following statements is most correct?

(A) James's derivative suit will probably be allowed, but he will ***not*** be permitted to recover his attorneys' fees and court costs (even if successful).

(B) James's derivative suit will probably be allowed, since shareholders cannot ordinarily ratify corporate waste.

(C) James's derivative suit will probably ***not*** be allowed because the shareholders have ratified the directors' action.

(D) James's derivative suit will probably ***not*** be allowed, ***unless*** he makes a formal demand on the directors to rescind the agreement.

76. Belton Corporation enters into an agreement to sell substantially all of its assets to Carlton Corporation. The consideration is 40% cash and an adequately secured promissory note for the balance. The transaction is properly approved by the directors of both corporations, as well as the necessary proportion of Belton's shareholders. However, the board of Carlton does not attempt to obtain the approval of Carlton shareholders. Johnson, a shareholder of Carlton, contends that she is entitled to exercise appraisal rights with regard to her shares. (You may assume that the applicable jurisdiction empowers shareholders with typical appraisal rights.)

Based on the foregoing, which of the following statements is most correct?

(A) Johnson is entitled to assert her appraisal rights with regard to her shares in Carlton Corporation.

(B) Johnson has no right to assert appraisal rights, but can probably obtain a court order enjoining the transaction (at least until the requisite proportion of Carlton shareholders authorizes the purchase).

(C) The transaction is invalid and can therefore be enjoined, since legislation in most states requires that a purchase of all (or substantially all) of another corporation's assets must be approved by the purchaser's shareholders.

(D) Johnson is entitled neither to assert appraisal rights nor to enjoin the transaction.

77. The directors of Ablon Corporation properly noticed a special meeting of the shareholders to approve the statutory merger of Ablon into Didon Corporation for stock of Didon. Amy, a shareholder of Ablon, wrote the boards of Ablon and Didon, advising both bodies that it was "unclear" to her whether or how the transaction would be beneficial to either corporation. Amy decided not to attend the shareholders' meeting pertaining to this transaction as a sign of her protest against the proposed merger.

At the meeting, the requisite proportion of Ablon's shareholders approved the transaction. The next day, Amy gave written notice to the board of Ablon that she intended to exercise her appraisal rights. (You may assume that the applicable jurisdiction empowers shareholders with typical appraisal rights.)

Within six days after the shareholders' meeting, the boards of both Ablon and Didon properly approved the merger, as did the Secretary of State.

Based on the foregoing, which of the following statements is most likely correct?

(A) Amy may exercise her appraisal rights because she communicated her disapproval to the board in a prompt manner.
(B) Amy may exercise her appraisal rights, ***if*** she tenders her shares to Ablon within a reasonable period of time.
(C) Amy may ***not*** exercise appraisal rights because she is a shareholder of the corporation whose assets are being sold.
(D) Amy may ***not*** exercise appraisal rights because she failed to vote against the sale.

78. The board of directors of Gibble Corporation passes a resolution whereby its assets will be conveyed to Helton Corporation, concurrently with Helton's transfer of its stock to Gibble shareholders. Pursuant to the terms of this ***statutory*** merger, Gibble will dissolve after the transaction is authorized by the Secretary of State. The board of Helton passes a resolution which approves the transfer of its stock in exchange for Gibble's assets. The requisite shareholder approvals are obtained at the annual shareholder meetings of both corporations, and the Secretary of State approves the transaction.

Bo, one of ***Helton's*** shareholders, notified the board of his opposition to the transaction and voted against it. (You may assume that the typical appraisal rights are recognized in the applicable jurisdiction.)

Based on the foregoing, which of the following statements is most likely correct?

(A) It was not necessary for Helton's board to obtain shareholder approval to undertake this transaction.
(B) Bo, being a shareholder of the acquiring corporation, is ***not*** entitled to assert appraisal rights in this situation.
(C) Creditors of Gibble can pursue Helton for any obligations owed to them by Gibble, whether or not Helton expressly assumed Gibble's debts.
(D) Assuming Bo is entitled to assert appraisal rights, he would receive the fair market value of Helton shares as of one month subsequent to completion of the merger.

79. Melton Corporation agrees to sell all of its assets to Nolton Corporation. The consideration for this sale will be Nolton stock. Since all of Nolton's originally authorized stock has been sold, its Articles of Incorporation must be amended to allow the issuance of additional shares. As part of the transaction, the Melton board has promised to distribute the Nolton stock it receives to its shareholders and then cause Melton's dissolution. (You may assume that the *de facto* merger doctrine is recognized in the applicable jurisdiction.)

Based on the foregoing, and assuming the transaction is consummated, which of the following statements is most likely correct?

(A) Nolton will ***not*** be liable for Melton's debts.
(B) The stockholders of Nolton need not approve the authorization of additional shares.
(C) Shareholders of both corporations may assert appraisal rights.
(D) Assuming there is nothing in the Articles of Incorporation or bylaws to the contrary, Nolton's shareholders may assert preemptive rights with respect to the newly authorized shares.

80. Megon Corporation, which is listed on the New York Stock Exchange, has entered into an agreement to merge into Polton Corporation, which is also listed on the New York Stock Exchange. This statutory merger is subject to approval by the shareholders of both corporations. The board of Megon solicits proxies from its shareholders and obtains a positive vote approving the merger.

Elwood, a Megon shareholder, believes that the proxy solicitation contained fraudulent, materially misleading information. (You may assume this contention could be proved successfully at trial and that the applicable jurisdiction recognizes the typical appraisal rights.)

Based on the foregoing, which of the following statements is most likely correct?

(A) Elwood can obtain rescission of the merger under SEC Rule 10b-5, ***if*** he bought (rather than inherited) his shares.
(B) Elwood can exercise his appraisal rights ***regardless*** of whether he votes at the shareholders' meeting.
(C) Assuming Elwood has an action under SEC Rule 10b-5 or Section 14 of the Securities Exchange Act, it can be commenced in either federal or state court.
(D) Elwood could probably commence an action under state law to rescind the merger or exercise his appraisal rights.

81. Felton Corporation and Carlton Corporation agree to effectuate a ***statutory*** merger, pursuant to which Felton will exchange 10% of its outstanding shares (which previously were held as treasury stock) for Carlton's assets.

The transaction is approved by the appropriate state authority. You may assume that there would be ***no*** change in Felton's Articles of Incorporation as a consequence of this merger.

Based on the foregoing, which of the following statements is most likely correct?

(A) Only the shareholders of Carlton must approve the transaction.
(B) The shareholders of both Carlton and Felton have appraisal rights.
(C) Felton would be liable for Carlton's outstanding obligations.
(D) The transaction described above is sometimes referred to as a short form merger.

82. ABC Corporation has authorized and issued 1,000 shares of its common stock. The board of ABC has concluded that it would be beneficial to the corporation to raise additional capital by the issuance of a new class of preferred stock. These shares would be nonvoting, but would have priority with regard to the distribution of dividends. The ABC board passes a resolution approving the issuance of this new class of preferred stock.

Based on the foregoing, which of the following statements is most correct?

(A) ABC's Articles of Incorporation probably require unanimous shareholder approval for the resolution to be effective.
(B) Approval of an amendment to the Articles of Incorporation by the holders of ABC common stock is ***not*** required in this situation.
(C) It is illegal to create a class of shares that has priority in the distribution of dividends, unless the issuance of these shares is authorized in the original Articles of Incorporation.
(D) The holders of common stock must approve an amendment to the Articles of Incorporation before the preferred shares can be validly issued.

83. Ogden Corporation had a net profit of $30,000 last year. However, its books and records reveal a deficit to earned surplus of $21,000. Nevertheless, the board of directors of Ogden declares a dividend of $1 per share. There are 1,800 shares issued and outstanding. (You may assume this dividend would ***not*** cause Ogden to become insolvent, and that there are no preferred shares which require priority in the payment of dividends.)

Based on the foregoing, which of the following statements is most correct?

(A) The dividend is valid because it will be paid out of Ogden's net profits.
(B) The dividend is invalid because dividend payments cannot be made while an earned surplus deficit exists.

(C) The dividend is valid because it will not cause Ogden to become insolvent.
(D) It is necessary to research applicable law to determine whether dividends may be paid under these circumstances.

84. Samuels, Tilden, and Underwood entered into a two-year voting trust which complied with all necessary requisites, and under which Watson was appointed as their trustee to vote all their shares with respect to certain specified matters, including the election of directors. Samuels and Tilden own 20% each of the corporation's shares, and Underwood owns 15%.

Watson decides to use the votes assigned to her under the trust to elect Martha as a director at the next shareholders' meeting. Watson believes Martha will do a good job as director of the corporation and that the interests of the beneficiaries would be served by her election. However, Samuels and Tilden do not like her and do not want her to be appointed. (You may assume that Martha is competent to handle this position.) Underwood is ***not*** opposed to Martha's election.

At the annual shareholders' meeting, Samuels and Tilden are present. They announce that they are repudiating the voting trust and attempt to vote their shares for a candidate other than Martha. Underwood makes no objection to Watson's voting his shares. (You may assume that the voting trust can be revoked by unanimous vote of the shareholder/beneficiaries.)

Based on the foregoing, which of the following statements is most correct?

(A) Watson can vote the shares for Martha's election as a director because she believes her election would be beneficial to the members of the voting trust.
(B) Watson can vote the shares for Martha because she is competent.
(C) Watson ***cannot*** vote the shares for Martha, because it would frustrate the purpose of the voting trust to ignore the wishes of two of the shareholder/beneficiaries.
(D) Watson ***cannot*** vote the shares for Martha, because her authority was revoked by Samuels and Tilden at the meeting and because of their express objection to Watson's voting their shares for Martha's election.

85. Mary, Katey, and Mandy are shareholders of Guildco Corporation. Mary owns 32% of the corporation's shares, Katey 11%, and Mandy 18%. They enter into a pooling agreement under which they each agree to vote their shares with regard to any matter as any two or more of them shall decide. The agreement is to be in effect for two years.

Prior to the next annual shareholders' meeting, Katey and Mandy decide to vote against a derivative action which another shareholder seeks to commence. Learning of their intention prior to the meeting, Mary declares that the pooling agreement is rescinded, and advises Katey and Mandy that she (Mary) is not bound by their decision. (You may assume that the pooling agreement was ***not*** filed with Guildco for inspection and that there is nothing on the face of Mary's shares that makes reference to the pooling agreement.)

Based on the foregoing, which of the following statements is most correct?

(A) Mary can vote her shares as she wishes, since she holds a majority of the stock that is subject to the pooling agreement.

(B) Mary can vote her shares as she wishes, since the pooling agreement was not filed with the corporation.

(C) Mary can vote her shares as she wishes, since no reference to the pooling agreement appears on the face of Mary's shares.

(D) Katey and Mandy can probably enforce the agreement by obtaining a decree of specific performance, if necessary.

86. Congolea Corporation is interested in acquiring control of Beldola Corporation. For cash, Congolea acquires a 72% interest in Beldola by purchasing the shares of Beldola's two largest stockholders, Bob and Beula Simpson. Congolea now plans to initiate a "short form" merger with Beldola.

Fred Farkel, a minority shareholder of Beldola, opposes this transaction. (You may assume that the purchase of Beldola shares was ***unanimously*** approved by Congolea's five-member board of directors. You may also assume that neither corporation is subject to federal securities laws.)

Based on the foregoing, which of the following statements is most correct?

(A) Fred can invalidate the transaction because it was not approved by Congolea's shareholders.

(B) Fred can invalidate the transaction because it was not approved by Beldola's board.

(C) Fred cannot invalidate the transaction because it was ***unanimously*** approved by Congolea's board.

(D) Fred will not be able to challenge the transaction.

87. Harrold owns a controlling interest (62% of the shares) in Ajax Corporation. Ajax is in the car wash business. Ianco Corporation is a competitor of Ajax, and it owns a car wash located a short distance from one operated by Ajax. Ajax shares have a fair market value of $30 per share.

Ianco, after a properly approved resolution by its board of directors, offers to purchase Harrold's stock for $40 per share.

Frances, a minority shareholder of Ajax, objects to the control premium which Harrold will receive. Frances can show that once the transaction is completed, Ianco is likely to (1) reduce the price of car washes at the Ajax facility, to bring it in line with the price charged at Ianco's premises, and (2) reduce advertising for the Ajax site, so that more business will accrue to Ianco's facility. (You may assume that the applicable jurisdiction recognizes appraisal rights in both merger and *de facto* merger situations. You may also assume that this jurisdiction follows the holding and rationale of *Perlman v. Feldman.*)

Based on the foregoing, which of the following statements is most correct?

(A) Frances has ***no*** right to receive a *pro rata* portion of Harrold's premium, since there is no proof that Ianco intends to loot Ajax.
(B) Frances has ***no*** right to receive a *pro rata* portion of Harrold's premium, since she has appraisal rights.
(C) Frances can invalidate the sale, since it has not been approved by Ajax's board.
(D) Frances ***cannot*** invalidate the transaction, but can probably obtain a *pro rata* portion of Harrold's premium.

88. Biltmore Corporation wishes to acquire a controlling interest in Park Place ("PP") Corporation. To achieve this objective, Biltmore purchases all of the shares of PP owned by Joe Randolph. This purchase represents 58% of PP's outstanding shares. Randolph receives a $15 per share control premium for selling his interest to Biltmore.

As part of the transaction whereby the purchase of Randolph's PP stock is to occur, Randolph promises to cause the seriatim resignation of PP's directors and the appointment of new directors, so that Biltmore will effectively have control of PP's board.

There is ***no*** reason to believe that (1) Biltmore's management intends to loot or otherwise undertake acts detrimental to PP, or (2) Biltmore's control of PP will result in any lessened profitability to PP.

Based on the foregoing, which of the following statements is most correct?

(A) The minority shareholders of PP are entitled to a *pro rata* distribution of Randolph's premium.
(B) The minority shareholders are ***not*** entitled to receive a *pro rata* distribution of Randolph's premium, but the directors' resignation and the appointment of new directors is invalid.

(C) The minority shareholders of PP are ***not*** entitled to receive a *pro rata* distribution of Randolph's premium, and the seriatim resignation and appointment of new directors is valid.
(D) The seriatim resignation of the present board and appointment of new directors is invalid.

89. Carla and John decide to incorporate for the purpose of operating an airport shuttle service. Each pays $10,000 to the corporation and receives 1,000 shares of stock. In addition, John lends $5,000 to the corporation, which is manifested by a promissory note. The $5,000 is used for the down payment on a van the corporation purchases.

One week after the shuttle service begins, the van is involved in an accident, resulting in two wrongful death judgments against the corporation. These judgments exceed the corporation's liability insurance (which was $250,000) by $500,000. The corporation then files a voluntary bankruptcy petition.

Based on the foregoing, which of the following statements is most likely to be correct?

(1) Carla and John are personally liable for the corporation's debts.
(2) Assuming strict adherence to the necessary formalities for incorporation, Carla and John have no personal liability.
(3) John's promissory note may be subordinated by a court to the claims of the corporation's other creditors.

(A) (2) only.
(B) (1) only.
(C) (1) and (3).
(D) (2) and (3).

90. There are seven directors of XYZ Corporation. Prior to the annual directors' meeting, Art, Sam, and Kelly (three of the directors) agreed to vote in favor of retaining Oscar as President, even though XYZ had just experienced a very mediocre fiscal year. (The President of XYZ is chosen by a majority of the directors.) Later, but still prior to the meeting, Art became ill and gave Sam a proxy to cast his (Art's) vote for Oscar.

At the meeting, Carla (another director) argued so forcefully against retaining Oscar, that Kelly decided to vote for Elmer as President. Elmer was the candidate proposed by Carla. Elmer received the four votes necessary to become President. The other three directors voted for Oscar (Sam cast his own vote and voted Art's proxy for Oscar).

Based on the foregoing, which of the following statements is most correct?

(A) Art and Sam can successfully maintain an action against Kelly for breach of their agreement.
(B) Sam was entitled to cast Art's vote for the election of Oscar.
(C) The agreement among Art, Sam, and Kelly was unenforceable and the proxy was invalid.
(D) Oscar is entitled to have Elmer's election rescinded under third-party beneficiary principles.

91. The Articles of Incorporation of XYZ Corporation provide that shareholders must, prior to any sale or conveyance of their shares, offer them for sale to the other shareholders for their fair market value (as determined by an independent appraiser). The shares issued by XYZ contain the following legend: "These shares may be subject to a restriction contained in the Articles of Incorporation."

Joe, one of XYZ's shareholders, agrees to sell his shares to Bertha for an amount per share that exceeds the fair market value. Bertha agrees to purchase these shares without actually seeing the certificates. On the date of the sale, Bertha tenders payment to Joe and he hands Bertha a certificate evidencing his shares, along with a power of attorney. When Bertha delivers the share certificate and power to XYZ's Secretary, he refuses to transfer the shares to her name.

Based on the foregoing, which of the following statements is most correct?

(A) Bertha can obtain an order compelling XYZ to transfer the shares to her name because she was unaware of the restriction when she entered into the agreement with Joe.
(B) Bertha can obtain an order compelling XYZ to transfer the shares to her name because the notation on the share certificate did not recite the specific restriction contained in the Articles of Incorporation.
(C) Bertha can obtain an order compelling XYZ to transfer the shares to her name because, regardless of her constructive knowledge of the restriction, the provision pertaining to transferability is invalid.
(D) Bertha cannot compel XYZ to transfer the shares to her name because the restriction is noted on the share certificate.

92. Under the laws of State X, any attorney who acts as incorporator in the Articles of Incorporation must attach an affidavit affirming his authority to practice law. John Avocat was one of three incorporators who signed the Articles of Incorporation for ABC Corporation. John knew that his license was ***not*** in force because he had failed to file the annual certificate evidencing malpractice insurance coverage, required by the state bar authorities, or to pay his required annual fees, but he signed the affidavit nevertheless. The other incorporators, A and B, had no reason to suspect John's fraudulent affidavit.

The Articles were filed with the Secretary of State, shares were issued, directors elected, and officers appointed. Shortly thereafter, a customer of ABC sued A and B personally in contract, claiming that he had been delivered a defective product.

Based on the foregoing, which of the following statements is most correct?

(A) ABC is a *de jure* corporation.
(B) ABC is a *de facto* corporation.
(C) ABC can successfully assert the "corporation by estoppel" doctrine against the customer.
(D) ABC would probably be viewed as a partnership for purposes of any recovery by the customer.

93. Gerber, Hall, and Jackson are the ***original*** shareholders, directors, and officers of Island Corporation. Included in the bylaws of Island is a provision requiring that, in the event any of the three ceases to be employed by Island, his or her shares must be offered to the other two at fair market value (as determined by an independent appraiser), before the stock may be sold to anyone else. The bylaws also provide that once this value is determined, it may be paid by the purchasing shareholder(s) over a three-year period, with interest at 5% per annum.

Hall decides to leave Island, but wants to sell her shares to Natalie. Hall honestly believes that Natalie would greatly complement the managerial skills of Gerber and Jackson.

Based on the foregoing, which of the following statements is most correct?

(A) Hall does not have to offer her shares to the other shareholders because the bylaw provisions are unreasonable.
(B) Hall does not have to offer her shares to the other shareholders because she is acting in good faith.
(C) Hall must offer her shares to the other shareholders because the bylaw provisions are reasonable.
(D) Hall does not have to offer her shares to the other shareholders because the agreement restricting transferability is not shown on the stock certificates.

94. Anticipating the production needs of the new company, Alex, a promoter for Bennett Corporation, entered into a pre-incorporation contract with Castleton Industries for the purchase of grain. Alex did not expressly tell

Castleton that he would not be personally liable on the contract if the Bennett board failed to approve it. After Bennett was validly incorporated, Castleton delivered the grain to Bennett's premises. Believing that the grain was delivered pursuant to a valid agreement between Castleton and the President of Bennett, Bennett's employees used 15% of the grain in the week following delivery.

When Bennett's board learned that the grain was delivered under the contract with Alex, it refused to approve the contract and returned the unused grain to Castleton.

Based on the foregoing, which of the following statements is most correct?

(A) Alex has no liability to Castleton because Bennett used some of the grain.
(B) Alex can recover in *quasi* contract for the grain that was used by Bennett.
(C) Bennett is liable to Castleton for the grain it consumed.
(D) By using some of the grain, Bennett became liable to Castleton for the entire contract price.

95. Able, a promoter of Benson Corporation (a corporation not yet formed) purchased a parcel of land in her own name for $50,000. Able purchased the parcel because she believed Benson would probably require the site for the retail toy store business it intended to operate. Able transferred the parcel to a partnership called Belbow Brothers, which she controlled. Subsequently, Benson was validly formed.

Shortly afterward, Belbow and Benson entered into an agreement under which Benson was to purchase the realty for $75,000. The partnership was ***not*** represented by Able but by another partner. One week after the land purchase agreement was made, the directors of Benson learned of Able's interest in Belbow Brothers.

Based on the foregoing, which of the following statements is most correct?

(A) Able has no liability to Benson because she was not a director or officer of the corporation when the purchase agreement occurred.
(B) Able is not liable to Benson because the transaction was negotiated by a partner of Belbow other than Able.
(C) Able is liable to Benson for her profit because she failed to disclose her interest in the property.
(D) Able is not liable to Benson for her profit, if she can prove that the fair market value of the land was $75,000 at the time the directors of Benson entered into the transaction with Belbow Brothers.

96. Minefield Incorporated is a corporation which is empowered by its Articles to acquire, operate, and sell minerals extracted from the earth. The bylaws of Minefield provide that the Treasurer has the authority to receive funds, provide receipts therefore, and make deposits into the corporate bank account.

A little over one year ago, Jack, the Treasurer of Minefield, entered into a one-year agreement with a boarding house for the employees of Minefield. The contract authorized the purchase of food by the boarding house for the account of Minefield. The food was to be used to feed Minefield employees. When Minefield's board became aware of this agreement, it instructed Jack to make ***no*** contracts for the corporation in the future.

However, with the knowledge the President of Minefield, Jack entered into a one-year renewal of the contract with the owner of the boarding house. The renewal was performed by both parties over several months. When the contract was brought to the attention of the board of directors by a disgruntled employee, the board passed a resolution repudiating the agreement. The owner has sued Minefield to compel the corporation to honor the contract.

Based on the foregoing, which of the following statements is most likely correct?

(A) The agreement is enforceable because it was within Jack's implied authority.
(B) The agreement is enforceable because it was within Jack's apparent authority.
(C) The agreement is enforceable because it was ratified by the board of directors of Minefield.
(D) The agreement is unenforceable under the *ultra vires* doctrine.

97. Joanne was a C.P.A. with Wilkes & Wilkes. Belmont Incorporated was a client of the accounting firm. One day, while Joanne was at Belmont's premises performing work on behalf of Wilkes & Wilkes, she reviewed a company file disclosing an offer by Ajax Corporation to acquire all of the outstanding shares of Belmont. Without disclosing this nonpublic information to anyone, Joanne purchased 1,000 shares of Belmont stock. After the purchase, Joanne owned 3% of Belmont's outstanding stock. About two months later, Ajax publicly offered to acquire all of Belmont's outstanding shares, resulting in a $2 per share increase in Belmont stock.

Based on the foregoing, which of the following statements is most correct?

(A) Joanne has no liability, since she was not a corporate insider.
(B) Joanne has no liability because she made no material misrepresentations with respect to her acquisition of Belmont stock.
(C) Joanne is liable under SEC Rule 10b-5 because she failed to disclose the information to the seller of her stock.
(D) Joanne is liable to the sellers of the shares under the "special facts" doctrine.

98. X, a Vice-President of ABC Corporation, overheard the President advise the Secretary in the company corridors that the corporation had just been awarded a valuable government contract. This fact would definitely make ABC stock more valuable. X immediately purchased 300 shares of ABC stock from Y (another ABC shareholder). After news of the government contract became public two weeks later, ABC stock increased in value by $5 per share. ABC Corporation sued X to recover the profit he had made as a consequence of his purchase of ABC shares from Y.

Based on the foregoing, which of the following statements is most correct?

(A) The corporation should be successful under SEC Rule 10b-5, ***if*** an instrumentality of interstate commerce was used in the X-Y transaction.
(B) The corporation should be successful under SEC Rule 10b-5, ***if*** ABC shares are sold on a national stock exchange.
(C) The corporation should be successful in its action against X under SEC Rule 10b-5, whether or not an instrumentality of interstate commerce was used or ABC stock is sold on a national stock exchange.
(D) The corporation may be successful in its action against X under the "special facts" doctrine.

99. Barnes is the President of Acme Corporation. On June 1, Acme purchased 1,000 shares of Caswell Incorporated common stock. Caswell stock is ***not*** traded on a national stock exchange. At the September 1 shareholders' meeting following Acme's acquisition of Caswell stock, Barnes was elected to Caswell's board of directors. Unknown to Acme or Barnes, Caswell had just patented an important medical device.

On November 11, Barnes acquired knowledge of this patent as a consequence of being a director of Caswell. On November 15, news of the patent became public, and Caswell stock increased by $5 per share. On November 22, Acme sold its Caswell stock, making a profit of $5 per share. (You may assume that Caswell has assets in excess of $6 million and 512 holders of Class A common stock. You may also assume that Caswell is engaged in interstate commerce.)

Based on the foregoing, which of the following statements is most likely correct?

(A) Acme has no liability to Caswell because it is neither an officer, director, or 10% shareholder of Caswell stock.

(B) Acme has no liability to Caswell because the corporation is ***not*** traded on a national stock exchange.

(C) Acme is liable to Caswell for the profit it made from the sale of its Caswell shares.

(D) Acme is liable to Caswell for the profit it made from the sale of Caswell shares, ***if*** it became at least a 10% shareholder as a consequence of its purchase of Caswell stock.

100. Abby and Brandon entered into an agreement with Carlson, the President of Davis Corporation, under which Abby and Brandon each agreed to purchase 50 shares of Davis stock at $30 per share. The par value of Davis stock as set forth in the Articles of Incorporation was $25 per share. The subscription agreement was executed by Carlson on behalf of Davis Corporation. Abby and Brandon agreed to complete the purchase "within three months." Two months after the agreement, Abby and Brandon sent the board of Davis a letter repudiating their obligations under the subscription agreement.

Davis Corporation is authorized to issue 10,000 shares of common stock. It had issued 8,000 prior to the date of the subscription agreement with Abby and Brandon.

Based on the foregoing, which of the following statements is most correct?

(A) Abby and Brandon could revoke the subscription agreement if the agreement was not ratified by Davis's board.

(B) Abby and Brandon may repudiate the subscription agreement because it requires them to pay an amount in excess of the par value of the shares as set forth in the Articles of Incorporation of Davis.

(C) Abby and Brandon must purchase the shares because their agreement with Davis is enforceable.

(D) The subscription agreement is enforceable against Abby and Brandon, only ***if*** they owned Davis stock at the time the subscription agreement was made.

Multiple-Choice Answers

1. **A** Where shares are ***not*** issued for money paid, labor done, or property actually transferred to the corporation, the transaction is ordinarily voidable by the corporation. Since the majority view is that an unsecured promissory note does not constitute "money paid," the transaction is voidable (not void) by ABC. Thus, the corporation can rescind its sale of the shares. In some jurisdictions, ABC alternatively could require Bill to make the payments due under the note. (*See* ELO Ch.12-I(B)(3)(b).) Choice **B** is incorrect because judgment creditors of ABC would not be permitted to enforce the note unless ABC was in bankruptcy (which it is not). Choice **C** is incorrect because ABC's shareholders cannot enforce the note. Rescission or demand for payment must be made by ABC through its officers and directors. In fact, in many jurisdictions, the corporation cannot obtain a ***monetary judgment*** for stock issued for inadequate value. It must either rescind or affirm the transaction. Finally, Choice **D** is wrong because Choice **A** is a correct answer.

2. **D** If stock is issued in good faith and with the reasonable belief that the stated par value is equal to the value of the property received in exchange, the shares are ***not*** watered. While there may be some evidence that the property received was not exactly equal in value to the shares, this fact alone is insufficient to characterize the shares as being watered. The evidence of the expert as to the worth of the property goes to its ***present*** value. It is entirely possible that the property had a higher value one year ago, when it was received in exchange for the shares. (*See* ELO Ch.12-I(B)(4)(c).) Choices **A**, **B**, and **C** are incorrect because the shares, having been issued in good faith with the reasonable belief that their par value was equal to the value of the property, are ***not*** watered. We do not have to consider whether creditors and/or stockholders would have standing to recover from Jackie because the stock is not watered.

3. **A** The watered amount of shares can ordinarily be recovered by judgment creditors of the corporation. Under the trust fund theory, all judgment creditors of a corporation can usually recover the watered amount of shares measured at the time of issue. Under the misrepresentation theory, only persons who extended credit to ABC ***after*** the transaction with Jackie could recover the $2,000 difference. The fact that Jackie no longer owns the stock is irrelevant. (*See* ELO Ch.12-I(B)(2)b).) Choices **B** and **C** are incorrect because the shareholders cannot personally recover the watered amount. Their remedy would be to commence a derivative action on behalf of ABC to rescind the transaction to the extent the stock was watered. Choice **C** is incorrect

also because the shareholders could only recover $2,000, not $5,000. Finally, Choice **D** is incorrect because judgment creditors of ABC can recover the watered amount from Jackie.

4. A Under the common law, a subscriber can repudiate his or her obligation under a subscription agreement at any time prior to formation ***and acceptance by*** the corporation. Although X Corporation was formed, no resolution was passed affirming the subscription agreement prior to A's repudiation. (*See* ELO Ch.12-I(A)(3)(i).) Choice **B** is incorrect because the corporation must be formed ***and*** must accept the subscription agreement for it to be binding on the subscriber. Choice **C** is incorrect because B's failure to join A in revoking the subscription agreement is irrelevant (unless, of course, the subscription agreement specifically provided that B's promise was contingent on performance by A). Finally, Choice **D** is incorrect because, once the corporation was formed, the board of X was the proper party for A to notify of her revocation, not the promoter.

5. C Once a subscription agreement is accepted by the corporation, the subscribers are ordinarily liable to pay for the shares they have promised to purchase. Although there is a minority view that a subscriber is relieved of liability if the corporation has become insolvent prior to delivery of the shares (i.e., there has been a material failure of consideration by reason of the corporation's insolvency), the majority view still holds the subscriber liable. (*See* ELO Ch.12-I(A)(3)(b).) Choice **A** is incorrect because A became liable under the subscription agreement when the contract was affirmed by the corporation. Choice **B** is incorrect because, in most jurisdictions, a subscriber remains liable even though the corporation becomes insolvent prior to delivery of the stock. Finally, Choice **D** is incorrect because the subscriber is liable to judgment creditors of an insolvent corporation. The trustee-in-bankruptcy enforces the rights all creditors of the corporation.

6. A When a promoter signs a contract on behalf of a corporation "to be formed," he is usually personally liable under that agreement. In the absence of proof of a contrary understanding, it is ordinarily assumed that the obligee expects the promoter to be bound by the contract because the corporation (1) may never be formed, or (2) may fail to ratify the agreement. Thus, in the absence of a specific disclaimer to the contrary, Zeek is personally liable to Paula. (*See* ELO Ch.2-III(B)(4).) Choice **B** is incorrect because, under the circumstances,

Zeek is liable to Paula. Choice **C** is incorrect because Amco would be liable to Paula ***only if*** it affirmed the agreement. Finally, Choice **D** is wrong because Choice **A** is a correct answer.

7. C Ordinarily, a promoter is ***not*** relieved of liability under a pre-incorporation contract simply by reason of ratification of that agreement by the corporation. Although Amco approved the agreement, Zeek is ***not*** automatically relieved of personal liability. The subsequent ratification by Amco is likely to be viewed as merely an implied assignment by the original obligor (Zeek) to Amco. (*See* ELO Ch.2-III(B)(4)(c).) Choice **A** is incorrect because, by approving the contract, Amco became liable under the agreement along with Zeek. Choice **B** is incorrect because Zeek is still liable under the contract. Finally, Choice **D** is wrong because Choice **C** is a correct answer.

8. B When a corporation knowingly accepts the benefits of a contract, it may have implicitly approved the agreement. In the alternative, the corporation may be liable under *quantum meruit* principles for the value of the benefit bestowed upon it. Since Alice worked at the corporation for five months, Exco would appear to have implicitly ratified the entire agreement. (*See* ELO Ch.2-III(C)(2)(c).) In the alternative, Alice should at least be able to recover the reasonable value of the benefit of her services under *quantum meruit* principles. Choice **A** is incorrect because John specifically exculpated himself from personal liability (i.e., " … but not for himself personally"). Choice **C** is incorrect because, although John is not liable, Exco may be liable for the entire agreement (if it implicitly ratified the contract) or at least for the reasonable value of the services Alice bestowed on it over five months. Finally, Choice **D** is wrong because Choice **B** is a correct answer.

9. C A *de jure* argument cannot be made successfully until the Articles of Incorporation have been filed. Thus, Choice **A** is incorrect. Under the common law, a *de facto* corporation exists where there has been (1) a good faith attempt to comply with the statutory filing requisites, and (2) some significant use of the corporate form (e.g., directors elected, officers appointed, stock issued, business conducted). Since there has been virtually no use of the corporate form (the facts fail to indicate that any directors have been elected, officers appointed, or stock issued), a *de facto* corporation argument would probably be unsuccessful. (*See* ELO Ch.2-IV(B).) While there was a reference to the corporate form in the A-with-Billie transaction, A alluded only to the future formation of Exco. Thus, Choice **B** is incorrect. Finally, Choice **D** is incorrect because the corporation-by-estoppel doctrine is applicable only where the plaintiff believed, or had reason to believe, he or she had transacted business with a corporation. Chuck had no such belief prior to the accident with B. Therefore, Choice **C** must be correct.

10. C Under the corporation-by-estoppel doctrine, if a person reasonably believes he or she is dealing with a corporation, a corporate structure is deemed to exist ***for purposes of that transaction***. Since Billie presumably believed she was dealing with a corporate entity (A signed the agreement, "A, future President of Exco Corporation"), the corporation-by-estoppel doctrine would arguably apply. While A's use of the word "future" makes the corporation-by-estoppel argument more problematic, this contention nevertheless represented his best means of avoiding personal liability. (*See* ELO Ch.2-IV(D).) Because the Articles of Incorporation were never approved by the Secretary of State, a *de jure* corporation does not exist. Thus, Choice **A** is incorrect. Under the common law, a *de facto* corporation exists where there has been (1) a good faith attempt to comply with the statutory filing requisites, and (2) some significant use of the corporate form (e.g., directors elected, officers appointed, stock issued, business conducted). As stated *supra*, Question 9, a *de facto* corporation argument would probably be unsuccessful. Thus, Choice **B** is incorrect. Finally, Choice **D** is incorrect because (1) A will be entirely relieved of personal liability if the corporation-by-estoppel doctrine is applicable, and (2) there is no factual basis to assert that he is personally liable for one-third of Billie's claim.

11. B Prior to the time a corporation is properly formed, the entity created by the proposed incorporators exists as a partnership. Each partner is ordinarily jointly and severally liable for the obligations of a partnership. (*See* ELO Ch.1-III(D)(2)(a).) Neither a *de jure* nor a *de facto* corporation existed at the time of the accident. Thus, A, B, and C were acting as a partnership. As such, A is jointly and severally liable for Chuck's damages. In some jurisdictions, only those partners who have assumed a management role are personally liable. However, even under that view, A would be jointly and severally liable to Chuck, since he (A) entered into a contract on behalf of Exco. The corporation-by-estoppel doctrine is ***not*** applicable because Chuck could not be aware that a corporation might be involved. While A is liable for the full amount of Chuck's injuries, as a partner, he can seek reimbursement from B and C for their proportionate (i.e., one-third each) shares of liability. Choice **A** is incorrect because A is liable to Chuck as B's partner, even though B was the driver of the vehicle involved in the accident. Finally, Choices **C** and **D** are incorrect because each partner is jointly and severally liable to the tort victim for the full amount of his injuries.

12. D Under SEC Rule 10b-5, a corporate insider who fails to disclose nonpublic, material facts in connection with a purchase or sale of securities is liable to the seller or purchaser, as the case may be. An insider is generally one who is advised of material, nonpublic information as a consequence of (1) his or her position with the corporation, or (2) being retained by the corporation to perform a confidential function. X is probably ***not*** an insider. He merely overheard a conversation between the geologist and the President of ABC; he was not advised of the facts by anyone. He is ***not*** liable to the sellers of ABC stock under SEC Rule 10b-5. (*See* ELO Ch.8-III(G).) Therefore, Choice **C** is incorrect. See *SEC v. Switzer*, 590 F. Supp. 756 (W.D. Okla. 1984). Choice **A**, which relies on SEC Rule 16(b) liability, is incorrect because the facts indicate that X was a mail person (not an officer or director) who was not already a 10% shareholder at both the purchase and sale of the stock. Choice **B** is incorrect because, in addition to X not being an insider, ABC Corporation was not the seller of the shares X purchased.

13. A A director, officer, or 10 percent shareholder of a corporation which (1) is traded on a national exchange, or (2) has a net worth of at least $5 million and at least 500 shareholders, is strictly liable ***to that corporation*** for any profits derived from a (1) sale and purchase, or (2) purchase and sale, of the corporation's securities within any period of less than six months. X, as an officer of ABC, is liable to the corporation for profits she derived from the purchase and sale of its stock, even though X may have lacked scienter. SEC Rule 16(b) is a ***strict liability*** measure. (*See* ELO Ch.8-VI.) Choice **B** is incorrect because (1) X lacked scienter (i.e., she did ***not*** act on nonpublic information known to her as a consequence of her corporate position), and (2) the facts ***do not*** indicate that ABC was directly involved in these transactions. Choice **C** is incorrect because X lacked scienter. Finally, Choice **D** is incorrect because, there being no misuse of insider information, X has no liability to ABC under the special facts doctrine.

14. D Under the special facts doctrine, when, as a consequence of her corporate position, one obtains material, nonpublic information about the stock, there is a fiduciary duty to disclose those facts ***to existing shareholders*** in connection with a sale or purchase of the corporation's shares. In some jurisdictions, the corporation can assert an action under this theory, ***if*** the aggrieved buyer or seller fails to do so; *Dia-*

mond v. Oreamono, 248 N.E.2d 910 (N.Y. 1969). Assuming (1) Bob does ***not*** assert an action against X, and (2) this jurisdiction permits a corporation to seek recovery if the aggrieved buyer or seller fails to commence an action, X may be liable to ABC for the profit obtained in her transaction with Bob. (*See* ELO Ch.8-II(C)(2).) Choice **A** is incorrect because, although X is the Vice-President, the facts fail to indicate that she has sold the stock she purchased from Bob. Choice **B** is incorrect because under SEC Rule 10b-5, only the aggrieved buyer or seller may commence an action. Finally, Choice **C** is incorrect because no instrumentality of interstate commerce was used during the transaction between X and Bob. Thus, a jurisdictional requirement for application of SEC Rule 10b-5 is absent.

15. C A director, officer, or 10 percent shareholder of a corporation which (1) is traded on a national exchange, or (2) has a net worth of at least $5 million and at least 500 shareholders, is strictly liable to that corporation for any profits derived from a (1) sale and purchase, or (2) purchase and sale, of the securities of that corporation within any period of less than six months. Under SEC Rule 16(b), all transactions within any six month period are analyzed for purposes of determining whether a profit was made. Since Ossie was a director when he sold 100 shares for $50 per share and purchased 100 shares only one month later for $10 per share, for purposes of SEC Rule 16(b) he has achieved a profit of $40 per share. Thus, he would be liable to ABC for $4,000. (*See* ELO Ch.8-VI(F).) Choice **A** is incorrect because Ossie, as a director of ABC, has liability under SEC Rule 16(b), even though he actually lost money in his overall transactions involving ABC stock. Choice **B** is incorrect because the correct calculations are those involving the sale of ABC stock for $50 per share and the subsequent repurchase of those shares for $10 per share. No liability would result to Ossie from the relationship between the transaction occurring on January 4 and the sale of the stock three months later for $50 per share. On these two transactions, Ossie derived no profit for SEC Rule 16(b) purposes. Finally, Choice **D** is incorrect because, for SEC Rule 16(b) purposes, Ossie's profit is $4,000. The first and last purchases are ***not*** compared. Liability under SEC Rule 16(b) must be based on (1) purchase and sale, or (2) sale and purchase.

16. C For purposes of liability under SEC Rule 16(b), one need be a director or officer only at the time of ***either*** the purchase or sale of the securities. Since Ossie was a director at the time of the sale of the shares he had acquired within the six-month period, Ossie is liable to ABC under SEC Rule 16(b) for $3,000. (*See* ELO Ch.8-VI(D)(1).) Choice **A**

is incorrect because, as discussed above, Ossie is liable to ABC under SEC Rule 16(b). Choice **B** is incorrect because the facts fail to provide any basis for concluding that Ossie used any nonpublic, material information during these transactions, even assuming an instrumentality of interstate commerce was used. Finally, Choice **D** is incorrect because the facts fail to state any basis for liability to the original seller of the shares.

17. D Under SEC Rule 10b-5, an aggrieved buyer or seller may recover the damages he or she has incurred in a transaction, provided the defendant had the intent to deceive, manipulate or defraud. Neither Smith & Smith nor ABC had any actual knowledge that negative data had been omitted. Since scienter is lacking, neither party is liable to Joan under SEC Rule 10b-5. (*See* ELO Ch.8-III(H).) In fact, since ABC retained an established and prominent accounting firm, the negligence of the firm cannot be attributed to it. Choices **A**, **B**, and **C** are incorrect since they each assert that either Smith & Smith or ABC is liable to Joan under either SEC Rule 10b-5 or the special facts doctrine. (It should be noted that Joan may have an action against Smith & Smith under common-law negligence principles.)

18. D Under SEC Rule 10b-5, it is unlawful for an insider to use any fraudulent or manipulative means ***in connection with the sale or purchase*** of securities by means of an instrumentality of interstate commerce. (*See* ELO Ch.8-III(D)(1).) Since Amy kept her stock, she could not sue Paul under any of the doctrines described in Choices **A**, **B**, or **C**. Choice **A** is incorrect because SEC Rule 10b-5 is applicable only where the aggrieved party has purchased or sold stock. Choice **B** is incorrect because SEC Rule 16(b) constitutes a basis for recovery ***by the corporation*** whose stock was traded by an officer, director, or 10 percent shareholder within a six-month period. Finally, Choice **C** is incorrect because (1) there is no indication that Paul is an insider, and (2) he did not purchase or sell ABC stock. The special facts doctrine usually applies only to purchases or sales of stock between an existing shareholder and an insider who possesses material, nonpublic information.

19. A A director, officer, or 10 percent shareholder of a corporation which (1) is traded on a national exchange, or (2) has a net worth of at least \$5 million and at least 500 shareholders, is strictly liable ***to that corporation*** for any profits derived from a (1) sale and purchase, or (2) purchase and sale, of that corporation's securities within any period of less than six months. Since Arlo is a director, she would be liable to ABC if she had purchased her shares within six months and made a profit from their sale. (*See* ELO Ch.8-VI.) Choice **B** is incorrect because, as an insider, Arlo would have an obligation to disclose negative financial information about ABC. Choice **C** is incorrect because Arlo would be liable under SEC Rule 10b-5 regardless of the price she paid for her shares. Her liability would be determined by the buyer's losses. Finally, Choice **D** is incorrect because, as discussed above, Arlo would have liability under SEC Rule 16(b) ***if*** she had purchased the stock for less than $20 per share within the preceding six months.

20. D One is an insider for purposes of SEC Rule 10b-5 where he or she learns of material, nonpublic information as a consequence of (1) his or her position with the corporation, or (2) being retained by the corporation to perform a confidential function. In addition, one may become an insider by reason of having established a relationship of trust with the plaintiff; *UTE Citizens of Utah v. United States*. Under these circumstances, Gale probably has no liability. (*See* ELO Ch.8-III(G).) Choice **A** is incorrect because there is no indication that SEC Rule 16(b) is applicable. Choice **B** is incorrect because Gale did not learn of the material, nonpublic information as a consequence of a position with the corporation. Thus, she is not an "insider" for purposes of SEC Rule 10b-5. In addition, Gale probably has no liability as a tippee. A tippee is only liable if the tipper would have been culpable. An insider is liable for "tipping" material, nonpublic information to someone who purchases or sells without disclosing the "tipped" facts ***if*** disclosure was made by the tipper to (1) acquire some type of personal gain or advantage, or (2) bestow a gift upon the tippee. Since Arlo made only an absent minded comment, there is no evidence that she sought to acquire any type of personal gain from her statement or to benefit Gale. Finally, Choice **C** is incorrect because Gale was ***not*** an officer, director, or key employee.

21. D For purposes of liability under SEC Rule 16(b), one must be at least a 10 percent shareholder at ***both*** the time of the (1) purchase and sale, or (2) sale and purchase. (*See* ELO Ch.8-VI(D)(2).) Choice **A** is incorrect because Mark was not at least a 10 percent shareholder when he bought the shares which he sold one month later, i.e., he was not at least a 10% shareholder ***both*** prior to, and at the time of, the purchase and sale of his ABC stock. Choice **B** is incorrect because Mark is ***not*** a tippee for the same reasons Gale is not a tippee in Answer 20, above. Finally, Choice **C** is incorrect because Mark did not learn of ABC's financial downturn by reason of his position with the corporation.

22. D M is liable to Zeta Corp. because shc was a 10% stockholder prior to her first purchase and her last sale. The amount recoverable under SEC Rule 16(b) is computed in a manner that maximizes the profits recoverable (e.g., the lowest purchase and highest sale prices within the six-month period are matched, then the second lowest purchase and sale prices are matched). M is liable to Zeta Corporation for $800. This amount is computed as follows. Since the greatest disparity is between the 200 shares of stock purchased at $6 per share and the stock sold at $8 per share, this calculation is done first (200 shares times $2 per share equals $400). Next, the remaining 400 shares sold by M on 5/5 are matched against those purchased at $7 per share, resulting in another $400 difference. (*See* ELO Ch.8-VI(F).) Choice **A** is incorrect because M, as a holder of more than 10% of Zeta's common stock prior to the times of purchase and sale, is liable to that corporation under SEC Rule 16(b). Finally, Choices **B** and **C** are incorrect because they fail to state the proper recovery by Zeta under SEC Rule 16(b).

23. B An individual doing business as a sole proprietorship is personally liable for all debts incurred. Since Jackson is doing business as a sole proprietorship, he is personally liable for any obligation incurred by that entity. In fact, a sole proprietorship is not really a separate, distinct entity from the individual operating that business. (*See* ELO Ch.1-III(A)(1).) Choice **A** is incorrect because the individual is personally liable for contractual obligations created by his or her sole proprietorship. Choice **C** is incorrect because Jackson is personally liable for the proprietorship's contractual obligations, regardless of whether he guaranteed those debts. Finally, Choice **D** is wrong because Choice **B** is a correct answer.

24. D Each partner of a general partnership is generally jointly and severally liable for the obligations of the partnership. (*See* ELO Ch.1-III(D)(2)(a).) (A few jurisdictions limit personal liability to those partners who actively participate in the management or operation of the entity.) Cook is probably jointly and severally liable for ***all*** partnership obligations, whether contractual or tortious in nature. Choice **A** is incorrect because Cook is personally liable to the full extent of all partnership obligations. She would, however, have a right of contribution from the other partners to the extent that her total satisfaction of a partnership obligation exceeded her proportionate interest in that entity. Choice **B** is incorrect because Cook is liable to contractual creditors of the partnership. Finally, Choice **C** is incorrect because Cook is personally liable to tort claimants of the partnership.

25. D Majority or controlling shareholders of a corporation have a fiduciary duty to refrain from exercising their position in a manner that takes undue advantage of, or oppresses, minority shareholders. (*See* ELO Ch.7-VI.) In addition, directors owe a duty of good faith to their corporation. This obligation requires directors to place the interests of shareholders before their personal interests. Since the minority shareholders did not purchase or sell any of their Ardvark stock, they ***cannot*** obtain recovery under SEC Rule 10b-5. Choices **A** through **C** are potentially successful causes of action. In engineering a negative vote with respect to the sale to Ant Corporation, Martin arguably took undue advantage of the other shareholders, so that he could subsequently sell his shares to Zoo for a premium. While a majority shareholder may ordinarily obtain a premium for selling a controlling interest, when a director rejects a *bona fide* offer made to all the shareholders in order to obtain greater personal profit, he or she may have violated the obligation of good faith. The individual shareholders may also have personal actions against Martin, since his rejection of Ant's offer arguably resulted in direct financial loss to them (measured by the difference between $35 and the present $30 per share value of Ardvark stock). Thus, Choice **B** is a correct statement. Choices **A** and **C** are correct statements because a director must act in good faith with regard to his or her corporation and all shareholders. Martin should have disclosed his negotiations with Zoo and refrained from voting or influencing other directors with regard to this matter. Also, if Zoo's operation of Ardvark might result in Ardvark shares becoming less valuable, Ardvark has been harmed.

26. C A corporation's net worth is equal to its total assets minus its aggregate liabilities. Since Fox's assets are $500,000 and its liabilities are $300,000, its net worth after the second year is $200,000.

27. B The book value of outstanding shares is ordinarily determined by dividing the stated capital and any surplus by the total number of outstanding shares. The stated capital ($150,000) and retained earnings surplus ($50,000) are divided by the 1,000 outstanding shares of stock. This results in a book value of $200 per share.

28. B Under straight voting, each shareholder may vote his or her total number of shares for each candidate for a directorship. Under cumulative voting, a person's shares are multiplied by the number of directors being elected, but these shares can be cast only once. Since Jones would possess one-third (rather than one-fourth) of the corporation's outstanding shares as a consequence of this transaction, Jones's personal voting rights are ***not*** adversely affected. This would be the case whether the corporation had cumulative or straight voting, and regardless of the number of directors chosen at the annual shareholders' meeting. Thus, Choice **B** is the correct answer. (*See* ELO Ch.3-II(B).)

29. D In a retained earnings jurisdiction, dividends may only be paid out of earned surplus (also known as "retained earnings"). The balance sheet reveals that, after year one, Fox Corp. had negative retained earnings (a deficit of $10,000). As a consequence, ***no*** dividends may be paid to any of the shareholders. (*See* ELO Ch.11-I(C)(2).)

30. C The fair market value of shares takes into consideration the appreciation and depreciation of the corporation's assets, as well as the future prospects of the business activity involved. While the Nevada real estate is reflected in Fox's balance sheet as being equal to $400,000, this is merely the price Fox Corp. ***originally*** paid for this asset. Its fair market value (i.e., the price at which a willing buyer and willing seller, each being under no pressure to buy or sell, would conclude the transaction for this land) may have appreciated or depreciated significantly due to market conditions. Thus, it is impossible to determine whether the sale of the Nevada real estate for $175,000 after year one increased or decreased the fair market value of Fox Corp. shares. Thus, **C** is the correct answer. Choices **A** and **B** are incorrect because there is not enough information provided to give a definite answer either way. Choice **D** is incorrect because the effect of cumulative or straight voting was reflected in the fair market value of Jones's shares independently of the sale of the Nevada real estate.

31. B Under straight voting, each shareholder may vote his or her total number of shares for each candidate for a directorship. Under cumulative voting, each stockholder's shares are multiplied by the total number of directors, but may be voted only once. Jones's rights are not adversely affected by whether Fox Corp. has straight voting or cumulative voting. Jones's rights will ***not*** be impacted in a positive manner either. With each shareholder holding 250 shares, Jones can elect ***no*** directors under a straight voting scheme. Even if each shareholder held 275 shares, Jones could still not elect any directors under a straight voting approach. Under cumulative voting, Jones can elect only one director regardless of whether she has 250 or 275 shares. (*See* ELO Ch.3-II(B).) The other three Choices are wrong since they are all premised on an adverse effect on Jones' s voting rights.

32. A In most nimble dividend states, a corporation may issue dividends from the current year's profits, even though an overall deficit (i.e., negative retained earnings) remains after the dividends are paid. Recently, some jurisdictions have permitted dividends as long as the corporation's total assets exceed its total liabilities by a stipulated proportion (e.g., total assets exceed 125% of total liabilities). After its first year of operation, Fox Corp. has ***no*** net profits. In fact, it has a deficit (i.e., negative retained earnings) of $10,000. Even if this jurisdiction has recently enacted legislation permitting dividends when assets exceed liabilities by 25%, Fox Corp. is still unable to issue dividends. Multiplying Fox's liabilities ($615,000) by 25% yields a result of $153,750. This amount, when added to $615,000, exceeds Fox's total assets of $710,000. Thus, even under this formula, no dividends are proper under these circumstances. (*See* ELO Ch.11-I(D)(7), I(D).)

33. D The board of directors may repurchase outstanding shares of the corporation's stock, if (1) a legitimate corporate purpose is served by this action, and (2) the repurchase will not cause the corporation to become insolvent or impair its ability to operate. (*See* ELO Ch.11-III(B),(D).) Since Fox Corp. has a net worth of $200,000, the purchase of Jr. Fox's stock will ***not*** cause the corporation to become insolvent. In addition, the facts stipulate that none of the transactions would impair Fox Corp.'s ability to operate. However, because other factors must be considered, it ***cannot*** be stated unequivocally that Fox Corp. could repurchase Jr. Fox's shares for $100,000, so Choice **A** is incorrect. More facts are needed to resolve this inquiry, such as (1) whether this is an excessive price for Jr. Fox's shares (we know the aggregate book value of Jr. Fox's shares is $50,000, but we do not know the stock's fair market value), and (2) what corporate purpose will be achieved by purchasing Jr. Fox's shares (the mere fact that Jr. Fox would like to sell his stock is no reason for Fox Corp. to incur a $100,000 obligation). Choice **B** is incorrect because the fact that the purchase price exceeds $50,000 is not, *per se*, a reason to conclude that the purchase is improper. Finally, Choice **C** is incorrect because Fox Corp. would ***not*** become insolvent as a result of this transaction.

34. A Profits earned by the corporation since its inception are retained earnings or earned surplus. Dividends can always be paid from this sum (assuming the payments will not cause the corporation to become insolvent or impair its ability to operate). Remember that the introductory paragraph preceding this series of questions (preceding Question 26) stated that none of the transactions would impair Fox Corp.'s ability to operate. Since Fox Corp. has retained earnings or earned surplus of $50,000, it can issue dividends in the amount of $10,000 to each shareholder. Actually, it could issue dividends in an amount up to $12,500 to each shareholder, if it chose to do so. (*See* ELO Ch.11-I(C)(2).) Choices **B**, **C**, and **D** are all incorrect because the dividend payments described in those answers would exceed Fox Corp.'s retained earnings of $50,000.

35. B Under the Deep Rock doctrine, when a corporation has become insolvent, its obligations to a shareholder may be subordinated to the claims of other creditors, if it would be inequitable (e.g., the shareholder/creditor was, in some manner, responsible for the corporation's inability to satisfy its debts) for the shareholder/creditor to participate equally with the corporation's other creditors. Since Barbell caused CG to (1) incur substantial obligations to him, and (2) enter into several high risk transactions, situations that combined to result in CG's bankruptcy, Barbell's debt will probably be subordinated to the claims of other creditors. (*See* ELO Ch.2-VI(C).) Choice **A** is incorrect because there is no *per se* rule invalidating corporate obligations to its corporate officers. Choice **C** is similarly incorrect because there is no *per se* rule subordinating debts owed to shareholders. Finally, Choice **D** is incorrect because, in view of the fact that Barbell's actions were in large part the cause of CG's insolvency, Barbell will probably not be allowed to enforce his claim on par with CG's other creditors.

36. C At the dissolution of a corporation, its assets are distributed in the following priority. First, secured creditors are paid to the extent their obligations are collateralized by specific property of the corporation. Next, unsecured creditors are paid. (If a secured creditor's collateral is insufficient to satisfy the obligation owed, he or she becomes an unsecured creditor for the balance.) Next, preferred shareholders are paid in accordance with their rights and preferences. Finally, the other shareholders receive whatever remains. Choice **C** most closely coincides with the order of priority set forth above. Choice **A** is incorrect because unsecured creditors are paid before shareholders. Choice **B** is incorrect because secured and unsecured creditors are paid before preferred shareholders. Finally, Choice **D** is incorrect because it fails to point out that (1) secured creditors take prior to unsecured creditors, and (2) preferred shareholders are ordinarily satisfied prior to common shareholders.

37. A At common law, either the corporation or the other party to the contract could disaffirm an *ultra vires* contract that was fully executory. The contract is *ultra vires,* since XYZ is authorized only to operate a restaurant. Thus, XYZ can assert the defense of *ultra vires* before either side commences performance of the agreement. (*See* ELO Ch.2-II.) Choice **B** is incorrect because, even if Paula had read the Articles of Incorporation prior to entering into the transaction with XYZ, XYZ could still assert the *ultra vires* doctrine. If this had occurred, Paula would have been on notice that XYZ could repudiate the transaction. Choice **C** is incorrect because, at common law, a corporation can assert the *ultra vires* doctrine. (The shareholders can assert this theory only if the corporation fails to do so.) Finally, Choice **D** is incorrect because, even if the shareholders had ratified the transaction, Paula would ***not*** prevail. Shareholders are incapable of approving an *ultra vires* act. It should be pointed out that some courts take the view that shareholder ratification, if accomplished by vote of the shareholder votes necessary to change the Articles of Incorporation, constitutes an implied amendment of that document. In such a jurisdiction, the transaction would not be *ultra vires* and Paula would prevail.

38. C At common law, when there was part performance of, or reliance upon, a transaction by either party, the other party was ordinarily estopped from asserting the *ultra vires* doctrine. The $25,000 payment made to Paula constitutes part performance of the agreement. In addition, the two-year contract with Oliver probably constitutes substantial reliance on the transaction by XYZ. As a result, XYZ may enforce the agreement. (*See* ELO Ch.2-II(B)(1).) Choice **A** is incorrect because, although the contract is *ultra vires*, there has been part performance and reliance by XYZ. Choice **B** is incorrect because mere return of the consideration Paula had received is not a basis for allowing her to avoid the contract. Finally, Choice **D** is incorrect because XYZ can prevail with or without stockholder approval.

39. A When a corporation should recognize that a third party will, based on ***prior*** dealings with the corporation, be likely to view an officer or agent as possessing authority to enter into the agreement in question, the corporation ***cannot*** avoid that transaction. However, even though Simone had undertaken similar transactions in the past, the growers with whom she contracted after the resolution was passed were ***not the ones with whom she had previously dealt.*** Thus, any "apparent authority" argument ***would not*** prevail in this instance. Although there is no indication that the growers were aware of the resolution limiting the monetary amount of contracts into which Simone could enter, a corporate treasurer is ordinarily ***not*** empowered to bind the corporation contractually. (*See* ELO Ch.3-II(C).) Choice **B** is incorrect because the growers would ***not*** be deemed to be on constructive notice of the resolution setting Simone's contractual limits. Choice **C** is incorrect because there is no basis in the hypothetical to assume that the growers in question knew of the transactions Simone had previously entered into on behalf of Fruitco. Finally, Choice **D** is incorrect because the "implied authority of office" doctrine would only allow the growers to assume that Simone had the normal powers of a corporate treasurer. As already noted, a treasurer does ***not*** ordinarily have the authority to bind the corporation to a contract.

40. C Each corporate officer has the implied authority to enter into transactions which are reasonably related to the performance of the normal duties of his office. A corporate secretary ordinarily certifies the records of the corporation, including the board's resolutions. He does not enter into contracts to buy land or inventory. ABC can probably rescind the transaction to acquire the steel because the vendor should have recognized that a corporate secretary lacks the authority to bind his or her corporation contractually. (*See* ELO Ch.3-II(C)(4).) Choice **A** is incorrect because a secretary lacks the implied authority of office to bind the corporation to land or inventory contracts. Choice **B** is incorrect because the facts fail to indicate that the steel vendor was aware of the transaction with Elmer, or that she believed that the corporation had approved of it. Finally, Choice **D** is incorrect because ABC's right to avoid the second transaction is not contingent upon repudiation of the initial one. The vendor of the land could raise Matt's lack of authority, if he chose to do so.

41. D Acts of a corporate officer or agent which are beyond his or her authority may be implicitly ratified by the board by its action or inaction. By approving a resolution to obtain bids for remodeling the premises subsequent to acquiring knowledge of the lease and by taking no action to repudiate the lease, the XYZ board probably implicitly ratified the contract. Thus, even though the secretary of a corporation ordinarily lacks authority to bind the company contractually, XYZ implicitly ratified the lease by passing a resolution which approved steps in furtherance of the lease. (*See* ELO Ch.3-II(C)(6).) Choice **A** is incorrect because, while Charles lacked authority to enter into the lease, the board implicitly approved the transaction by instructing XYZ's President to obtain bids for remodeling the premises. Choice **B** is incorrect because, once having approved the lease, the board could no longer repudiate that contract. Finally, Choice **C** is incorrect because there is nothing to indicate that the lessor had reason to believe Charles had authority to enter into the lease.

42. A When a corporation sells all, or substantially all, of its assets, the transaction must be approved by the board and a majority (in some jurisdictions even a greater proportion) of its shareholders. Since the transaction involves the sale of ***all*** of Bilko's assets, it must be approved by the shareholders of Bilko. (In some states, the shareholders of Apex must also approve the transaction.) (*See* ELO Ch.10-I(E).) The facts do not indicate that the Bilko shareholders knew of the transaction or approved it. Choice **B** is incorrect because Joan is the proper officer to enter into this type of transaction for Bilko (subject to shareholder and director approval). Choice **C** is incorrect because approval by the Apex and Bilko boards is not enough; the transaction must be approved by Bilko's shareholders. Finally, Choice **D** is incorrect because ***both*** Bilko's board and its shareholders must approve the transaction.

43. D Resolutions ordinarily need be passed only by a majority vote of directors present at a properly called meeting at which a quorum exists. The facts indicate that that's what happened here. A corporation ordinarily has the implied power to perform acts which are reasonably necessary to accomplish its express or authorized purposes (and which are not otherwise prohibited or unlawful). Undertaking farming operations until the necessary permits could be obtained would arguably, under these circumstances, be viewed as reasonably necessary to Buildco's main purpose of subdividing land for the purpose of constructing tract homes. Otherwise, the land would be totally unproductive during the period before the permits could be obtained. The fact that the nonattending directors would have voted against the resolution does ***not*** undermine its validity, so long as the meeting was properly called and a quorum was present. The directors had the power to call another meeting to overturn the resolution. (*See* ELO Ch.3-II(E)-(F).) Choice **A** is incorrect because undertaking farming operations while awaiting the necessary permits would appear to be reasonably necessary to preserve Buildco's express purposes, and therefore ***not*** *ultra vires*. Choice **B** is incorrect because only a majority vote of a duly constituted quorum is usually necessary to pass a resolution. Finally, Choice **C** is incorrect because the resolution was properly passed at a meeting at which a quorum was present.

44. D If the time of regular meetings is stipulated in the Articles of Incorporation or bylaws, no additional notice is required. (*See* ELO Ch.3-II(E)(2).) Directors are ordinarily deemed to be on constructive notice of their corporation's Articles of Incorporation and bylaws. Since corporate bylaws ordinarily require only that a majority of directors be present for a proper quorum, the meeting was properly held. Because a majority of those attending voted in favor of the resolution, it is valid. Choice **A** is incorrect because Carson is on constructive notice of Ajax's bylaws. Choice **B** is incorrect because the board was under no obligation to give additional notice to Carson of a regularly scheduled meeting. Finally, Choice **C** is incorrect because there was no obligation to give specific notice to Carson. Thus, it is wrong to state that she failed to receive ***proper*** notice.

45. C A corporation cannot use as a defense against parties with whom it has contracted and who acted in good faith that it failed to give adequate notice to its directors for a meeting at which the transaction was approved. Those parties ordinarily have a right to assume that facially valid resolutions were properly undertaken. Although the resolution was not properly passed because three of the directors failed to receive the written notice required for a special meeting, Nancy had the right to rely on the resolution presented to her by the president. Choice **A** is incorrect because Nancy had a right to rely upon a facially valid resolution. Choice **B** is incorrect because the President was ***not*** relying on his actual or apparent authority to enter into the agreement with Nancy. Rather, he relied on an express resolution by the board approving the transaction. Finally, Choice **D** is incorrect because Oilco would have been able to rescind the transaction but for the fact that Nancy was presented with a resolution which appeared to be valid. If a meeting is improperly noticed, any action undertaken by the board at the meeting is invalid (even if it appears that votes of the absentee directors would have had no impact upon the resolution). It is possible that if the non-noticed directors had attended, they would have been able to persuade the other directors to vote in a different manner.

46. B Under the director's duty of due care, directors must exercise the same degree of care and skill with respect to corporate matters as a reasonably prudent person would with respect to his own affairs. A director's reasonable business judgment which proves, in retrospect, to have been erroneous, is ***not*** actionable, because of the protection afforded by the business judgment rule. (*See* ELO Ch.6-II, III.) However, on these facts, the directors who failed to approve the resolution requiring the purchase of insurance are probably jointly and severally liable for the losses resulting from their decision. It is ordinarily unreasonable to neglect to carry insurance on a substantial corporate asset. This error is compounded by the fact that funds which could have been used to purchase the insurance were retained for a non-business purpose (the payment of dividends). Choice **A** is incorrect because, while wide latitude is given to the business judgment of directors, the failure to obtain fire insurance under these circumstances is probably actionable. Choice **C** is incorrect because the directors who voted against the acquisition of fire insurance would be jointly and severally liable (not proportionately) for the losses resulting from their action. Finally, Choice **D** is incorrect because directors who voted in favor of purchasing the insurance would be absolved from liability.

47. D Under the director's duty of due care, directors must exercise the same degree of care and skill with respect to corporate matters as would a reasonably prudent person with respect to his or her own affairs. Directors must make a reasonable effort to inform themselves of the facts necessary to make a proper decision. Prior to acquiring a lease, a reasonably prudent business person would verify whether there were any delinquencies or outstanding liabilities by the transferor-lessee. This is especially true when, as here, the directors know that the landlord has alleged a breach by the tenant. Thus, the directors who approved the transaction are probably liable for the losses which may be sustained by Beta. (*See* ELO Ch.6-II.) Choice **A** is incorrect because the fact that officers of Alpha may have misrepresented their liability to the lessor does not relieve Beta's directors of their obligation to make a reasonable inquiry with regard to all breaches under the lease. Choice **B** is incorrect because the business judgment rule would probably ***not*** protect the directors in this instance. Finally, Choice **C** is incorrect because the directors of a corporation that is acquiring the assets of another entity for cash are ordinarily ***not*** required to seek approval by their shareholders.

48. D Under cumulative voting, each stockholder's shares are multiplied by the total number of directors to be chosen. However, these votes can be cast only once. In most states, if cumulative voting for directors is required, a director may ***not*** be removed ***without good cause*** if the votes ***against*** removal are sufficient (if voted cumulatively) to have elected that director. If cumulative voting is applicable in Acme's state, Mitchell ***cannot*** be removed. Because only 334 votes are necessary to elect Mitchell, the votes against his removal are sufficient to preclude this action. (*See* ELO Ch.3-II(B)(3)(g).) Choices **A** and **B** are incorrect because the Articles of Incorporation specifically allow shareholders to remove directors without cause. Finally, Choice **C** is incorrect because, even if cumulative voting was applicable, there were a sufficient number of votes cast against Mitchell's removal to prevent this action. (Editor's note: the student may wonder why, if we are hypothesizing a state in which cumulative voting is required, the Articles and bylaws would contain a provision inconsistent with that hypothesis — i.e., that a director can be removed without cause.)

49. C Ordinarily, the directors of a corporation appoint its officers. Since shareholders cannot ordinarily appoint officers, their election of Adolpho to be president was improper. Actions (1) and (4) are proper, since the shareholders do elect directors. (*See* ELO Ch.3-I(B).) The fact that the directors had made an interim appointment of Edward is irrelevant; their action is superseded by the shareholder action. The action described in (3) is proper because, although shareholders cannot make management decisions pertaining to the operation of their corporation, they may ordinarily ratify transactions when a disinterested quorum of directors does ***not*** exist.

50. B Fundamental management decisions and the appointment of corporate officers ordinarily ***cannot*** be delegated by the board of directors. Since the contract with Kent authorizes him to select officers and determine corporate expenditures, the employment agreement is probably invalid. The fact that he can be dismissed for incompetence or the failure to satisfy specific performance standards does not detract from the breadth of his initial authority. (*See* ELO Ch.3-II(J).) Choice **A** is incorrect because the agreement's invalidity is ***not*** predicated on the fact that it exceeds one year. Today, most jurisdictions permit a board to approve contracts which exceed the terms of the existing directors. Choice **C** is incorrect because a board can certainly approve a transaction which will bind the corporation beyond the date of the next board election; a contrary rule would inhibit a corporation unreasonably. Finally, Choice **D** is incorrect because the contract with Kent is invalid for the reasons described above.

51. C When an independent litigation committee or consultant advises against a derivative action, the action is ordinarily barred. Because an independent, disinterested attorney-consultant appointed by ABC's board of directors has advised against a derivative action, a lawsuit by Shawn (or any shareholder) is barred. (*See* ELO Ch.9-IV(D).) Choice **A** is incorrect because there is no requirement that a derivative action be commenced to compel recovery when an employee has committed a crime. Choice **B** is incorrect because the shareholders cannot override the recommendation of independent counsel. Finally, Choice **D** is incorrect because her presence during the vote to refrain from commencing an action against the employee would ***not***, in itself, preclude Shawn from pursuing a derivative action.

52. C Choice **C** is the correct answer because it is the only choice which is incorrect on the facts. When a derivative action is commenced in federal court on account of diversity, the complaint must allege the plaintiff's efforts to obtain action from the directors, or explain her reasons for not making the efforts; FRCP 23.1. Because Alice commenced the action in federal court, she is required to allege the efforts she made to obtain action by the directors (i.e., demanding that the directors sue Ted and Michael), or explain why she failed to make the efforts. Choice **A** is a correct statement because only a derivative action can be commenced against Ted and Michael. Alice can not sue them in her own behalf, because the losses resulting from their allegedly improper actions were incurred primarily by ABC, not by individual shareholders. (*See* ELO Ch.9-II(A)(2).) Choice **B** is a correct statement because Alice is excused on these facts from making a demand on the directors. Since two of the three directors are involved in the alleged wrongdoing, no disinterested majority exists upon whom such a demand can be made. (*See* ELO Ch.9-II(B)(2).) Finally, Choice **D** is a correct statement. Because Alice's derivative action is premised upon diversity jurisdiction (rather than upon a federal claim), she must post a bond if required to do so under applicable state law. (*See* ELO Ch.9-V(A).)

53. C A derivative action is appropriate when the harm complained about was done ***primarily*** to the corporation, rather than to the plaintiff/shareholder. The actions of the directors described in (1) and (4) resulted primarily in financial loss to ABC. Although the action described in (1) was allegedly premised on an intention to obtain Mike's shares at a discounted value, the complaint alleges the sale of corporate assets at less than market, and the harm which resulted was incurred primarily by the corporation. On the other hand, the refusal to let Mike vote his shares and the dilution of his ownership interest in ABC were actions that impacted primarily on Mike, personally. The actions described in (2) and (3) did not ***primarily*** affect ABC and may not be made the subject of a derivative action. (*See* ELO Ch.9-II(A).)

54. D To maintain a derivative action, the plaintiff must ordinarily have been a shareholder at the time the harm to the corporation occurred. However, the date of acquisition for a plaintiff who acquires her shares through operation of law (e.g., inheritance, intestacy) is the date upon which her decedent acquired the shares. While the facts tell us that Alex inherited her stock from her father, they do ***not*** disclose whether her father was a shareholder at the time the directors breached their duty of loyalty. If Alex's father acquired his shares ***after*** that time, Alex could not commence a derivative action for that breach. While Alex could bring a derivative action based upon the directors' negligence with regard to her second assertion, since she was a shareholder at the time of the negligence, it still would be necessary to ascertain when her father acquired the XYZ shares to determine whether a derivative action alleging a breach of the duty of loyalty (for the first assertion) can also be maintained. (*See* ELO Ch.9-III(C)(6).)

55. C When a derivative action is based on SEC Rule 16(b), it is ***not*** necessary for the plaintiff to have been a shareholder at the time of the alleged wrong. Also, when a derivative action in federal court is based on a ***federal claim***, state laws requiring a bond or other security are superseded. Since Moe's claim is based on SEC Rule 16(b), any otherwise applicable state law requiring a bond or other security is superseded. (*See* ELO Ch.8-VI(B)(3).) Choice **A** is incorrect because, under federal law, one does not have to have been a shareholder at the time of an alleged wrong to maintain an SEC Rule 16(b) action. Choice **B** is incorrect because, in view of the fact that all three directors were the alleged wrongdoers, it would be futile to demand that they take action against themselves. Finally, Choice **D** is incorrect because, if Moe's derivative action is successful, the entire recovery will be paid to the corporation. (Moe could, however, recover his reasonable attorneys' fees and court costs.)

56. A In many states, the plaintiff must request that a majority of the ***disinterested*** shareholders ratify a derivative action. However, where the derivative action is premised upon acts which are prohibited by statute, shareholder approval is usually unnecessary. In most states, the circumstances under which dividends may be paid are statutorily mandated. In these states, the shareholders cannot approve or ratify an improper or illegal dividend distribution. (*See* ELO Ch.9-III(F)(3)(c).) Choice **B** is incorrect because all of the directors participated in the allegedly improper conduct. Chris must, however, describe in her pleadings the reason why a demand would be futile. Choice **C** is incorrect because state bond or security requirements are applicable when a derivative action in federal court is predicated upon ***diversity*** jurisdiction. Finally, Choice **D** is incorrect because, under these circumstances, Chris had no choice but to accept any dividend payment which was tendered to her. Her acceptance of the dividend cannot be used to justify improper distribution by the board.

57. D When a director or officer has a direct financial interest in a transaction, he or she is ordinarily obliged to disclose that interest and refrain from voting on the matter. If, after his disclosure, the transaction (1) is approved by a majority of the disinterested directors, and (2) is fair to the corporation, it is ordinarily valid. A majority of disinterested shareholders may ordinarily ratify a transaction so long as it is not statutorily prohibited, wasteful, or patently unfair to the corporation. Because the transaction was ***not*** approved by a majority of ***disinterested*** directors (i.e., excluding the votes of the four interested directors, the directors voted 1-1 for approval of the transaction), approval by a majority of disinterested shareholders was necessary. However, because the transaction was patently unfair to Alpha (i.e., would constitute a waste of corporate assets), it cannot be validly ratified even by the disinterested shareholders. (*See* ELO Ch.7-II(D)-(F).) Choice **A** is incorrect because, while the resolution was not approved by a majority of disinterested directors, a majority of disinterested shareholders can nevertheless ratify a transaction which is not prohibited or patently unfair to the corporation. Choice **B** is incorrect because the shareholders may ratify a transaction even if approval by the board was defective because it was voted by interested directors. Since (1) the owner/director and his family should have refrained from voting, and (2) the disinterested directors split 1-1 on the transaction in question, shareholder ratification was appropriate (subject to the *caveats* above). Finally, Choice **C** is factually incorrect because the vote of the ***disinterested*** directors was 1-1.

58. D A director or officer cannot exploit for personal gain information acquired or made available to him as a consequence of his corporate position, ***unless*** the corporation (1) declines to pursue the same opportunity after full disclosure, or (2) is, and would continue to be (despite any reasonable efforts), unable to take advantage of the opportunity. If the officer breaches this rule, the corporation can obtain either equitable relief or damages equal to the profit derived by the wrongdoer. Because Charles has appropriated a corporate opportunity by purchasing the manufacturing plant in his partnership, Tilden can either rescind the purchase or recover the $150,000 profit made by Unger. (*See* ELO Ch.7-IV(D).) Charles also breached his duty of loyalty by failing to inform the Tilden board of his personal interest in the transaction. Choice **A** is incorrect because Charles' failure to vote on the matter does ***not*** absolve him of culpability. Choice **B** is incorrect because the board can rescind the transaction to prevent unjust profit to Charles even if it finds that the purchase price of the facility was fair. Finally, Choice **C** is incorrect because, even if the other general partners of Unger were unaware of Charles' personal interest, his misdeed would probably be attributed to the partnership, of which he was an agent; further, the equities would still favor Tilden.

59. A Actions based upon SEC Rule 10b-5 or SEC Rule 16(b) ***must*** be commenced in federal court. Since the SEC Rule 10b-5 action was commenced in ***state*** court, a motion by Green to dismiss the case will be successful. Choices **B** and **C** are incorrect because a state court action does not lie even if a valid state claim is asserted or an allegation is made that interstate commerce was not involved. Finally, Choice **D** is incorrect because ***no*** additional facts are necessary to conclude that Green's motion will be successful.

60. D When an action against a director or officer based on an act or omission in connection with his or her duties is settled prior to judgment, the corporation may indemnify the defendant for his or her attorneys' fees and litigation expenses (provided a majority of disinterested directors or shareholders determines that the defendant was acting in good faith). Notwithstanding this general rule, because the basis of the action in this case is not a lawsuit, act, or omission ***connected with*** Green's duties as President of Drugco, Drugco should refuse to indemnify her for any amount whatsoever. (*See* ELO Ch.9-IX(D)(3)(e).) Thus, Choices **A**, **B**, and **C** are all incorrect.

61. C When a director or officer in a derivative suit is adjudged to have breached a duty owed to the corporation, indemnification is ordinarily not permitted. Since Joe was exonerated of negligence in selecting the employee who embezzled money from Island, he is entitled to be indemnified for his attorneys' fees and litigation expenses. (*See* ELO Ch.9-IX(D)(4).) Choice **A** is incorrect because Todd may ***not*** be indemnified for his litigation expenses and attorneys' fees. Choice **B** is incorrect because Joe may be indemnified for his litigation expenses and attorneys' fees by Island. Finally, Choice **D** is incorrect because Todd, who was found to have breached his duty to Island, is ***not*** entitled to indemnification. In a few jurisdictions, a director who is found liable may nevertheless be reimbursed for his attorneys' fees and litigation expenses ***if*** he is adjudged to be "fairly and reasonably" entitled to indemnification. However, in this instance the facts tell us that no such finding was made.

62. B If a lawsuit against a director or officer does ***not*** allege a knowing breach of duties, and the suit is settled prior to trial, the officer or director may be indemnified by the corporation ***if*** a majority of disinterested directors determines that the defendant acted in good faith and for a purpose reasonably believed to be in the best interests of the corporation. Since the board approved a resolution stating that Karl had acted in good faith and for purposes which he reasonably believed to be in Acro's best interests, all of his expenses (including the settlement amount to the extent paid by Karl) may be reimbursed by the corporation. (*See* ELO Ch.9-IX(D)(3).) Choice **A** is incorrect because the fact that Karl was named personally in the action does ***not*** preclude reimbursement. Choice **C** is incorrect because in the vast majority of states it is not necessary for Karl to have been successful on the merits to obtain reimbursement from Acro; in the interest of avoiding litigation, a reasonable settlement is always encouraged. Finally, Choice **D** is incorrect because Karl may, under these circumstances, be indemnified for his attorneys' fees and litigation expenses.

63. D Civil lawsuits against a director or officer which do ***not*** allege a knowing breach of duties, and which are settled prior to trial, may ordinarily be reimbursed by the corporation if a majority of the disinterested shareholders determines that the defendant acted in good faith and for a purpose reasonably believed to be in the best interests of the corporation. However, where a criminal action is involved, the director or officer must satisfy a third requirement — he must show that he had no reason to believe that his action was unlawful. If a majority of the disinterested shareholders determines that this tripartite test in a criminal action is satisfied, reimbursement may occur. (*See* ELO Ch.9-IX(D)(3).) Choice **A** is incorrect because a mere charge of that a criminal offense has been committed does not preclude indemnification. Choice **B** is incorrect because indemnification under these circumstances is ***not*** contingent upon prevailing on the merits. Finally, Choice **C** is incorrect because it does not satisfy the third part of the tripartite test — the shareholders must also conclude that the directors had no reason to believe that their actions were unlawful.

64. A At common law, when a ***new*** issue of shares occurred, an existing shareholder had the right to acquire the number of shares necessary to maintain her proportionate interest in the corporation. Underhill may assert preemptive rights in up to 30% of the newly issued shares (excluding the 500 that will be tendered to Smith). Thus, Underhill may purchase an additional 300 shares. (*See* ELO Ch.9-IX(D)(2), (D)(4).) Choice **B** is incorrect because Underhill may not assert preemptive rights with respect to the 500 shares that will be delivered to Smith. At common law, preemptive rights did ***not*** extend to newly issued shares that were to be exchanged for property other than cash. Choice **C** is incorrect because preemptive rights extend ***only*** to shares ***not*** previously authorized at the time the shareholder acquires his or her stock. Finally, Choice **D** is incorrect because, while Underhill may not assert preemptive rights in the 500 shares to be given to Smith, she does retain those rights with regard to the remaining 1,000 shares of newly issued stock.

65. A In most states, preemptive rights ordinarily do ***not*** extend to the resale of treasury stock. Since Arthur purchased 5% of the originally issued shares, he is entitled to exercise preemptive rights in up to 5% of the ***newly*** authorized 500 shares of stock. But, he has ***no*** preemptive rights with regard to the treasury shares which were previously redeemed by Ajax and which are now being sold by Ajax. (*See* ELO Ch.12-I(D)(4)(b).) Choice **B** is incorrect because Arthur (1) is only entitled to 25 shares, and (2) would be obliged to pay the offering price of $150 per share. Choice **C** is incorrect because Arthur has preemptive rights only with regard to the 500 newly issued shares, not the 500 treasury shares. Finally, Choice **D** is incorrect because, as described above, Arthur is entitled to purchase only 25 shares of the newly authorized stock at $150 per share.

66. D At common law, if there was an issue of new shares, an existing shareholder had preemptive rights, i.e., the right to acquire the number of shares necessary to maintain his proportionate interest in the corporation. Williams has preemptive rights with respect to the newly issued shares. In addition, because the shares were not necessary for a valid business purpose, but were apparently issued only to enhance the ownership interest of the other two stockholders, Williams may be able to obtain a court order rescinding the issue of the newly authorized stock. She might seek such an order if purchasing 40% of the newly authorized stock would pose a financial hardship for her. (*See* ELO Ch.12-I(D)(2), (D)(6).) Choice **A** is incorrect because preemptive rights extend ***only to shares that were not authorized*** at the time the plaintiff originally acquired her stock. Choice **B** is incorrect because it would be essentially unfair to require Williams to expend the money necessary to buy her rightful share of the stock when there was no valid business purpose for the issue. Finally, Choice **C** is incorrect because, at common law, preemptive rights were implied into the corporate relationship whether or not they were specified in the corporate charter.

67. C A proxy is ordinarily revocable by the proxy-giver who attends a shareholders' meeting, provided either (1) she expressly revokes the proxy, or (2) votes the shares subject to the proxy herself. Mere attendance is not enough to accomplish revocation. Mervin's attendance at the shareholders' meeting would not prevent Joan from voting the shares that were subject to the proxy. However, if Mervin indicates in any manner that he no longer intends the proxy to be operative, the proxy is revoked. Choice **A** is incorrect because Joan can vote the shares unless Mervin expressly or implicitly revokes the proxy, notwithstanding his attendance at the meeting. Choice **B** is incorrect because a proxy is ***not*** inoperative merely because the original reason for its issuance has ceased to exist. Finally, Choice **D** is incorrect because, even if the Articles of Incorporation expressly authorize proxy voting, Mervin can still revoke the proxy given to Joan.

68. C A proxy is irrevocable when it is given by the seller of shares to her buyer. Only stockholders on the record date (or those who have received proxies from these stockholders) may vote at a shareholders' meeting. Since Mindy had sold her shares to Sally, her proxy was irrevocable. If Mindy attempts to revoke the proxy at the shareholders' meeting, she will be unable to do so. Choice **A** is incorrect because Mindy cannot repudiate the proxy she gave to Sally. Choice **B** is incorrect because, while Sally was not the shareholder of record for purposes of the meeting, she received an irrevocable proxy from Mindy at the time of sale. The proxy was valid because it was issued by the record owner. Finally, Choice **D** is incorrect because, without the proxy from Mindy, Zebco could prevent Sally from voting the shares she purchased from Mindy, on the grounds that Sally was not a shareholder on the record date.

69. A Under SEC Rule 14a-8, shareholders who (1) own at least 1 percent or \$1,000 in present value of the corporation's securities, and (2) have held their shares for at least one year, may submit a single proposal for inclusion in management's proxy materials to be voted on at the upcoming shareholders' meeting. The shareholder's proposal and supporting statement may not exceed 500 words. The proposal that Jones be appointed Chief Financial Officer may be rejected because it is ***not a proper subject for shareholder action*** (corporate officers are usually appointed by the directors). The second proposal — to install a coffee room for employees — can also probably be excluded because it relates to the company's ordinary business operations and is too routine a management matter to constitute a proper subject for stockholder action. (*See* ELO Ch.4-V(C)(e).) Choice **B** is incorrect because major corporate officers are ordinarily chosen by the board of directors. Choice **C** is incorrect because, even if Elmer has owned his shares for a year, management is not required to include these kinds of proposals in its solicitation materials. Finally, Choice **D** is incorrect because the second proposal relates to Fairway's ordinary business operations and is too routine a management matter to permit shareholder intervention.

70. B Under SEC Rule 14a-8, shareholders who (1) own at least 1 percent or $1,000 in present value of the corporation's securities, and (2) have held the shares for at least one year, may submit a single proposal for inclusion in management's proxy materials to be voted on at the upcoming shareholders' meeting. The shareholder's proposal and supporting statement may not exceed 500 words. Because Emma's proposal seems to be an appropriate one for consideration by the shareholders, management must include it in its solicitation materials, if the statement and its supporting materials do not exceed 500 words. The facts stipulate that Emma has been a shareholder for more than one year and that the value of her stock exceeds $1,000. (*See* ELO Ch.4-V(C).) Choice **A** is incorrect because the proposal and its supporting statement may ***not*** exceed 500 words, regardless of its content or significance. Choice **C** is incorrect because under these circumstances, Belton ***cannot*** charge Emma for any costs associated with including her proposal in its proxy solicitation to the corporation's shareholders. Finally, Choice **D** is incorrect because the board is ***not*** required to provide Emma with a mailing list of its shareholders or to mail her proposal at Belton's expense to the shareholders, except as a part of its own solicitation.

71. A When a proxy solicitation contains a material misstatement or omission, the court may rescind any corporate action that was undertaken on the basis of those proxies. A successful plaintiff can ordinarily recover her attorneys' fees and litigation expenses. On these facts, the solicitation of proxies for the re-election of Ralph without describing his past contacts with the criminal justice system would probably be a material omission. Thus, Mary could have Ralph's election set aside and recover the attorneys' fees and expenses incurred in her action. (*See* ELO Ch.4-IV(B), (E).) Choice **B** is incorrect because any shareholder may complain when proxies have been solicited on the strength of material omissions or misstatements, regardless of the amount of stock she owns. In a few jurisdictions, the shareholder will not have standing unless she has actually given her proxy in response the solicitation. This is not an issue here, because Mary did give her proxy. Choice **C** is incorrect because the fact that Mary did not commence her action until after Ralph's election is not significant (unless she delays an unreasonably long period of time). Finally, Choice **D** is incorrect because Ralph's contacts with the criminal system are probably material, despite the absence of an actual conviction.

72. C Corporate action must ordinarily be undertaken pursuant to validly authorized resolutions validly adopted. The appointment of corporate officers must ordinarily be undertaken by resolution of the directors. The fact that a majority of directors have signed a typewritten resolution appointing Cindy as Secretary is not controlling. Although recent legislation in many jurisdictions permits directors to act without a formal meeting, these statutes still ordinarily require that (1) ***all*** of the directors have waived notice of the meeting, and (2) the board's action be approved unanimously. In this instance, none of the directors waived notice of a meeting, nor was the resolution signed by ***all*** of the directors. (*See* ELO Ch.3-II(G)(2)(a).) Choice **A** is incorrect because shareholders ordinarily ***cannot*** appoint a corporate officer by agreement with the officer directly. Choice **B** is incorrect because there was no properly held meeting of the board to consider Cindy as Secretary. Finally, Choice **D** is incorrect for two reasons — officers must be appointed by the board rather than the shareholders; and the board does not need unanimous agreement to appoint an officer. A majority of directors is sufficient, provided all formal requirements for notice and/or waiver are met.

73. B Under the common law, shareholders may inspect corporate books and records, including board minutes, minutes of shareholders' meetings, bylaws, books of account, contracts, and other similar documents pertaining to the company's affairs. The inspection must be done in good faith, at a reasonable time, and for the purpose of advancing the interests of the corporation or its shareholders. Since Paula is asking to inspect Weldon's books of account and contracts for a proper purpose (to determine why the corporation has not been more profitable when others have), she should be permitted to examine these items. (*See* ELO Ch.4-I.) Choice **A** is incorrect because, her purpose being a proper one, there is no basis to preclude Paula from viewing the contracts entered into by Weldon. Choice **C** is incorrect because no assertion of wrongdoing by management is necessary before a shareholder is permitted to view corporate books and records. Finally, Choice **D** is incorrect because, her purpose being a proper one, Paula may view both Weldon's books of account and its contracts.

74. A When a statute restricting the inspection of corporate books and records exists, it is usually construed narrowly to avoid encroaching on common law rights — in this case, the common law rights to inspect all relevant books and records. Since the statute in this case is limited to inspections of corporate ***books of account***, it will probably be construed as applying only to that category of records. Therefore, John can still assert his common-law right to review the corporation's books, records and documents ***other than*** its books of account, even though he has been a stockholder for only seven months. Because John's purpose in soliciting the shareholder lists is a proper one (i.e., to become a director for the purpose of determining whether fraud by members of the board has occurred), he should be able to view this data. (*See* ELO Ch.4-I(A)(5).) Choice **B** is incorrect because he has owned Boolon stock for only seven months (not the one-year period of time required by the statute to inspect the books of account). Thus, John cannot inspect the books of account. Choice **C** is incorrect because John can properly inspect the shareholder lists; and the solicitation of proxies in an effort to unseat existing management is not an improper purpose. Finally, Choice **D** is incorrect because John's common-law rights of inspection would probably still extend to corporate documents ***other than*** the books of account.

75. B A derivative action to overturn an act of the board which is either unlawful or constitutes a waste of corporate assets cannot be prevented by stockholder ratification of the director's act — not even by a majority of disinterested stockholders. James's derivative suit should be allowed if Josephine's compensation is so excessive as to constitute waste of corporate assets. Because, on these facts, both the board and a majority of disinterested shareholders have approved the contract with Josephine, James will probably have the burden of showing that the contract was unfair. He may succeed in doing this if he can show that her contract was much more costly than the contracts of officers with comparable authority and duties in the same industry. (*See* ELO Ch.7-II(F)(4)(a).) Choice **A** is incorrect because, if James's suit is successful, he should be permitted to recover his attorneys' fees and court costs. Choice **C** is incorrect because even disinterested shareholders cannot ratify corporate waste. Finally, Choice **D** is incorrect because in view of the fact that the directors had voted unanimously in favor of Josephine's compensation, a demand on the board would presumably be futile.

76. D The sale of all or substantially all the assets of one corporation to another for cash or for cash and secured debt is usually followed by the liquidation of the seller and the distribution of its assets to its shareholders. The stockholders of the two corporations involved are not treated equally. The stockholders of the selling corporation must approve the sale. (*See* ELO Ch.10-I(C)(4)(b).) The shareholders of the purchasing corporation do not ordinarily have to approve the sale. Because the outstanding stock of the purchasing corporation is not affected by the purchase, appraisal rights do not apply. Therefore, Johnson does not have appraisal rights, and she cannot complain that the shareholders of Carlton have not been asked to approve the transaction. Choice **A** is incorrect because Johnson is not entitled to appraisal rights. Choice **B** is incorrect because consent by the Carlton stockholders is not required. Choice **C** is incorrect because most states do not ordinarily require approval by the stockholders of the purchaser.

77. D To exercise her appraisal rights, a shareholder must do the following: (1) give notice to the corporation ***prior to the shareholder vote*** that she demands payment of the fair value of her stock interest; (2) vote against the transaction or refrain from voting in its favor; and (3) as soon as possible (some states require that this be done before the vote), deposit her shares with the corporation. Since Amy failed to vote against the sale, she will probably ***not*** be permitted to exercise her appraisal rights. (*See* ELO Ch.10-II(B)(11).) Choice **A** is incorrect because communication of disapproval is not enough; Amy failed to vote against the transaction. Choice **B** is incorrect because, having failed to appear at the shareholders' meeting, Amy forfeited her right to exercise her appraisal rights. Choice **C** is incorrect because appraisal rights were designed to protect the interests of shareholders in the selling corporation and Amy would be entitled to these rights, except for her failure to follow the required steps.

78. C When a statutory merger occurs (i.e., the transaction is effectuated pursuant to the applicable statutory requirements), the surviving corporation (Helton) automatically assumes the obligations of the target company (Gibble). Because a statutory merger has occurred, the creditors of Gibble can enforce collection against Helton for any obligations owed to them by Gibble. This principle applies regardless of whether (1) Helton expressly assumed Gibble's debts, or (2) the obligations were known or unknown by Helton. (*See* ELO Ch.10-I(F)(1).) Choice **A** is incorrect because a statutory merger requires approval by the boards of both the target and the survivor. Choice **B** is incorrect because, when a ***statutory*** merger occurs, the shareholders of ***both*** corporations may assert appraisal rights. In some states, the appraisal rights of the shareholders of the acquiring corporation will be unavailable if the resulting increase in outstanding stock is less than 20%. Finally, Choice **D** is incorrect because, while Bo has appraisal rights as a stockholder in the target company, his recovery is the value of the stock as of the date immediately ***preceding*** the merger.

79. C When, as consideration for a sale of all (or substantially all) of its assets, the transferor corporation receives stock of the transferee and is required to dissolve soon afterward, many courts treat the transaction as a *de facto* merger. In these situations, the principles applicable to statutory mergers (e.g., approval of the directors and shareholders, appraisal rights, assumption by the survivor of the target corporation's debts) are applicable. Since we know that the *de facto* merger doctrine is operative in this jurisdiction, the shareholders of both corporations possess appraisal rights. (*See* ELO Ch.10-II(C).) (Except that the appraisal rights of shareholders in the acquiring corporation may not be as broad as those of the transferor-shareholders.) Choice **A** is incorrect because, assuming the transaction is viewed as a *de facto* merger, Nolton is liable for Melton's debts (regardless of whether Nolton has expressly agreed to assume these obligations). Choice **B** is incorrect because stockholders of the acquiring corporation would be obliged to approve the issuance of additional shares. Ordinarily, an increase in the amount of authorized stock is viewed as an "organic" change in the corporation and requires an amendment to the Articles of Incorporation. Finally, Choice **D** is incorrect because preemptive rights are ordinarily ***not*** applicable to situations where stock is exchanged for specific property other than cash.

80. D Instead of resorting to the federal courts, a shareholder whose proxy has been fraudulently solicited may ordinarily commence an action for rescission against the culpable party in a state court, under applicable state law. (*See* ELO Ch.4-IV(E)(2).) Or, instead of his other remedies, an aggrieved shareholder in a merger or *de facto* merger, can assert his appraisal rights. However, he can assert his appraisal rights only if he has ***voted against the merger.*** Choice **B** is therefore incorrect. Choice **A** is incorrect because, whether Elwood purchased his shares or inherited them, he must be a buyer or seller of securities ***in the transaction under scrutiny*** to assert SEC Rule 10b-5. The facts do ***not*** indicate that Elwood purchased his shares in reliance on the misleading information contained in the proxy. Finally, Choice **C** is incorrect because, an action under SEC Rule 10b-5 or § 14 of the Securities Exchange Act ***must*** be initiated in federal court.

81. C In a statutory merger, the general rule is that shareholders of both the target and surviving corporations must approve the transaction. (*See* ELO CH.10-I(F)(1)(b),(c).) However, in a whale-minnow merger, approval of the shareholders of the surviving corporation is not required. (See our discussion of appraisal rights of the Fenton shareholders). Choice **A** is, therefore, incorrect. Choice **B** is incorrect because both groups of shareholders do not have the same appraisal rights, either. If we view this as a whale-minnow merger (applicable here because Fenton, the whale, is giving up only 10% of its stock for all the assets of the minnow, Carlton), then this is an exception to the general rule requiring approval of the shareholders of the acquiring corporation. Under RMCBA § 11.03(g)(3), the shareholders of the surviving corporation do not get appraisal rights if the increase in outstanding stock of the survivor is less than 20%. (*See* ELO Ch.10-II(B)(4)(b).) Choice **D** is incorrect because a short form merger occurs when, prior to the transaction, the survivor owned a substantial proportion (e.g., often at least 90%) of the target's stock. There is ***no*** indication from the facts that this is the case. The correct answer is **C**. In a statutory merger, the surviving corporation is responsible for the debts of the target corporation.

82. D Unless the class is provided for in the original Articles of Incorporation, the holders of outstanding common stock must approve an amendment to the Articles of Incorporation before the issuance of a new class of stock that has priority in the distribution of dividends. Since ABC seeks to create a class of preferred stock having priority in the distribution of dividends, the requisite percentage of holders of common stock — usually, a majority — must approve an amendment to the Articles of Incorporation. (*See* ELO Ch.2-I(C); Ch.10-III(A).) Choice **A** is incorrect because ***unanimous*** approval by shareholders to create a new class of preferred stock is not necessary unless the Articles require it. Choice **B** is incorrect because an amendment to the Articles of Incorporation is necessary in this situation. Changes in the right of shareholders to receive dividends are ordinarily viewed as being "organic" or "basic" in nature. Finally, Choice **C** is incorrect because, provided it is accomplished with the necessary percentage of common shares, the Articles of Incorporation can be amended to create a new class of stock that has priority in the distribution of dividends.

83. D To determine whether Ogden can pay dividends under these facts, it is necessary to research the law pertaining to dividends in the applicable jurisdiction. While most states still require that dividends be paid only from positive earned surplus, jurisdictions that allow nimble dividends permit distributions to be made from annual net profits. Nimble dividends are dividends paid from the corporation's net profits for the fiscal year in which the dividend is declared and/or the preceding fiscal year. Most nimble dividend jurisdictions required, however, that the dividend not result in corporate insolvency. Some jurisdictions have enacted statutes which permit dividends to be paid only as long as a corporation's total assets are at least a stipulated proportion of total liabilities (e.g., 125%). (*See* ELO Ch.11-I(C)(7), (D).) No decision on payment of dividends can be made without knowledge of the local laws. Choice **A** is incorrect because only a minority of jurisdictions recognizes the payment of nimble dividends. Choice **B** is incorrect because some jurisdictions do allow dividend payments to be paid out of current operating profits despite a deficit in the earned surplus account. Finally, Choice **C** is incorrect because dividends cannot automatically be paid simply because the corporation won't be insolvent after the distribution.

84. A A voting trust is ordinarily enforceable according to its terms. The trustee has a fiduciary duty to act in the best interests of the beneficiaries (i.e., the participating shareholders). She need not adhere to the wishes of any of the beneficiaries. Watson can vote the shares for Martha's election, assuming she possesses a good faith belief that this action is beneficial to the shareholders of the trust. Since the trust is to operate for two years, the opposition of Samuels and Tilden to Martha's appointment is inoperative. (*See* ELO Ch.5-II(C)(4).) Choice **B** is incorrect because Martha's competence is not sufficient. Watson must believe that Martha's election to the board will be beneficial to the trust's beneficiaries. Choice **C** is incorrect because Watson's obligation is to vote the shares in a manner which promotes the interests of the shareholder/beneficiaries as she sees them. She cannot disregard her judgment because it conflicts with the preferences of some of the beneficiaries. Finally, Choice **D** is incorrect because Samuels and Tilden cannot revoke the trust by appearing at the stockholders' meeting at the meeting or by objecting to the election of Martha. The trust can be terminated only by ***unanimous*** vote of the trust beneficiaries, and Underwood does ***not*** oppose Martha's election.

85. D A valid pooling agreement — i.e., an agreement among stockholders to vote their stock together as a unit on certain or all matters — can ordinarily be enforced by a decree of specific performance. Since Katey and Mandy intend to vote in favor of the resolution preventing the derivative action, Mary ***must*** vote her shares in the same way because their agreement provides that a two-out-of-three vote will control. If Mary does not do so, Katey and Mandy can probably obtain a decree of specific performance. (*See* ELO Ch.5-II(B)(4)(b).) Choice **A** is incorrect because the fact that Mary owns more shares than the combined total of Katey and Mandy is irrelevant; their agreement controls. Choice **B** is incorrect because it is not necessary that the corporation receive a copy of the agreement before the agreement can be enforced against the original parties. Failure to file the agreement with the corporation might affect the rights of a bona-fide purchaser from one of the three parties, but not the original parties. Finally, Choice **C** is incorrect because the omission of any reference to the pooling agreement on the stock certificates is irrelevant among the original parties to the agreement. This omission would be significant if one of these parties transferred her shares to a person who did ***not*** know of the agreement; UCC § 8-204.

86. D The courts in some states have applied the *de facto* merger doctrine although all of the requirements of a statutory merger are not met, if the transaction is enough like a merger to be treated as one. (*See* ELO Ch.10-II(C)(1).) When the doctrine of *de facto* merger is applied, the stockholders of the target corporation get appraisal rights and, in some cases, the stockholders of the selling corporation get the right to vote on the transaction. Because Congolea purchased a controlling interest in Beldola from shareholders of Beldola ***for cash***, it is extremely unlikely that any court would apply the *de facto* merger doctrine to this transaction. Fred is in no worse position than if another person, or several persons, had purchased a majority interest in Beldola. But Fred may be able to assert appraisal rights when the "short form" merger of Beldola into Congolea occurs. (*See* ELO CH.10-I(F)(1)(f).) Choice **A** is incorrect because, barring application of the *de facto* merger doctrine, approval by Congolea's shareholders is unnecessary. Choice **B** is incorrect because the transaction involved a purchase of stock for cash directly from ***shareholders*** of the target; thus, approval of Beldola's board was unnecessary. Finally, Choice **C** is incorrect because Fred's rights are not governed by the actions of the Congolea board. It doesn't matter whether the Board approved the merger unanimously, or by a simple majority.

87. D In a jurisdiction which applies the reasoning in the *Perlman* case, the courts will scrutinize any case in which a controlling stockholder sells all his stock to an acquiring corporation at a premium. This would be especially so when the two corporations are direct competitors, because the instinct of the acquiring corporation is likely to be to reduce the impact of the competition, thereby injuring the minority stockholders in the Target corporation. Because Harrold has violated his fiduciary duty by usurping a corporate opportunity and prevented the minority stockholders from buying his shares, Frances will be entitled to her *pro-rata* share of the premium. The correct answer is **D.** When the seller knows, or has reason to know, that the transfer will impair the value of shares held by the other shareholders, he is obliged to share the control premium with those other stockholders. (*See* ELO Ch.7-V(D).) Choice **A** is incorrect because the right under *Perlman* to obtain a *pro rata* share of the premium is ***not*** contingent upon proof that the new controlling shareholder intends to loot the corporation. As long as the seller has violated his fiduciary duty by negating the corporate opportunity, *pro rata* distribution of the control premium should apply. Choice **B** is incorrect because there is no basis on which Frances could assert appraisal rights in this situation. Finally, Choice **C** is incorrect because Harrold's sale of his shares does ***not*** require approval by Ajax's board.

88. C In most states, a shareholder who obtains a premium for selling a majority or controlling portion of the corporation's stock ordinarily does ***not*** have to account to minority shareholders for this premium. Also, as part of the acquisition of a controlling interest in a corporation, the seller and purchaser may arrange a seriatim change in the directors elected by the seller. Since there is no reason on these facts to believe that Biltmore's control of PP will be detrimental to PP, its minority shareholders are ***not*** entitled to receive a *pro rata* portion of the "control" premium received by Randolph. In addition, the seriatim resignation and appointment of new directors is valid under these circumstances. (*See* ELO Ch.7-V(C).) The courts will not interfere with the seriatim transfer of control even though majority control is being sold for a premium. Choice **A** is incorrect because there is no indication that Randolph has breached his fiduciary duty to the corporation or the minority shareholders. Choice **B** is incorrect because seriatim transfer of control through orderly resignations of existing directors will not be disturbed by the courts. Biltmore may arrange for the replacement of the directors with individuals of its choosing.

Finally, Choice **D** is incorrect because, concurrently with obtaining control of a corporation, the acquiring party can arrange for the seriatim resignation and replacement of existing directors.

89. D When a corporation is capitalized with assets that are grossly inadequate to meet reasonably foreseeable obligations, considering the nature and purpose of the business, the corporate veil may be "pierced" (i.e., the shareholders may be held personally liable for the corporation's debts). This is especially true with respect to claims by involuntary creditors, as opposed to creditors who chose to do business with the company. However, the majority of states will not pierce the corporate veil unless there has been fraud or misdoing, or a gross failure to follow corporate formalities. Since neither of those factors is present here, Carla and John should be able to avoid personal liability, especially since they did secure liability insurance. Statement (2) is therefore correct. (*See* ELO Ch.2-V(B)(4).) If Statement (2) is correct, then Statement (1) is incorrect. Statement (3) is correct because in the bankruptcy proceeding, John's note will probably be treated as insider capital and will, therefore, be subordinated to the claims of general creditors. The correct choice is therefore D, which adopts Statements (2) and (3), but not Statement (1).

90. C Ordinarily, board members may ***not*** give proxies to other directors for the purpose of voting on corporate matters. A director must exercise his own independent judgment on all corporate matters and may ***not*** transfer his right to vote as a director to anyone else, including another director. The original agreement among Art, Sam, and Kelly was unenforceable. The proxy given by Art to Sam was also invalid. Directors may not vote by proxy. (*See* ELO Ch.3-II(H).) Choice **A** is incorrect because the original agreement among Art, Sam, and Kelly was invalid and unenforceable by any party. Choice **B** is incorrect because directors may not give or receive, or vote by, proxy. Finally, Choice **D** is incorrect because Kelly had an absolute right to vote as she thought best for the corporation.

91. D Generally, a shareholder may transfer her stock, subject to any reasonable restrictions as to its alienability. These restrictions may be found in the Articles of Incorporation, bylaws, or in shareholder agreements. A restriction on transfer of a security is ineffective against any person without actual knowledge of it, unless the restriction is conspicuously noted on the security; U.C.C. § 8-204. On these facts, the notation on Joe's stock certificate would be sufficient to place Bertha on notice of the restriction, even though the notation makes reference to another document which sets forth the terms of the restrictions. The restriction described here (a right of first refusal by current shareholders at the stock's fair market value) is ordinarily viewed as reasonable. (*See* ELO Ch.5-V(C)(1), (E).) Choice **A** is incorrect because Bertha was not bound to complete the purchase when she was tendered the certificate bearing the legend. Until that time, she had suffered no damage. Choice **B** is incorrect because Bertha is deemed to have knowledge of the limitations on the transferability of the stock contained in the Articles of Incorporation by virtue of the legend on the certificate. She had the duty to pursue the reference by reading the Articles. Finally, Choice **C** is incorrect because a restriction that gives existing shareholders a right of first refusal at the fair market value of shares is ordinarily considered to be reasonable and valid.

92. C The common law *de facto* corporation, created to protect stockholders against personal liability whenever there was an innocent defect in the Articles of Incorporation or in the filing of the Articles (e.g., when a lawyer neglected to file the Articles), is in disfavor among modern lawmakers and judges. (*See* ELO Ch.2-IV(C).) The Revised Model Business Corporation Act has abolished the *de facto* doctrine entirely and many states have adopted the RMBCA approach. Under this approach, promoters who act on behalf of the corporation when they know there is in fact no corporation, are liable jointly and severally to any creditor of the corporation. However, the courts will protect investors who have no knowledge of the defect and do not take an active role in the management of the corporation. On these facts, A and B would probably not be liable to the customer because they were entitled to rely on Avocat's affidavit and there is no showing that they did anything other than act as incorporators. The best answer is **C.** Most courts have held that even when the defect in incorporation is so severe that the *de facto* doctrine does not apply, creditors of the corporation are estopped to deny the corporate existence. Choice **A** is incorrect because the Articles of Incorporation are probably invalid and ineffective because an important statutory requirement was not complied with. Choice **B** is incorrect under the RMBCA and in those states which do not recognize *de facto* corporations. Choice **D** is incorrect because it would be inequitable to hold A and B liable as partners when they can rely on the defense of estoppel.

93. C Generally, a shareholder may transfer his or her stock freely, subject only to any reasonable restrictions. These restrictions may be found in the Articles of Incorporation, bylaws, or in shareholder agreements. A bylaw provision that requires a stockholder to give the other shareholders a right of first refusal when she leaves is probably valid (especially since the shareholder is entitled to receive the stock's fair market value). The provision requiring that payment be made over three years is not unreasonable, nor is the provision limiting interest to 5% per annum. (*See* ELO Ch.5-V(C)(1), (E).) Choice **A** is incorrect because the provision is almost certainly a reasonable one. Choice **B** is incorrect because the mere fact that Hall is acting in good faith does ***not*** exempt her from compliance with valid restrictions in the bylaws. Finally, Choice **D** is incorrect. As one of the original shareholders/directors/officers. she is deemed to have actual knowledge of the bylaws adopted by the corporation.

94. C A corporation is ***not*** liable for contracts made on its behalf by promoters prior to incorporation, unless the contracts are expressly or implicitly ratified by it after formation. (*See* ELO Ch.2-III(C).) A corporation may, however, be liable under *quasi* contract principles if it has derived a benefit from a contract that the board of directors subsequently rejects. Since Bennett consumed approximately 15% of the grain, it is liable to Castleton for the reasonable value of the benefit it derived from the grain. Choice **A** is incorrect because Alex remained liable to Castleton under the contract, despite the fact that Bennett began using the grain. He failed to disclaim personal liability in his negotiations with Castleton. Choice **B** is incorrect because Alex will not be able to recover in *quasi* contract until Castleton obtains a judgment against Alex for the contract price. At that point, Alex may be able to recover an amount equal to the benefit that Bennett derived from the grain. Finally, Choice **D** is incorrect because Bennett used only 15% of the grain prior to the time it discovered Alex's agreement, and then without any knowledge by its employees that the contract was not negotiated by an officer after incorporation. This would probably ***not*** be sufficient to constitute implied ratification of the entire contract.

95. C A corporate promoter owes a fiduciary duty to the corporation in formation. This duty includes the obligation to refrain from exploiting a corporate opportunity. Because Able purchased the land in anticipation of reselling it to Benson and did not divulge her interest in the partnership, she is probably obliged to remit the $25,000 profit to the corporation. This is true even if she paid a fair market price and earned her profit only because of an increase in property values generally. (*See* ELO Ch.2-III(D).) Choice **A** is incorrect because promoters owe a fiduciary duty to their prospective corporations. The fact that Able was not a director or officer of Benson when the purchase agreement was made is irrelevant. Also, the fact the transaction was negotiated by a Belbow partner other than Able is irrelevant. The facts tell us that the partnership was controlled by Able. Finally, Choice **D** is incorrect because Able is liable for the profit, even if Benson was contracting with Belbow to pay what was then a fair market price.

96. B A corporate treasurer is not ordinarily empowered to negotiate contracts for the purchase of commodities required in the operation of the business. His duties usually consist of the collection and deposit of funds and the preparation of financial reports and documents. Each officer of the corporation has certain duties implied by the nature of his office. The Treasurer does not have the implied authority to enter into contracts of the kind involved here. (*See* ELO Ch.3-III(C)(4).) Choice **A** is therefore incorrect. Choice **C** is factually incorrect because the board did ***not*** ratify the second agreement with the boarding house owner. In fact, the directors repudiated that agreement as soon as they all became aware of it. Choice **D** is incorrect because it is reasonable to conclude that a corporation engaged in mining operations — often in a remote area — would probably have to provide food and housing for its employees. Thus, the contract itself is not *ultra vires*. The correct answer is **B.** If the board is aware that an officer has routinely exercised authority beyond the normal scope and that third parties have come to rely on the appearance of authority, the corporation will be liable on the theory of apparent authority. Here, Jack renewed the contract with the approval of the president and the knowledge of several directors. Furthermore, the renewal was performed by Minefield over several months and the board is probably charged with notice.

97. C A person is an insider for purposes of SEC Rule 10b-5 when she learns of material, nonpublic information as a consequence of either (1) her position with the corporation, or (2) her performance of a confidential function on behalf of the corporation. Also, she may become an insider by establishing a relationship of trust with the plaintiff. An insider is liable to an aggrieved party when she fails to disclose nonpublic, material information in connection with the purchase or sale of stock. Although Joanne was not an officer or director of the corporation, she was a "constructive insider" for purposes of SEC Rule 10b-5, because her company had been retained by Belmont to perform a confidential function (i.e., Belmont's accounting work). (*See,* ELO Ch.8-III(G)(3), (9)(c).) As an insider, Joanne was obliged to disclose nonpublic, material information to the persons from whom she purchased Belmont stock. Choice **A** is incorrect because Joanne was an "insider" for purposes of SEC Rule 10b-5. Choice **B** is incorrect because the fact that Joanne made no material misrepresentations is irrelevant. Her liability arises from her failure to disclose to the seller the material, nonpublic information she had obtained. Finally, Choice **D** is incorrect because the special facts doctrine has traditionally been applied only to officers, directors, or key employees of a corporation. Joanne does not satisfy any of these designations. In addition, the culpable party must have transacted business with another stockholder of the corporation. On these facts, it is unclear from whom Joanne purchased her shares.

98. D Because the other answers are clearly wrong, the best answer is **D.** It must be noted, however, that the corporate remedy described in **D** is permitted only in a limited number of states, including New York. Under the special facts doctrine, when, as a consequence of his corporate position, a person acquires material, nonpublic information affecting the stock's value, there is a fiduciary duty to disclose those facts to an existing shareholder in conjunction with a sale or purchase of that shareholder's stock. In the few jurisdictions which follow New York, the corporation can bring an action under this theory if the aggrieved buyer or seller fails to do so (*Diamond v. Oreamuno*, 248 N.E.2d 910 (N.Y. 1969)). Assuming this jurisdiction adheres to this holding, ABC could recover X's profit under the special facts doctrine. (*See* ELO Ch.8-II(C)(2).) Choice **A** is incorrect because the remedy provided in SEC Rule 10b-5 is available only to the buyer and seller of stock. Since ABC was not directly involved in the transaction between X and Y, it cannot recover under this doctrine (even if an instrumentality of interstate commerce was used). Choice **B** is incorrect because SEC Rule 10b-5 does ***not*** require that the security involved be sold on a national stock exchange. However, as we have noted, the Rule can be asserted only by buyers or sellers of the security. Finally, Choice **C** is also incorrect for the same reason — ABC was not involved in the purchase or sale of the shares in question and SEC Rule 10b-5 can be asserted only by buyers or sellers of the security.

99. C When a person or entity uses his or its shares to elect an individual to sit on the board — in effect, ***deputizing*** that individual — that person or entity is deemed to be the director for purposes of SEC Rule 16(b), a rule which controls short-swing sales made within six months of stock acquisition. Upon the election of Barnes to the board of Caswell, Acme became (in effect) a director of Caswell for purposes of Rule 16(b). Because Acme sold its Caswell shares while (in effect) a director within six months of its purchase, Caswell can recover Acme's profit under SEC Rule 16(b). (*See* ELO Ch.8-VI(C)(3).) Choice **A** is incorrect because the SEC Rule deems Acme to be a director of Caswell. Rule 16 16(b) is applicable to a corporation which is ***either*** traded on a national exchange, ***or*** has assets greater than $5 million and a class of stock held by at least 500 stockholders. Choice **B** is incorrect because, although Caswell is not traded on a national stock exchange, it has assets in excess of $5 million and more than 500 shareholders of at least one class of stock. It is also engaged in interstate commerce. Thus, the transactions are subject to SEC Rule 16(b). Finally, Choice **D** is incorrect because Acme's liability is premised on its position as constructive director and not on its percentage of stock ownership. It's not necessary to apply the 10% rule under these facts.

100. C When subscribers enter into a contract to purchase the shares of an ***existing*** corporation, and the shares in question are issued and tendered under proper authorization, the agreement is enforceable. Because Abby and Brandon have agreed to purchase validly authorized shares from an existing corporation, the subscription agreement is enforceable against them. Choice **A** is incorrect because the shares involved were validly authorized, issued and tendered by an existing corporation. It's not necessary for Davis's board to accept or ratify the agreement. Ratification would be necessary only if the agreement had been made before the incorporation of Davis. Choice **B** is incorrect because a corporation may charge more for its shares than the par value specified in its Articles of Incorporation. The par value stated in the Articles is ordinarily only the minimum price at which the shares may be sold. Finally, Choice **D** is incorrect because the obligations of Abby and Brandon are ***not*** contingent upon their prior ownership of Davis stock. Their obligation to perform is not diminished because they are strangers to the corporation.

Index

References are to the number of the question raising the issue.
"E" indicates an Essay Question; "M" indicates a Multiple-Choice Question

Products for 1997-98 Academic Year

Emanuel Law Outlines

Steve Emanuel's Outlines have been the most popular in the country for years. Twenty years of graduates swear by them. In the 1996–97 school year, law students bought an average of 3.0 Emanuels each – that's 130,000 Emanuels.

Civil Procedure ◆	$18.95
Constitutional Law	23.95
Contracts ◆	17.95
Corporations	18.95
Criminal Law ◆	14.95
Criminal Procedure	14.95
Evidence	17.95
Property ◆	17.95
Secured Transactions	14.95
Torts (General Ed.) ◆	17.95
Torts (Prosser Casebook Ed.) Keyed to '94 Ed. Prosser, Wade & Schwartz	17.95
Also, Steve Emanuel's First Year Q&A's (see below)	$18.95

The Professor Series / Smith's Review

All titles in these series are written by leading law professors. Each follows the Emanuel style and format. Each has big, easy-to-read type; extensive citations and notes; and clear, crisp writing. Most have capsule summaries and sample exam Q & A's.

Agency & Partnership	$14.95
Bankruptcy	15.95
Environmental Law (*new title)*	15.95
Family Law	15.95
Federal Income Taxation	14.95
Intellectual Property	15.95
International Law	15.95
Labor Law	14.95
Neg. Instruments & Payment Systems	13.95
Products Liability	13.95
Torts	13.95
Wills & Trusts	15.95

◆ *Special Offer...*First Year Set
All outlines marked ◆ *plus* Steve Emanuel's First Year Q & A's *plus* Strategies & Tactics for First Year Law. Everything you need to make it through your first year.

Complete Set — *$97.50*

Latin for Lawyers
A complete glossary and dictionary to help you wade through the complex terminology of the law.

New title — *Price TBA*

Question & Answer Collections

Siegel's Essay & Multiple–Choice Q & A's

Each book contains 20 to 25 essay questions with model answers, plus 90 to 120 Multistate-style multiple-choice Q & A's. The objective is to acquaint the student with the techniques needed to handle law school exams successfully. Titles are:

Civil Procedure	Evidence
Constitutional Law	Professional Responsibility
Contracts	Real Property
Corporations	Torts
Criminal Law	Wills & Trusts
Criminal Procedure	

Each title — *$15.95*

The Finz Multistate Method

967 MBE (Multistate Bar Exam)–style multiple choice questions and answers for all six Multistate subjects, each with detailed answers – *Plus* a complete 200 question practice exam modeled on the MBE. Perfect for law school and ***bar exam*** review.

$33.95

Steve Emanuel's First Year Q&A's

1,144 objective–style short-answer questions with detailed answers, in first year subjects. A single volume covers Contracts, Torts, Civil Procedure, Property, Criminal Law, and Criminal Procedure.

$18.95

For any titles not available at your local bookstore, call us at 1-800-EMANUEL or order on-line at **http://www.emanuel.com**. Visa, MasterCard, American Express, and Discover accepted.

Law In A Flash Flashcards

Flashcards

Civil Procedure 1 ◆	$16.95
Civil Procedure 2 ◆	16.95
Constitutional Law ▲	16.95
Contracts ◆▲	16.95
Corporations	16.95
Criminal Law ◆▲	16.95
Criminal Procedure ▲	16.95
Evidence ▲	16.95
Future Interests ▲	16.95
Professional Responsibility (953 cards)	32.95
Real Property ◆▲	16.95
Sales (UCC Art.2) ▲	16.95
Torts ◆▲	16.95
Wills & Trusts	16.95

Flashcard Sets

First Year Law Set (includes all sets marked ◆ *plus* the book Strategies & Tactics for First Year Law.)	95.00
Multistate Bar Review Set (includes all sets marked ▲ *plus* the book Strategies & Tactics for MBE)	165.00
Professional Responsibility Set (includes the *Professional Responsibility* flashcards *plus* the book Strategies & Tactics for the MPRE)	45.00

Law In A Flash Software

(for Windows® 3.1 and Windows® 95 only)

Law In A Flash Interactive Software combines the best features of our flashcards with the power of the computer. Just some of the great features:

- Contains the complete text of the corresponding *Law In A Flash* printed flashcards
- Side-by-side comparison of your own answer to the card's preformulated answer
- Fully customizable, savable sessions – pick which topics to review and in what order
- Mark cards for further review or printing
- Score your answers, to help you spot those topics in which you need further review

Every *Law In A Flash* title & set is available as software.

Requirements: 386, 486, or Pentium-based computer running Windows® 3.1 or Windows® 95; 16 megabytes RAM; 3.5" high-density floppy drive; 3MB free space per title; Windows-supported mouse and printer (optional)

Individual titles	$19.95
Professional Responsibility (covers 953 cards)	34.95
First Year Law Set*	115.00
Multistate Bar Review Set*	195.00
Professional Responsibility/MPRE Set*	49.95

* These software sets contain the same titles as printed card sets *plus* the corresponding *Strategies & Tactics* books (see below).

Strategies & Tactics Series

Strategies & Tactics for the MBE

Packed with the most valuable advice you can find on how to successfully attack the MBE. Each MBE subject is covered, including Criminal Procedure (part of Criminal Law), Future Interests (part of Real Property), and Sales (part of Contracts). The book contains 350 actual past MBE questions broken down by subject, plus a full-length 200-question practice MBE. Each question has a ***fully-detailed answer*** which describes in detail not only why the correct answer is correct, but why each of the wrong answer choices is wrong.

☛ Covers all the new MBE specifications tested on and after July, 1997.

$34.95

Strategies & Tactics for the First Year Law Student

A complete guide to your first year of law school, from the first day of class to studying for exams. Packed with the inside information that will help you survive what most consider the worst year of law school and come out on top.

☛ Completely revised for 1997.

$12.95

Strategies & Tactics for the MPRE

Packed with exam tactics that help lead you to the right answers and expert advice on spotting and avoiding the traps set by the Bar Examiners. Contains actual questions from past MPRE's, with detailed answers.

$19.95

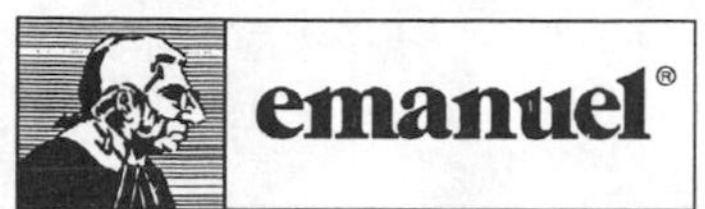

We'd like to know . . . .

Siegel's on Corporations (2nd ed.)

We value your opinions on our study aids. After all, we design them for *your* use, and if you think we could do something better, we want to know about it. Please take a moment to fill out this survey and feedback form and return it to us. We'll enter you in our monthly drawing where 5 people will win the study aid of their choice! If you don't want to identify yourself, that's OK, but you'll be ineligible for the drawing.

Name: ______________________ **Address:** ______________________

City: ____________________ **State:** ______ **Zip:** __________ **E-mail:** ____________

Law school attended: ______________________ **Graduation year:** __________

Please rate this product on a scale of 1 to 5:

General readability (style, format, etc.)	*Poor*	①	②	③	④	⑤	*Excellent*
Length of book (number of pages)	*Too short*	①	②	③	④	⑤	*Too long*
Essay questions	*Poorly written*	①	②	③	④	⑤	*Well written*
Multiple-choice questions	*Poorly written*	①	②	③	④	⑤	*Well written*
End-of-book aids (tables & index)	*Not useful*	①	②	③	④	⑤	*Useful*
Book's coverage of material presented in class	*Incomplete*	①	②	③	④	⑤	*Complete*
OVERALL RATING	***Poor***	①	②	③	④	⑤	***Excellent***

Suggestions for improvement: ______________________

☛ **What other study aids did you use in this course?** ______________________

☛ **If you liked any features of these other study aids, describe them:** ______________________

☛ **What casebook(s) did you use in this course?** ______________________

☛ **What study aids other than Emanuel do you use, and what features do you like about them?** ______________________

☛ **Please list the items you would like us to add to our product line:**

Outline subjects: ______________________

Flashcard subjects: ______________________

Other products (e.g., software, multimedia, etc.): ______________________

☛ **If you win our drawing, what one study aid would you like?** ______________________

Send to: *Emanuel Law* **Survey**
1865 Palmer Avenue, Suite 202
Larchmont, NY 10538

OR Fax to: *(914) 834-5186*

Please complete & return the Survey Form on the other side